VAMPIRE UNIVERSE

VAMPIRE UNIVERSE
The Dark World of Supernatural Beings
That Haunt Us, Hunt Us, and Hunger for Us

JONATHAN MABERRY

CITADEL PRESS
Kensington Publishing Corp.
www.kensington.com

CITADEL PRESS BOOKS are published by

Kensington Publishing Corp.
850 Third Avenue
New York, NY 10022

All Kensington titles, imprints, and distributed lines are available at special quantity
discounts for bulk purchases for sales promotions, premiums, fund-raising, educational, or institutional use. Special book excerpts or customized printings can also be
created to fit specific needs. For details, write or phone the office of the Kensington
special sales manager: Kensington Publishing Corp., 850 Third Avenue, New York,
NY 10022, attn: Special Sales Department; phone 1-800-221-2647.

CITADEL PRESS and the Citadel logo are Reg. U.S. Pat. & TM Off.

First printing: September 2006

10 9 8 7 6 5 4 3 2 1

Printed in the United States of America

Library of Congress Control Number: 2006926711

ISBN 0-8065-2813-3

As always . . . this is for Sara Jo, my own immortal beloved.

Contents

Acknowledgments

Vampire Universe and the books to follow have been a massive undertaking, and a host of people have generously provided information, assistance, insights, and support. Thanks to:

My agent, Sara Crowe of the Harvey Klinger Agency; and my editor at Citadel, Michaela Hamilton.

To the folks who helped shape the book: Sara Jo West, Sam West-Mensch, and Arthur Mensch.

David Kramer, for doing the first serious edit on this book.

My "crew," for support and feedback: Fran and Randy Kirsch, Gina and Charlie Miller, Gary and Donna Berkowitz, Cindy and Steve Rubino, Marylou and Frank Sessa, Marge and Frank Makos, and Carol and David Gabay.

Geoff Strauss and David Kramer (again) for designing my websites www.ghostroadblues.com and www.vampireuniverse.com.

My team at Career Doctor for Writers www.careerdoctorforwriters.com: Jerry Waxler, John Moskowitz, Mark and Gretchen Gunn, Keith Strunk, Raquel Pidal, Justin Bowers, Edie Moser, Kim Nagy, Toni Lopopolo, Susan Korman, and Lisa Papp.

HWA: The Horror Writers Association; and the GSHWA: Garden State Horror Writers.

To Kim Zagoren, editor of *Forever Underground*, for first publishing my column on Supernatural Predators.

PWC: Philadelphia Writers Conference—to my fellow board members and the many conferees I've come to know, many thanks!

To the Wild River Gang who work with me to produce *The Wild River Review*, the world's coolest literary magazine—www.wildriverreview.com.

And to the wonderful artists who provided the amazing art that graces this book (please check out the Artist Index in the back to learn more about them).

— *Introduction* —
THE NATURE OF THE BEAST

THEY ARE OUT THERE IN THE DARK, always watching, always hungry. They have always been there, preying on humanity since before recorded history. Eternal. Patient. Ravenous.

Scary thought, isn't it?

We humans have always believed in monsters, in strange beings whose exact nature is unknown and whose intent is decidedly alien. Prehistoric man painted cave walls with half-human half-animal figures. The walls and columns of ancient temples around the world are carved with semi-humans, monsters, demons, and bestial gods. Clerics in the churches and temples of a thousand religions have warned of unnatural monsters that wanted to corrupt or destroy mankind. Stories of them have been handed down through the millennia, and are still told today, sometimes in jest ... and sometimes with a tremble in the voice and a flick of the eye toward the nearest shadow. In the whole history of humanity on Earth there has not been one single culture that has not had legends of predatory supernatural monsters. They are everywhere.

And they are certainly in here ... in these volumes of the *Vampire Universe* series. In these pages, and in the books that follow, you will meet many hundreds of these weird and pernicious beings. Although there are other single volumes that have attempted to collect all of these monsters, there are just too many for one book. They exist in astonishing variety. Within that vast horde, however, there are a number of recurring types of supernatural predator, and these categories or paradigms include vampires, theriomorphs (shape-shifters), revenants (the living dead), hags, imps, faeries, sea monsters, beast men, and tricksters. Most people think that there is just a single example of each, that—for example—a vampire is a vampire and all vampires are alike. That couldn't be further from the truth. Even within a major grouping there are dozens, sometimes hundreds, of sub-species, each one unique. This creates a pretty severe problem for a monster hunter because what might stop one vampire might not stop another. It is vital to understand as many of the monsters as possible, otherwise the intrepid vampire slayer might become the main course of a gruesome feast.

Vampires, you see, come in all shapes and sizes, and they exist in such exotic variety that the term "vampire" itself is only used here for convenience. Vampirism isn't limited just to the blood-sucking living dead, because only about a third of the world's vampires are hematophageous, meaning they hunt for blood. Many vampires attack humans in order to feed off life essence, breath, or sexual essence; some even feed off emotions such as hope or love, or qualities like fidelity. Some vampires possess no physical form and prey on their victims as a flashing ball of light, or come in the form of a destructive plague. Some are even necrophageous (flesh eaters).

So, what defines a creature as a vampire?

Quite simply, vampires are supernatural beings that *take* what is not theirs to takes—blood, life, breath, or some other vital part of their human victims; and they take it by force. It is the taking without permission that characterizes the vampire. Even in cases of vampire seduction, the vampire is using supernatural powers to seduce its victim, which is no more a consensual act than spiking a woman's cocktail with a "date rape" drug.

One aspect of this book that will surprise many readers is that nearly everything the average person knows about vampires is wrong. Most of the qualities of the vampire and the methods of destroying them in the popular consciousness is not drawn from any of the world's many cultural beliefs, but are instead the creation of writers of horror fiction, such as Bram Stoker and his many successors. For example, vampires, as a rule, do not fear sunlight or the cross, they are not prohibited from entering a house unless invited, they can cross running water, they don't always sleep in their graves, and very few of them can be killed by a stake through the heart.

Also, vampires come in all shapes and sizes (though generally they do not appear in the form of Eastern European nobility, wearing tuxedos and opera cloaks). Many species of vampires can shape-shift; but they generally don't turn into wolves or bats (birds, insects, cats, and balls of light are far more common). Not all vampires are resurrected corpses—some have never died, some are immortal beings, and some are created through sorcery. Vampires are not created by an exchange of blood between the vampire and its victim—that is pure fiction. Moreover, not all vampires are evil. In short, if the average person living in modern times were to be confronted by a vampire, that person would be armed with all the wrong knowledge. "Oops!" hardly covers it.

Vampire Universe presents vampires in all their many forms and types; just as it does with the different species of werewolves, vengeance ghosts, wildmen, and others. It is the ultimate survival guide for anyone wishing to either take a stand against evil—or successfully flee from it.

For students of the weird and terrible, the book and its sequels have an additional benefit in that even some of the well-documented monsters presented here are seen from a different point of view. Often the entries include information from older and rarer sources than are commonly referenced in occult encyclopedias, which means that scholars, writers, and anyone fascinated by monsters will have some new information to chew on. Even more information can be found on the official website of this book (www.vampireuniverse.com).

The following are some of the major groupings and sub-groupings of monsters that will help you navigate the rest of the book.

⊰ VAMPIRES ⊱

Here are the major categories into which vampires are classified:

•**Astral Vampire**[1]: Vampirism in which the astrally projected[2] spirit of a living person preys on human victims, often draining them of life force or spiritual energy. This differs from psychic vampirism in that it is a deliberate method of attack, whereas most people who use psychic vampirism do so without conscious knowledge.

•**Essential Vampire:** Essential vampires feed on one or more of the following:

- *Life force.* Life force is often called Chi (Chinese), Gi (Korean), or Ki (Japanese). This life force is believed to be either electro-chemical, or made from pure energy and flows throughout the body along pathways called meridians that are laid out much like the circulatory system. This energy flow is the basis for healing arts such as acupuncture and acupressure, and it cultivated through various meditative practices, such as yoga. Humans generate this vital energy naturally, but essential vampires cannot and therefore must feed on humans to maintain their own existence.

- *Breath.* Many of the world's shape-shifting vampires, particularly those that transform into cats, will-o'-the-wisps, or flying insects, land on sleeping humans (usually children) and then drain away the breath leaving a child gasping or dead.

- *Sexual essence.* Some vampires seduce their victims in order to drain away a man's potency or a woman's fertility.

•**Human Vampire:** These are not supernatural beings but ordinary humans who embrace one or more aspects of the vampire life. There are a number of different kinds of human vampires:

---

1. A term coined by Theosophist Franz Hartmann.
2. Astral projection is the practice of deliberately separating one's consciousness from the physical body in order to move unhindered by any limitations.

– *Role players:* People involved in online vampire role-playing games such as *Vampire: The Masquerade, Vampire: The Eternal Struggle,* and *BloodLust.*

– *Lifestylers:* People who live the vampire life constantly and identify with vampires as kindred spirits.

– *Real vampires:* Self-named for their addiction to activities involving real blood, often involving sadomasochistic cutting (of themselves and their willing partners) and sometimes the ingestion of blood. To these real[3] vampires, vampirism is not a game but an actual way of life bordering on, and perhaps actually becoming, a religion.

•**Living vampire:** Supernatural creatures that have vampiric qualities but who are not dead; and because they are alive, they are hard to detect and can more easily infiltrate a community.

•**Psychic vampire:** Living humans who either deliberately or, more often, subconsciously use passive aggressive or codependent behavior to drain others of emotional, mental, and psychological energy.

•**Revenant:** A true "living dead" being that has risen from the grave as a vampire, ghost, zombie, or angel. In this book the term "revenant" is used to classify those vampires that are human corpses that have returned from the dead.

•**Nosferatu:** A Romanian word that is widely used in folklore to describe any of the many vampires around the world who spread disease. The word "nosferatu" translates as "plague carrier." In his novel, *Dracula,* Bram Stoker incorrectly translates it as "undead."

•**Sexual vampire:** A vampire that uses sexuality as a predatory tactic. Many sexual vampires are also essential vampires, but often there are other distinct qualities that set them apart. Within this group there are two primary subgroups.

---

3. Often called "true" vampires.

– *Seduction vampire:* These are creatures who use seduction merely as a tool to lure a victim close enough to attack. This sub-group is largely composed of blood-drinkers or meat-eaters. Most vampires in this category are female, though there are certainly examples of male vampires using the tactic of seduction.

– *Incubi/succubi:* These are (almost always) invisible spirits who visit sleeping humans at night and engage in sex for the sole purpose of feeding on sexual energy, potency, or in some rare cases, sexual fidelity. Incubi are male sexual vampires and Succubi are female.

– *Charismatic shape-shifter:* These vampires take the form of a compellingly beautiful woman or man in order to lure a victim into a tryst. Once alone, the creature then reverts back to its true form and attacks with great violence, feeding on blood or flesh.

•**Vampire:** A general name given by the English-speaking world to supernatural predatory monsters who feed on the blood, psychic energy, emotion, or life essence of others.

Another way to classify vampires is by what they consume, which creates a shorter and somewhat different list:

•**Blood-drinker:** These are the "classic" vampires, largely because of the source of their sustenance, but in folklore, blood-drinkers are varied and often wildly dissimilar, both to each other and to popular impressions of them.

•**Flesh-eater:** This is a much larger class of monsters and includes many species of vampire as well as all species of werewolves, various kinds of living dead, ghouls, and even some faerie folk, gnomes, and imps.

•**Breath-taker:** Are usually invisible, though not always. They come in various forms, are often small, and generally prey on the weak and sick; however, the legend of the Old Hag[4] falls partly into this category and partly into the next.

• **Waster:** This is another name for essential vampires. As most of the wasters appear at night they are frequently referred to, in folklore, as night wasters or night comers.

☙ THERIOMORPHS ☙

A "theriomorph" is a creature who possesses the ability to change its shape into that of another creature. Most often this is a human who can take the shape of an animal, bird, or insect. The most famous theriomorphs in folklore are werewolves, but there are many other kinds as well. In folklore it is more common for a vampire to turn into a bird or cat than into a wolf. Many of these shape-shifters become balls of light that fly through the air, also known as will-o'-the-wisps.

Unlike the transformations seen in films, in folklore the ability to shape-shift is a deliberate choice, even with werewolves. These creatures are not the victims of a tragic curse but evil-hearted predators who take animal form in order to deceive, elude, hunt, or attack. The cycle of the moon has nothing to do with the transformation, which means that theriomorphs of all kinds can change at will.

Theriomorphs abound in *Vampire Universe* and they truly do come in all shapes and sizes. When referring to the various kinds of theriomorph commonly known in modern culture as a werewolf, the term "lycanthrope" is often used since it refers to both versions of wolf monster, the *Wolf-Man* and the true *Werewolf*.

---

4. See the sidebar on page 211 for more on this monster.

⊰ CRYPTIDS AND HOMINIDS ⊱

Throughout the world there are many hundreds of creatures that have been seen—and which are widely believed to exist—but which have never been captured or classified. These *unknowns* are called cryptids, and debate has raged for years between folklorists and scientists as to whether they are real but unknown, supernatural, figments of wild imaginations, or simply unreliable accounts. Cryptids include many of the world's lake monsters (*Nessie* and her cousins), woodland monsters like the *Jersey devil* and the goat-sucking *Chupacabra*, and of course the many shaggy forest beast-men.

The *Wildmen*, as this latter group is called, form the biggest sub-group and range from the shy Bigfoot of the American Northwest to the murderous Yeren of the Himalayas. Unlike vampires and werewolves, there are frequent modern-day sightings of these wildmen, and some researchers have even collected artifacts such as plaster casts of footprints and bits of hair.

While cryptid is used generally for all of these unknown animals, the term "hominid" is used frequently in this book to describe possible species of wildmen. Hominids, in the strict scientific sense, refers to any member of the family of humans, *Hominidae*, which includes all of the species of humans and living apes, and are included in the super-family of all apes, the *Hominoidea*. Not all scientists use this broad a description, however, and there is some heated debate on the point ongoing in scientific circles. For our purposes, however, the term "hominid" will be used to describe the shaggy beast-men in all their variety mainly because they have not yet been properly and scientifically classified but who, if they exist, will probably prove to be cousins, however distant, of *Homo sapiens*.

Since wildmen are usually predatory in nature and are not truly human—or anything else represented in the fossil record—they are included here among other potentially supernatural monsters.

⊰ THE HUNGRY DEAD ⊱

Throughout the world there are tales of bodies brought back to life, often through black magic or sorcery. Mummies, zombies, and ghouls are just a few of the many kinds of living dead creatures that prey on humans. Some of these creatures share commonalities with vampires; others are unique and exotic.

The *Living Dead* films by George Romero brought these creatures to the public eye most successfully, but there are plenty of examples of flesh-eating corpses in folklore as well, and they have been included in this book.

⊰ EVIL GHOSTS ⊱

For the most part the typical ghost story, though often frightening, does not tell the tale of a predatory monster but of some lost soul, or perhaps a kind of spiritual echo that has no driving personality. In folklore, however, many of the spirits that return to the Earthly plane are quite vicious and do a lot more than moan in the night and rattle their chains. Some ghosts return to exact revenge or redress a wrong. Others are trapped on Earth because of some crime against Heaven; others exist for no known reason but appear to delight in causing torment. In many cultures, the line between a ghost and a vampire is completely blurred and some vampires are themselves, ghosts, and manifest bodies that are more illusion than substance.

There are quite a few modern versions of the "evil ghost" tales, most of which have become part of that vast wealth of stories known as urban legends. In these more modern tales, ghosts often appear to lure travelers to their deaths or to cause destruction.

⊰ A MISCELLANY OF MONSTERS ⊱

Aside from the traditional vampires, werewolves, zombies, and ghosts, a number of other creatures lie waiting for you in these pages. From life-sucking hags to vile faerie tricksters, there are all manner of rare and dangerous monsters lurking herein. The monsters here are not fictional creations for TV, books, or movies, but creatures that our ancestors grew up fearing. Perhaps our forebears were right all along and there are reasons to fear the dark, to close the closet doors firmly, and to shut the windows against the spirits that ride the night wind.

In the next volume we will explore further into the darkness, and there we'll meet demons, evil gods, creatures of mythology, and other beings that are far, far stranger and more deadly.

Right now we'll meet the vampires, werewolves, and other predators that haunt us, hunt us, and hunger for us.

So, grab your stake, string garlic bulbs around your neck, and follow me. . . .

~ *Chapter One* ~
VAMPIRES AND MONSTERS
A–F

A

Abatwa   The insect-size people of Zulu folklore are small enough to ride ants and hide under blades of grass, but despite their size they are great hunters and can work together to bring down large animals. These are wandering creatures who travel in tribes but have no home and occasionally build temporary homes—or hunting lodges—in anthills. They can be found in mountains or forests, but most often they follow the migration patterns of game. Humans observing the diminutive Abatwa during a hunt often learn the secrets of cooperative hunting that will make their own efforts more successful.

In the great majority of Abatwa tales, the little hunters are seen as either indifferent to the presence of the taller humans, or more often, as kindly guides and advisors; however, other stories tell of quick tempers and vengeful rage. For example, if a person steps on an Abatwa the little warrior is likely to lash out with a poison-tipped spear, piercing the sole of the taller human's foot. The poison can sometimes kill. Also, if a human steals an animal that has been killed by a tribe of Abatwa, then the little hunters are likely to come en masse and carry off the sleeping child of the thief.

Children under the age of four see the Abatwa most often, and usually that means that good luck will follow the child the rest of the day. If a pregnant woman sees a male Abatwa, then it is a sign that she'll give birth to a healthy boy. However, if a sick person sees three Abatwas walking side by side, then it is an omen of impending death.

Abchanchu   The Abchanchu of Bolivia in South America is a shape-shifting blood-drinking vampire who assumes the form of an old man who pretends to be lost and helpless, and when some kindly stranger comes along to help the old duffer home, then out come the fangs and the bloodlust. Wary travelers wear small amulets in which they've placed a drop of garlic oil, and this is enough to ward off this beast.

Abere   The Abere is a particularly vicious mermaid species from Melanesian legend. This monster has the typical mermaid's anatomy: the lower half of a fish and the upper half of a well-endowed woman with long golden hair; and it has a siren voice that can lure men right out of their boats. Once the men are in the water, the Abere drags them into the reeds and either drowns them in the shallows or slashes their throats with a sharp piece of oyster shell. She then feeds on the hot spewing blood, and then shares the flesh with her offspring, all of whom are female. How—or with whom—the Abere mates in order to pro-create is a matter for unsavory speculation.

Abnuaaya (also **Bekk-Bok, Almas,** and **Albasty**)   The Caucasus Region, comprising the newly independent states of Armenia, Azerbaijan, and Georgia in Asia, has many ancient tales of strange creatures and supernatural beasts, but chief among them is the legend of the Abnuaaya, the Yeti-like wild-men who some cryptozoologists[5] believe may be based on sightings of remnants of Neanderthal Man who survived as late as 500 years ago.

The Abnuaaya haunt the fierce and remote Caucasus Mountains of central Asia and have been described as manlike with a lot of coarse body hair, sloping brows, and faces that are an even blend of simian and human. The Abnuaaya have deep chests, sloping muscular shoulders, long arms, short bandy legs, and often wear clothes made from animal skins. In some reports these

5. Cryptozoology is the science of identifying creatures previously unknown to the fossil record.

ABERE Kelly Everaert

cryptids are not hirsute but were instead wearing clothing made from fur or hide. The description bears a striking resemblance to that of the Neanderthal as described by paleontologists. Neanderthals, of course, were a race of humanoid beings similar in many ways to Homo sapiens, but evolved parallel to the more genetically successful Cro-Magnon.

The great majority of the folktales of the Abnuaaya suggest that they are harmless, or at least timid, and very shy of contact with humans. But in remote areas some tales have been handed down from father to son telling of how during bad winters when food was scarce, the Abnuaaya would grow so hungry and desperate that they would come hunting for any kind of meat . . . including the flesh of men.

The Abnuaaya have been sighted for centuries, with reports of them entering into official records as early as 1420. This is, of course, very much at odds with the widespread belief in the scientific community that the Neanderthals became extinct about 30,000 years ago.

Many of the reports of wildmen surviving in remote areas bear similarities to the Neanderthal, raising the question as to whether these early cousins of mankind could have survived for tens of thousands of years longer than believed . . . or might still survive in small pockets in the world's most remote and inaccessible places.

≼ CRYPTIDS ≽

Cryptids are creatures that are believed to exist but for which there are no existing physical records or evidence. The science of Cryptozoology is built around discovering proof of these creatures so that they can be moved from the long list of "unknown" animals to proven additions to the ever-growing fossil record.

Accuser   One of a number of different names given to Satan. Others include Shaitan, the Father of Lies, and Lord of the Flies. Also known as the Evil One, the Accuser appears in one form or another in nearly every culture, often as the embodiment of everything corrupt, unnatural, and wicked.

Acheri   Vampires and the spread of disease is a common theme throughout the world, especially in third-world or underdeveloped countries where supplies of fresh water, availability of adequate medicines, and a lack of understanding of the nature of disease create an ideal breeding ground for germs of all kinds. In many of these cultures the spread of disease is believed to be the result of an evil and supernatural intent, as in the case of the Acheri of India.

The Acheri is the ghost of a little girl whom travelers sometimes encounter in India's vast mountainous regions. There are two primary versions of the Acheri's hunting practices. In one version she appears to other children and either walks with them or plays with them, seeming to be nothing more than an ordinary child herself. But when the human children leave her they carry with them a terrible disease. In the other (and more common) version, the Acheri comes down from the mountains during festival times and visits the villages in the lowlands where she joins in the celebrations as if she is part of the town, but will single out children as victims and poison them by casting her shadow over them. The very touch of the Acheri shadow is like the breath of someone with a highly communicable respiratory disease; infection occurs instantly and spreads rapidly throughout the community.

The disease can take many forms and generally manifests as a mysterious wasting sickness that is ultimately fatal. Whole families and sometimes whole villages are wiped out by the infection spread by the Acheri, who in turn feeds off of the sadness, pain, heartbreak, and death the disease creates, marking her as an essential vampire as well as a species of nosferatu.[6]

The Acheri, like many evil spirits, can be thwarted by sacred charms and the one used most effectively against them is woven red thread. This practice is common around the world, and charms of red, scarlet, or crimson are used throughout Asia and Europe, though in the case of the latter the practice has died out in the past few centuries.

Adlet   The Adlet of the Inuit peoples of Alaska and Canada is the hideous offspring of an unholy union of an Inuit woman and a demonically possessed red-haired dog. This unnatural coupling resulted in a litter of five monster hounds that seemed to embody evil. The woman, horrified by her offspring, bundled them onto rafts made from whalebone and animal hides and set

---

6. *Nosferatu* is a Romanian word meaning "plague carrier" and is used here to identify vampires who spread disease.

⊰ RED: THE COLOR OF ⊱ PROTECTION

The color red is purported to be the first color humans perceive, and since Neolithic times red has symbolized new life, health, fertility, and protection against evil.

Red string bracelets are worn by followers of the Kabbalah. (Even the singer Madonna sports one!)

India charms hung from red cords are proof against the dreaded Acheri.

To this day Australian Aborigines paint their weapons red in order to conquer evil.

Amulets set with rubies or garnets were used for thousands of years as charms against the Evil Eye.

During the Middle Ages, particularly in Germany, red linen on a bed was believed to protect against "red sicknesses" such as rashes, fever, anemia, and miscarriages.

In Greece, Albania, and Armenia new brides wear red wedding veils as charms to insure that they will be fertile and that their children will be healthy.

The red rose is the classic symbol of pure love and fidelity.

In biblical times the ancient Israelites painted their doorframes with red blood to ward off demons.

them adrift in the frozen arctic waters. The infant monsters did not die from the cold but rather drifted all the way to Europe where, according to the Inuit beliefs, they became the progenitors of all the white races on that continent. Since then at least one or more of the Adlet apparently returned to the icy lands of its mother and has since preyed on its mother's people.

Adze   In southern Togo (formerly the Slave Coast of Africa), on the west coast of that vast continent, there is a cult of sorcerers of the Ewe tribe who become voluntarily possessed by a vampiric spirit called Adze. The Adze is a deliberate theriomorph—shape-shifting by magic and will into various insect forms such as a firefly, common fly, or large mosquito. These diminutive forms are so common and innocuous that they can bypass any posted guard or watchful eye. This makes the Adze one of the world's most dangerous vampires in that it is nearly impossible to notice and therefore equally difficult to stop.

Though their base form is that of a human sorcerer, once the Adze spirit has been accepted the witch becomes a living vampire whose powers are sustained and even enhanced by a regular diet of innocent blood. Children—especially infants—are its special prey, and the Adze does more than feed on their blood. It is a carrier of disease as well.

In rare cases when the Adze is caught it will instantly revert back to its human form, and through keen observation or by methods of divination the villagers sometimes recognize the person as someone who is possessed of this inner evil. In human form, the Adze can be killed by any ordinary means, and is sometimes given over to the families of a child who has suffered from the monster's bite. The punishment the Adze suffers at the hands of vengeful family members is often quite terrible and does not end quickly.

If an Adze is denied its normal food of children's blood, it can sustain itself on coconut milk, palm oil, or juice from ripe fruits; but on this diet it will gradually become weaker. When its strength begins to fail, the Adze may go into a feeding frenzy and consume all of the coconut water in the district, leaving the villagers parched. Or it will drink up all of the palm oil, leaving the villagers with no oil for their lamps.

If an Adze is able to feed regularly, it sometimes settles into a pattern of taking only what it needs to survive. When denied or deterred, the creature's spiteful side emerges. In such cases it may seek to inhabit the body of a particularly virulent disease-carrying fly so that it will intentionally start the spread of a plague.

⊰ DIVINATION ⊱

"Divination" is a general term for any of a large number of methods by which cultures around the world glean information from supernatural or celestial sources. Divination is still practiced today in even the most modern of cultures. Tarot cards, palmistry, astrology, and many other forms are part of our everyday life. Here are just a few methods of divination:

AEROMANCY: Divination by the study of the sky.

ALEUROMANCY: The study of the patterns of flour in a bowl into which some water has been added.

ANTHROPOMANCY: Reading the future through human sacrifice where the entrails of a victim are studied.

ASTRAGLOMANCY: Divination in which dice bearing various letters and numbers are used.

AUSTROMANCY: The observation or study of the wind for purposes of divination.

BIBLIOMANCY: In which a book, usually the Bible or other sacred text, is opened and a passage is read at random and the passage studied for possible significance.

CARTOMANCY: Divination through the use of cards.

CATOPTROMANCY: The practice of gazing at a reflection of the moon in a mirror.

CAUSIMOMANCY: Divination by fire.

CEPHALOMANCY: Literally "head divination," this practice involves using the head of goat or donkey to predict future events.

CERAUNOSCOPY: The observation of thunder, lightning, and other features of the atmosphere to predict future events.

CLAIRAUDIENCE: Also "clear hearing," this is the perception of voices and sounds outside of the normal spectrum of hearing.

CLAIRVOYANCE: Meaning "clear seeing," the perception of visions beyond the normal spectrum of sight. Also a form of ESP.

CRYSTALLOMANCY: The observations of crystals for divination; also referred to as *scrying.*

DEMONOMANCY: When the aid of demons is used for purposes of divination.

DOWSING: The use of a "divining rod" or forked stick to find sources of water or precious minerals beneath the Earth's soil.

GELOSCOPY: Divination by examining the tones and nuances of someone's laughter.

HEPTASCOPY: Predicting the future by examining the entrails of various types of animals.

ICHTYOMANCY: Examing the entrails of fish to predict future events.

METAGNOMY: Practitioners of this craft study visions that come to them while in a trancelike state to predict future events.

METEOROMANCY: Divination by the notation and the study of the appearance and behavior of meteors.

NUMEROLOGY: The study of numbers, dates, times, and values assigned to various letters of the alphabet for purposes of divination.

OMPHALOMANCY: The practice of counting the amount of knots in the umbilical cord to predict how many children a woman may have in her lifetime.

OOMANTIA: Also called *ooscopy* and *ovomancy*, it is divination by the examination of various types of eggs.

OPHIOMANCY: Divination by observing the behavior of snakes.

PHYSIOGNOMY: This practice of divination works by examining a person's physical features.

SCIOMANCY: The employment and use of "spirit guides" to predict the outcome of future events.

TASSEOGRAPHY: The famous practice of "reading tea leaves."

TIROMANCY: Divination by the study of cheese.

XYLOMANCY: Despite its musical-sounding name, this practice of divination concerns observing the behavior of wood while it burns.

Agogwe   In the East African nation of Tanzania there is a legend of a creature that bears a strong resemblance to wildmen such as the Yeti and Bigfoot, though much smaller. The Agogwe stands only four feet tall and is completely covered in thick rust-colored hair like that of a yak. His shoulders and arms are heavy with muscle and his head sits low on a short, thick neck pitched forward like a gorilla's.

The Agogwe is rarely seen and most sightings date back seventy or eighty years, but every once in a while a child will go missing and there will be blood on the ground and the villagers will start whispering the name "Agogwe."

A similar creature, the *Sehité*, has been reported in the Ivory Coast.

Agta (also **Agra)**   Supernatural predators generally prey on humans, but not all of these predators are evil. The Agta of the Philippines is one such creature. This bizarre creature is known for smoking fat cigars and loitering around streams where fishermen tend to congregate; the Agta is a great boon to fishermen. The Agta is a very strange species of essential vampire that feeds off of the life energies of fish, which is why it hangs around fishing holes and often leads fishermen to the best spots. When a fish is hooked and killed, the Agta feeds off of the release of its life force just as the fisher will feed on the flesh. It is one of the strangest examples of symbiosis known to man.

One of the many quirky aspects of this creature is that the only way in which someone can actually *see* the Agta is if they bend over and look backward through their legs. No good spiritual reason for this has ever been revealed, but this quirk is shared by the *Dwende* as well.

Ahool   The Ahool is a gigantic batlike creature that has been spotted off and on for nearly a century in western Java. The Ahool has a head like an ape, huge dark eyes, and a fur-covered body that is about the size of a small child, and it flies around on powerful wings twelve feet across. The largest known bat, the flying fox, only has a six-foot wingspan.

The Ahool is generally timid, preferring to hunt for fish and small mammals, but there are reports of it chasing hunters and frightening fishermen so badly that they overturned their boats. The creature is said to live in caves behind waterfalls and may only be acting aggressively to protect its nest.

Akhkharu (also **Akakharu)**   Vampirism has been part of our worldwide human belief system since the earliest days of recorded history, and very likely for many centuries before that. Vampires—or creatures such as demons, witches, gods, and ghosts that have preyed viciously on humans—fill the ancient stories and songs of the first cultures.

Ancient Assyria, one of the oldest documented cultures, suffered from plagues of vampires 6,000 years ago, and these monsters of the ancient world were no less terrible than the fiends of more recent times. One of the oddest of the ancient Assyrian monsters was the essential vampire called the Akhkharu. This seductress vampire fed on the life essence of its victims, using sexuality as a true weapon and—for all intents and purposes—"loving" her victims to death. Like the Succubus of later myth, the Akhkharu was a creature of irresistible sexual appeal who would seduce her victim and over time drain him of all vitality, potency, breath, blood, and leave him a withered and dead husk.

The Akhkharu herself grew younger with each feeding and reached the point of perfect health at the moment of her victim's death. From then on she would begin to age again, slightly faster than a normal human, until she began feeding on another unwilling victim.

Algul　The Arabian deserts are often empty and desolate during the long days, but the cooler nights are filled with creatures of all kinds—both natural and supernatural. The night is the hunting time for most desert dwellers, and the Algul is as hungry and determined a night-hunter as anything that runs, slithers, or flies. The name means "horse leech," and this monster is not a resurrected corpse but an evil spirit, a *jinn*, who takes the form of a woman in order to win the confidence of untended children. But there are no traces of motherly concern in the Algul—she is a blood-drinking monster.

Much like a traditional vampire, the Algul often haunts cemeteries and places where death has occurred or where blood has been spilled; but she is not confined there, and by the dark of night she slips through windows or through tent flaps in search of sleeping children, taking either blood or breath—and sometimes both. At other times she plays the trickster and lures children into the dark where she can feast on their flesh as well. When the Algul can't get fresh blood, she'll feast on the flesh of newly buried corpses to sustain her, preferably the corpses of children or pregnant women.

The Algul is a wretched monster—heartless, cruel, and sly. One of her favorite tricks is to mimic the cry of a wounded traveler calling out for help and then attacking anyone coming to investigate. In the regions of the Algul, curiosity will kill more than just the cat.

The Algul has been written about for centuries, most notably in *The Thousand and One Nights*.

Allghoi Khorkhoi   With an imposing nickname such as the Mongolian Death Worm it's no wonder that the Allghoi Khorkhoi has earned such a dreadful reputation. This monster is a huge snakelike creature about three to four feet in length that can kill faster than a cobra. Stories vary as to just how the Allghoi Khorkhoi accomplishes its quick kills—surviving witnesses are few. Some report that it kills by spitting lethal venom that works like a neurotoxin; other tales suggest that it kills with an electric discharge not unlike an eel's. In either case, its attack is rumored to be potent enough to instantly drop a man or even a horse. Added to its lethal armament is a skin that secretes an oily poison that can kill any person unwise enough to touch it. Who would *want* to fondle such a beast is another matter.

The Allghoi Khorkhoi, first reported in 1929, is fortunately a rare creature that lives in the remote southern reaches of the Gobi desert. It lives deep in the hearts of sand dunes and generally preys only on desert animals, but will extend its diet to include unwary travelers if they happen by.

The literal translation of its name is "intestine worm," and it gets this gruesome appellation from the bruised reddish purple coloring of his hide, which looks like an intestine.

Though it may only be a naturally evolving creature that has not yet been added to the classifications of known animals, it also has ties to the supernatural in that many Mongolians believe that a mere mention of its name can bring bad luck resulting in sickness or death.

Alp (also **Alp, Doggele, Doggi, Druckerl, Drückermannchen, Drud**)

Every so often the difference between vampire, ghost, and demon is hazy. In many cases it overlaps, as in the case of the lethal German monster, the Alp. The world "Alp" translates as, "shining white one," and it is one of the most feared (and indeed most common) supernatural predators in Europe. Some myths maintain that the Alp is the returning spirit of a man who has died under horrific circumstances, such as murder or suicide; others suggest that it is the vampiric specter of a child who died before he could be baptized. There are also those who believe that the Alp is not a ghost at all but rather a particularly vicious demon, but whichever version of its origin is accurate, they all agree that the Alp is a voracious blood drinker and one that is nearly impossible to kill.

Like the Incubus, the Alp typically preys mainly on women, appearing first in dreams and then manifesting in the corporeal world to drink their blood or, in some cases, to nurse at their breasts in order to drink their breast milk. From this milk it derives tremendous power and at the same time deprives the woman's child of his or her rightful sustenance. Sometimes the Alp drinks both milk and blood from its victim's nipples, thereby weakening her and making her vulnerable to disease, depression, and despair. The Alp may also assault men and young boys for blood, similarly feeding at the nipple, though this is far less frequent.

When the Alp has fed but left its prey alive, the victims have suffered from horrific nightmares and in many cases, a wasting sickness.

In all of its many aberrant manifestations, the Alp wears a *tarnkappe* ("cap of concealment"), which gives it a variety of magical powers, including invisibility. If the hat is stolen, the Alp loses this power of concealment and its powers are reduced. In such cases the Alp can be driven out by prayers or spells, though actually destroying the creature appears to be impossible.

The Alp's most formidable weapon against its human prey is its "evil eye," with which the Alp can trouble the dreams of the living. The Alp is also a theriomorph. It most often appears as a moth or butterfly, but is able to assume a variety of animal forms, including birds, dogs, and wolves, and in some cases it can transform into a cold mist. Some folktales link the Alp to tales of werewolves because of this shape-shifting capability.

Since destroying the Alp is impossible, various methods have been devised to try to discourage this creature. Women are instructed to sleep with their shoes placed by the side of the bed with the toes facing outward toward the door. Scissors can also be placed under one's pillow with the points facing toward the head of the bed. Either method will deter the Alp because for some reason it will become confused, turn away from the sleeper, and back out the door. Another popular deterrent is to take a large sack of seed and pour some in the center of a crossroads with thin trails of them laid along the center of each of the four off-shooting ways. Like many vampires, the Alp will feel compelled to count them; because the seeds go off in all directions the Alp will get thoroughly confused and sit there weeping in frustration until dawn when it must slink away to seek a resting place. In those rare times when an Alp can be cornered or caught sleeping, it can only be deterred by filling its mouth with lemons. This does not kill it, but it weakens the creature considerably and it may not be able to resume the hunt for months or even years. It will, however, ultimately return and generally will not be in a forgiving mood when it reappears.

⊰ EVIL EYE ⊱

The Evil Eye is a wicked spiritual ability allowing a person to cause harm or illness to another merely by looking at them. It appears in one form or another throughout the world, and most cultures have some traditional charm or amulet that serves as a protective against this curse.

Alukah   The ancient Hebrews had trouble with a fierce predator called the Alukah, whose name translates as "horse leech." This monster was either a human who could change into a wolf or other predator, or a demon (very probably of Babylonian vintage) who took human form as a disguise.

The horse leech is also an actual insect parasite, often found in and around Palestine, that was lapped up by horses when they drank from contaminated wells or streams. It grew to larger size and lodged in the throats of the animals. Historians believe that legend of an evil, shape-shifting Alukah is nothing more than a less scientifically evolved culture attempting to explain the nature of this deadly parasite. Folklorists, on the other hand, contend that the Alukah *took* the form of a leech as one of its many disguises.

In either case, the Alukah has become the model for grasping behavior. In Proverbs 30:15–16 (KJV)[7] there is the following enigmatic reference to the monster:

> **15.** *The horseleach hath two daughters, crying, Give, give. There are three things that are never satisfied, yea, four things say not, It is enough:*
> **16.** *The grave; and the barren womb; the earth that is not filled with water; and the fire that saith not, It is enough.*

In either case, the Alukah is a destructive monster and one that has been feared for thousands of years.

Aluqa   Many of the demons that plague men act through a human agent, but there are some who take a far more personal approach. The Aluqa is one of the most ferocious of these. She is both a succubus—draining her victims of sexual essence and potency—and a psychic vampire—who drives her victims so mad with frustration and shame that they often commit suicide.

Many folktales of the Aluqa have been confusingly merged with those of the ancient Hebrew vampire Lilith,[8] but they are not at all the same creature.

---

7. Kings James Version.
8. See *Lilith*, page 198, for the complete story.

When depicted, Aluqa is often presented as a woman of surpassing beauty with a face that has the appearance of pure innocence, but a serpent coils in her heart. Being a demon she cannot be killed, but fervent prayers can drive her off. Sleeping with a nail under one's pillow has been shown to be a potent deterrent, lending even more weight to the belief that there is great defensive power in cold iron.

In a number of folktales the Aluqa legend is overlapped with that of the Alukah, and the name is often given the same translation, "horse leech." As with many of the legends of monsters, gods, and demons that grew out of ancient Assyria and Mesopotamia and evolved into the early stories of the Hebrew culture, the Aluqa and Alukah may indeed have sprung from the same historical sources. Then as cultures rose and peoples moved from place to place, the legends became splintered and over time evolved into their own enduring versions.

Andandará   A strange race of evil were-cats of sixteenth-century Spanish legend were said to seek out human women with whom to mate, producing both human and feline offspring. The Andandará kill with their lethal stare, though they can certainly use fangs and claws with equal effectiveness. The very presence of an Andandará can cause crop failure, disease, and ill fortune.

Angiak   In centuries past when hard times and famine struck the Inuit people of what is now Alaska, another young mouth to feed was a hardship that could endanger the survival of the entire family and the unwanted child was sometimes taken out into the remote snowfields and left to die. After the poor child died its spirit sometimes returned as a vengeful revenant called an Angiak who sneaks into the camp and suckles each night at its mother's breast while she sleeps. This feeding helps it gain strength, and when it becomes strong enough, it starts openly attacking the elders of the family, taking various fierce animal forms.

Animalito   The bizarre Animalito of Spain is a water predator, much like the *Dames Blanche* (White Ladies) of Fau in France, the *Grindylow* of Great Britain, and the *Kappa* of Japan. Animalito means "small animal" in Spanish, and as the name suggests the creature is diminutive and bestial, standing no more than two or three feet high, with a dark reptilian body and a canine snout for its mouth. Agile and swift, the Animalitos attack swimmers and bathers, biting at submerged body parts and feasting hastily and hungrily on the flowing blood.

In centuries past, when a common care for just about any ill would be to bleed a patient, wizard-healers would use Animalitos like leeches to rectify the humors. However, the creatures were known for developing an addiction to the blood of specific patients and would seek them out long after they were discharged from the healer's care.

Though supernatural, the Animalitos may be destroyed by any common method used to kill a small animal, and will also choke to death on waters polluted with oil. The difficult part is catching one of these elusive monsters, since they possess a cunning ruthlessness, swim with the supple trickery of otters, and are as ferocious as sharks.

Anito (also Mamangkiks and Cancaniaos)   These are "spirits of the mound," a kind of nosferatu from the Philippines who rise from the grave as formless vapors and spread sickness. For the most part the Anito stick close to their burial mounds and are therefore not much of a threat, but if some unlucky person were to disturb either the mound or the clinging vapor, then the Anito would breathe sickness into that person. The sickness manifests as a spread of boils, but soon infects the lungs and blood, and if the will of the Anito is strong enough, the sickness can be fatal.

There is a protective chant that announces to the creatures that a person has no intention of doing harm or interfering with the grave. That chant goes: "tabi-tabi po . . . makikiraan lang," which translates roughly as "Honored spirit, please step aside—I'm just passing through." This is spoken when a person is walking at night, just in case an Anito's spirit is blowing by on the breeze.

If a child accidentally collides with an Anito and incurs its anger, parents of the afflicted child place offerings of fruit near the mound they believe is home to the spirit.

As the Anito sometimes claims all of the territory around its mound as its own, great care is used before cutting down any trees near any mound—whether it is a burial mound or a simple hillock. Prayers of appeasement and offerings of fruit are used to secure the Anito's permission to cut the trees.

Aniukha   One of the rarest of the world's vampires is the little-known Aniukha of Siberia. This creature was most recently sighted by Jews exiled to the frozen forests and icy wastes of that remote land following World War II, and in their accounts the creatures ranged from the size of a large grasshopper to about the size of a rabbit. The Aniukha runs on all fours like a woodland mammal, but it can also stand erect and leap great distances much like a cat. Its body is covered in pale scales with patches of sparse dark brown fur. It has huge dark eyes, pointed ears, and a short snout filled with jagged teeth.

The creature, though odd-looking, is not physically powerful and relies on cunning and trickery in order to hunt, and also chooses the easiest prey: young children and the sick or very old.

The Aniukha is repelled by garlic, and those who dwell in those remote areas know that smearing garlic in a circle over the sternum will insure a safe night's sleep. Likewise, daubing garlic around doorways and windows will keep the creature out. However, nothing but fire can kill the beast.

Anjing Ajak   In the Indonesian nation of Java there is a ferocious lycanthrope called the Anjing Ajak who lives as a normal man by day but when the sun sets he undergoes a deliberate transformation into a vicious *Wolf-Man* that goes about on two legs and savages its victims with teeth and talons.

Though the Anjing Ajak is not particularly difficult to kill—a single bullet to the heart or brain will do the job—it is smart and tricky, and its viciousness is seldom paralleled in either the natural or supernatural world.

Apotamkin Among the Maliseet-Passamaquoddy Indian tribe of the Pacific Northwest there are legends of a race of ferocious wildmen with hairy bodies and long fangs that hunt on the fringes of tribal society. These creatures, called the Apotamkin, hunt singly or in packs, and though their prey is often deer and other game, they do consider humans to be part of their diet.

The Apotamkin stand taller than a man, with heavy shoulders, long arms, and thick orange-brown hair that covers their entire bodies. They have faces that are often described as apelike, though in some tales they are given snouts like wolves. The cry of the Apotamkin can cause a heart to freeze and die in the chest, and the sight of one is sometimes enough to cause heart attacks or strokes. Parents use tales of the Apotamkin as a kind of Bogeyman story to caution children about the dangers of straying too far from home or talking to strangers.

Among the Alsea, also of Oregon and surrounding areas, there is a similar legend, that of *Asin,* a female monster who bears such a strong resemblance to the Apotamkin that some believe that she may be one of their young. Young or not, however, the Asin is every bit as bloodthirsty and ferocious as the adult Apotamkin.

Asasabonsam (also **Asanbosam)** Imagine walking through the darkened paths of the jungle, perhaps heading back to your village after seeing to the livestock, and suddenly a creature reaches down out of the trees and drags you off the ground before tearing at you with long taloned fingers and biting with wickedly sharp teeth made of iron! The Asasabonsam also has strange hook-like legs, much like those of a praying mantis, with which it holds its victims while it feeds. In all other ways, though, the Asasabonsam looks human and at times can even blend in with a group of humans, especially if the light is poor. That is the hunting tactic of the Asasabonsam, the fierce vampire predator spoken of in legends of the Ashanti people of Ghana as well as in chilling accounts from Togo and the Ivory Coast.

The creatures dwell in the forests of West Africa and are masters of concealment, hiding in the leaves of the trees and waiting for travelers or farmers to pass by. Or they may hide in bushes and shrubs that line the paths through the woods and grab the ankles of passers-by. In either case, the Asasabonsam then drags the victim off to a secluded spot and uses its iron teeth to tear out the throat, open the chest, and begin feeding. First it drinks the blood as it spurts, then as the heart stills and the blood no longer flows, the Asasabonsam sets to eating the flesh of its prey. What it can't finish in one sitting it casts to the ground, leaving body parts like scraps for wild animals.

The Asasabonsam is a malicious being and enjoys the hunt as much as the kill, often prolonging the moment of attack so that it can entertain itself by hunting a fleeing human. Like a cat, the Asasabonsam sometimes catches, releases, and catches again, delighting in the power it has over its prey.

Some Asasabonsam use other kinds of trickery, such as mimicking the plaintive cry of a child in the manner of a *Calling Ghost,* waiting in the dark for a concerned parent, a Good Samaritan, or another child to come to investigate, and then killing the good-natured helper. It is a well-known trick of the Asasabonsam to use imitations of human calls—child or adult—to lure villagers or travelers away from their campfires at night. The unwise person who goes to investigate is seldom seen again, or at least seldom seen *alive* again.

In some parts of the same region of Ghana there is a different version of the Asasabonsam story. In this alternate version the Asasabonsam seldom kills outright but instead comes at night to bite the thumb of a sleeping person, taking some blood but not enough to kill. The creature may return the following night, and many nights thereafter, until the victim has been slowly drained of blood and, eventually, of life. These nighttime visits often have a secondary effect in that the bite of the Asasabonsam is either poisonous or it carries disease, the latter being the most likely.

This habit of biting the thumb links the Asasabonsam with the feeding habits of some species of vampire bats. Though bats rarely prey on humans, in the rare cases when they do the thumb is a likely target for a bat bite because its large, exposed, and bleeds freely. Bats are a well-documented disease vector, and depending on your personal stance on the existence of supernatural vampires, the hunting tactics of the bat and the Asasabonsam of Ghana are either similarities from species that share common qualities, or evidence of how a superstition can grow out of a natural event.

Asema   Throughout the Caribbean there are a number of very similar vampiric creatures that are more or less human by day, but by night undergo a startling transformation. Known as the *Loogaroo* in Haiti and the *Sukuyan* in Trinidad, the Asema of Surinam is a bizarre creature that was probably brought to the New World with slaves captured from among the Fo peoples of Benin, where it is known as the *Aziman*. There are subtle differences culture to culture, but the essential creature is the same.

By day the Asema takes the form of an ancient crone who looks frail and helpless, but when the sun goes down the Asema sheds its skin and becomes a ball of fiery blue light that instantly takes to the air seeking prey. Once it locates a victim—generally someone out walking alone—the Asema descends like a thunderbolt, knocking the victim to the ground and feasting on blood and life essence.

Like many of the world's vampires, the Asema has a manic fixation with counting seeds. Consequently, a wary person will often strew seeds, grains, or rice and even small nails on the ground in a spot that is likely to attract the Asema, which feels compelled to stop and count each one and as a result wastes the whole of the night. If the Asema is caught by the rising sun it will evaporate into nothingness, making it one of the very few vampires in the world that can be destroyed by sunlight. Most European vampires are not so

⍃ BATS ⍄

Bats can be found nearly everywhere in the world except in areas of extreme heat or extreme cold, and they live on every continent except Antarctica. In the United States the greatest number of bat species can be found in the southwestern states. Texas alone has 32 different species; Arizona has 28. The 952 species of bats currently extant make up about 20 percent of all known living mammal species.

Though bats are tied to folklore, especially that of vampires, they are not particularly aggressive toward humans in real life. For example, they don't get caught in your hair (a silly old myth), they aren't blind, and they don't all carry rabies (they're actually quite clean little critters).

Bat species are divided into two major suborders, Megachiroptera and Microchiroptera. Megachiroptera has only one family, Pteropodidae, and about 166 species. All of them feed on plant material, either fruit, nectar, or pollen; Microchiroptera has 16 families (around 759 species) and these are predominantly insect eaters. One sub-family of this latter grouping has three species that are blood-drinkers. The classic vampire bat (*Desmodus rotundus*) is one of these.

easily dispatched, though they often share the obsession with counting seeds.

Another method of disposing of the Asema requires a little more effort and daring. If someone were to track down the Asema's lair and steal its skin, and then take that skin and boil it so that it shrinks, then the returning Asema will be unable to put its skin suit back on in time to avoid the rays of the rising sun.

A few of the various Asema legends argue a different view of sunlight and its effects on the creature. In more urban folktales of the Asema it is believed that the sunlight does little more than weaken the monster and that come sunset it regains its strength. In these beliefs it is stressed that only destruction of the skin will have any lasting effect because it needs to return to its skin in order to rest. Without that respite its energies will gradually become dissipated and it will fade into oblivion.

Asin   In the Pacific Northwest, home to the Alsea Indian people, there is a legend of a murderous creature called the Asin. The creature is variously believed to be a demon in human form or a female of a species of woodland monsters. In either case, the Asin appears as a monstrous girl—feminine in basic form, but covered with hair and possessing taloned fingers and teeth like those of a wolf.

The Asin preys on the fringes of communities, watching for children who stray too far from their homes or who are left unattended. When the Asin sees an opportunity she rushes in, snatches up the child, and vanishes back into the woods at great speed to feast on the helpless child.

One legend recounts that Asin bewitched the fruit of the huckleberry bush so that any child who ate them would become entranced and would wander off into the woods, where the Asin would be waiting. For that reason the Alsea banned anyone from eating huckleberries.

The Asin myth overlaps to some degree with that of the Apotamkin of the Maliseet-Passamaquoddy tribe, with the exception that the Apotamkin is often seen as a large hairy male, much in keeping with creatures such as the *Shampe* and *Sasouatch*.

Asuang (also Aswang and Aswang Mananaggal)   The Asuang is one of the fiercest of the Filipino monsters, and certainly the most clever. In its true form, the Asuang is an ordinary man or woman who has taken up the dark arts and learned the foulest secrets of sorcery. Through magical practices the Asuang acquires vast supernatural abilities, the most startling of which is its ability to change shape at will.

The Asuang can become a bull, dog, cat, bird, even an insect. Unlike werewolves who transform from human to a wolf of equal mass, the Asuang changes its actual mass. Where this extra mass goes to or comes from is unknown.

To determine if an animal is, in fact, a transformed Asuang requires a person to do the one thing that no one *should* do: get close and stare it right in the eye. The eyes of the Asuang are fiery and red-veined, and there is the unmistakable presence of human intelligence. Sadly, the discovery that Rover or Elsie the Cow is actually a shape-shifting monster is often the last discovery a person is likely to make, because the Asuang is a foul-tempered meat-eating predator.

The Asuang has often been described as a kind of vampire, but this is incorrect. It is far more closely related to the werewolf in that it changes shape and eats meat. Like the true werewolves

MANANAMBAL
(Enemy of the Asuang) Ken Meyer

of Europe, the Asuang keeps its human mind and memories when in beast-shape, though it does gain the animal's cunning and instinct as well, making it the most fearsome of predators.

When the Asuang makes a kill it generally drags its victim back to its lair and then settles down to a grisly feast, favoring the liver as the choicest delicacy. It will drink the blood to wash down the meat, but it is not primarily a blood-drinker: that's just a nasty side effect of consuming a living human.

The Asuang has its vulnerabilities, though, and chief among them is an absolute dread of garlic. The sight of a garlic bulb is enough to chase the Asuang off, the smell of garlic can render it powerless, and garlic oil is fatal. The Asuang also has an aversion to various kinds of metal, which is why travelers often keep a lucky coin in their pocket. Just the proximity of a single coin can make the Asuang so weak it cannot lift its prey.

If a witch has been an Asuang for a very long time it undergoes other changes, and in its most advanced form the creature can literally rip its head, torso, and entrails free from its body and fly through the air, dripping gore. In this most hideous of forms it is the most powerful and can kill with a shriek or a single bite. This head and entrails form is very similar to the *Kephn* of Burma, the *Mjertovjec* of Belarus, and the gruesome *Penanggalan* of India, as well as monsters in Vietnam and other torrid climates.

The unique cry of the Asuang, a strange *kik-kik* noise, has compelling supernatural properties, and when a person hears it they are drawn inexorably to the creature. Only by fingering a coin in one's pocket can a person escape.

Unlike other kinds of witch-monsters, the Asuang does not become a monster by choice: the Asuang curse is a side effect of certain kinds of magical practices—a kind of spiritual sickness from which there is no known cure. The descent into total evil is unstoppable.

A person can also be forcibly transformed into an Asuang by another of that species. To do this an Asuang creeps up on a person and breathes its foul breath down the back of the unsuspecting person's neck. This causes a kind of spiritual infection that sparks the transformation. Once the transformation from true human to Asuang has taken place, the Asuang retains all of its memories and personality traits, but these are governed by a new, supernatural intelligence. It is like two minds—one demonic and one human—becoming a single mind.

The Asuang is self-aware, of course, and never hunts in its own village. Instead, it flies through the sky to other towns to hunt. Some Asuang choose not to hunt at all, but use animal familiars (typically crocodiles) to hunt for them. These less active Asuang are called Hayopan.

Fighting the Asuang requires cunning and great knowledge, and the most effective enemy of the monster is also the antithesis of the sorcerer—a village shaman or healer, called a "Mananambal." This healer is skilled at potion making and can make drafts lethal to the monster; but more often the Mananambal focuses on preventative salves and charms, many of which are garlic based. Some Mananambal have even been known to cure the Asuang—separating the demon and the human, but this is a dangerous process that seldom works.

Atraiomen   The Carib[9] people tell a story of how they became scattered throughout so many islands, and at the heart of the tale is a terrible monster called the Atraiomen. This creature was once a "Callínemeti," a "very peaceful man," and was very popular among his people but his sons were deeply jealous of their father and shared none of his peaceful, easygoing ways. One day they ambushed him while he was getting ready to go fishing, murdered him, and threw his body into the ocean.

Something happened to this peaceful man as his body floated out to sea and decayed. His soul was released, but somehow it had become corrupted and twisted and the Callínemeti entered into the body of a fish, transforming it into a fierce man-killer called the Atraiomen.

In this awful form the Atraiomen pursued his sons with such wild aban-

9. "Carib" is a name given to these people by Europeans. They refer to themselves either as Callinago in the men's language and Calliponam in the "women's language," while Callínemeti was "a good peaceful man." A more common phonetic spelling is Kalinago.

don that anyone who got in his way was slaughtered. Fearing the wrath of this monster, the people deserted their islands and fled across the water, hoping to escape from its hunting grounds. And this is how the Caribs explain why their people are so widely scattered.

It is not known whether the Atraiomen ever caught up with his traitorous children, but the legends say that the monster still hunts the seas between the islands.

Aufhocker   The name "Aufhocker" means "leap upon" and that certainly describes this monstrous canine from German folklore. The Aufhocker is a hulking brute of a dog that walks about on its hind legs (much like a Wolf-Man) and tears the throats out of its victims. The creature is often found in the vicinity of a crossroads, waiting for hapless travelers.

The Aufhocker is a theriomorph who can also take the form of other animals and, in rare cases, of humans; and some folklorists claim that it has no true shape at all, being a spirit that only adopts animal form in order to kill.

The Aufhocker cannot be killed, but the rising of the sun or the tolling of a church bell can scare it away as it can abide neither.

$$\mathcal{B}$$

Bagat   Many of the world's supernatural predators either appear as a monstrous dog, or assume that shape through transformation. This pack of hellhounds includes the *Eng-Banka* of Malaysia, the *Kludde* of Belgium, the *Otgiruru* of Namibia, the *Qiqirn* of the Eskimo, the *Sukuyan* of Trinidad, the *Upor* of Poland and its close relative the *Upyr* of Russia, the fierce *Barghest* of Great Britain, the Transylvanian *Murony*, and several Filipino monsters, including the *Aswang*, the *Pugut*, and *Bagat*.

Unlike many of its cousins, the Bagat is not always evil or even malicious, but it is easily offended. If it—or any dog in its vicinity—is either deliberately injured or harmed through carelessness, the Bagat becomes enraged and will attack with terrible ferocity. A corpse found along the side of the road, savaged and torn, is generally believed to be the leavings of this hulking beast.

Luckily, the Bagat is a creature who favors lonely and remote places and one seldom encounters it. It loves to hunt at night and during the full moon, or during storms. If one should spot one of these monsters, a quick prayer and a change of direction are both advised.

Baital   India has hundreds of gods and demons, and many supernatural predators that may have qualities of one or the other. Some of these monsters are steeped in its ancient religions and some dwell only in regional folktales.

One of the strangest and most frightening of the Indian predators is the brutal Baital. This creature is a grotesque patchwork, half-bat and half-man. Though short in stature (the Baital only stands about four feet tall) it is fierce and clever, and it delights in drinking human blood.

The Baital is also something of a trickster and in the *Baital-Pachisi,* or *Twenty-Five Tales of a Baital,* an ancient Hindu text written in Sanskrit, there is a long account of how King Vikram (the Hindu equivalent of Britain's King Arthur, also called Vikramaditya) promised a Yogi that he would bring him one of the Baital. King Vikram found one of the creatures hanging from a tree and managed to subdue it, but maintaining control over the Baital was another matter. This trickster vampire challenged King Vikram to keep totally silent while the monster narrated a series of stories (both moral and philosophical); but as he finished each tale he asked the king for his opinion. Naturally, to answer meant to break silence and the Baital was released. The king had to go back, regain control, and start over again—each time with a new tale. Each time his attempt to answer the creature's questions resulted in the monster being released from Vikram's control.

Bajang   Vampires who either transform into cats or transform from cats into the semblance of human beings are to be found all throughout Asia. The

Bajang of Malaysia is one such monster, and it is a creature born from despair and sudden death into an unnatural life of murder and predation.

As far back as the oldest of recorded human cultures there have been legends built around the angry ghosts of stillborn male infants who return to the world of the living to cause great harm. The Assyrians and Mesopotamians had the horrible Ekimmu, and in recent centuries there are dreadful tales of the *Pontianak* of Java, the *Ohyn* of Poland, *Pret* of India, and the Bajang of Malaysia. The Bajang, however, does not just rise from the corpse of a stillborn baby, but is deliberately invoked and consigned to the form of a polecat or other hunting feline. In that beast-shape it becomes the eternal familiar of the witch or warlock who invoked it.

The Bajang has two methods of attack. When left to feed on its own, the creature will feed on flesh and blood; but when it is directed by its master to a specific target, it will infect its master's enemies with a terrible wasting illness that, if not diagnosed and treated correctly, is fatal.

After the Bajang has been called forth into flesh it is kept in a bamboo vessel called a *tabong*; and is protected by various spells and charms and closed by a stopper made from special leaves grown and carefully harvested and prepared by the witch. The creature is then kept as both a protector and as a weapon to be used against rivals and enemies. The creature is immortal and is handed down from one generation to the next. While the Bajang is imprisoned in its tabong its unholy appetite is controlled by regular feedings of eggs; but if its master does not keep it well-fed its growing hunger can give the Bajang increased strength and there are plenty of tales of these monsters shattering their bamboo cages and feeding on the flesh of their careless masters.

⊰ FAMILIARS ⊱

Familiars are creatures, either natural or supernatural, with whom a sorcerer or witch has created a psychic bond. Familiars are servants who are used for a variety of tasks ranging from attack to espionage, though most often they are used to carry out spells and bewitchments.

There are two basic kinds of familiars in folklore: animals and imps.

Animal familiars are the most common, especially in European folklore, and may be a cat, toad, owl, mouse, dog, hen, or other creature including insects. In European witchcraft trials if even so much as a housefly entered the court while someone was being tried as a witch it was suspected of being that person's familiar and often sealed the fate of the accused right there.

Imps are supernatural creatures, either demonic or a sub-species of faerie, that have been forced into servitude by the wizard. These creatures must serve their master and often possess potent magic themselves. If the sorcerer makes the mistake of weakening his control over his imp, then the tables are quickly and tragically turned. Imps are not particularly forgiving.

Some vampire species such as the *Nelapsi, Bajang,* and *Talamaur* have also been known to use familiars.

Baka   Shape-shifters are plentiful throughout the world, be they vampires changing into black hens or jaguars, humans becoming wolves, or in the case of the Baka of Benin, a spirit-creature that assumes the shape of any animal it chooses. The Baka is the spiritual essence of a dead person, usually a bokor (dark priest of Vodoun) or someone who demonstrated evil tendencies while alive. After death, the person's spirit undergoes a transformation into a being that is more substantial and powerful than a ghost but not necessarily a demon. This entity then returns to Earth and takes the form of an animal, but it does not act like an ordinary animal. This new creature is a predator that hunts humans and other animals, savages them, and drinks their blood.

The animal form it assumes does not necessarily have to be a powerful one, because the Baka is immensely strong in whatever form it takes. It could appear as something as harmless and unassuming as a chicken and yet still have the power to kill a grown man.

In some tales of the Baka it is not an evil spirit but a vengeance demon that comes back to Earth to kill whomever murdered him; and to accomplish this the Baka takes on the aspect of a nosferatu and spreads disease and pestilence throughout the village where the killer lives, choosing to kill everyone in order to guarantee that the guilty party perishes.

Bakechochin   In Japan there are spirits everywhere. Many of them are either benign or protective; while quite a few are predatory. In the Shinto religion there are a great number of rituals and objects designed to protect the living against the spiteful appetites of the dead. One such object is the Bakechochin, or "haunted lantern." Also called an Obake, the ghost lantern is usually fashioned with doleful eyes and a lolling tongue, and it is made as a kind of birdhouse for evil spirits so that they are drawn there instead of to the houses of the living.

The Bakechochin generally attract the most unsettled of ghosts; those whose spirits are greatly troubled by hatred and thoughts of murder. These impure thoughts prevent the spirits from moving onward into cleaner spiritual realms.

When an Obake is made it is not lit, because setting a candle alight inside one will chase the ghost out and it will immediately attack the first human it encounters. These ghosts are deadly and cruel, and when they attack the person is left looking like they have been mauled by tigers.

Some Bakechochin are both clever and deceitful and if released will kill a person so that it looks like the deed was done by another person, often resulting in an innocent person being arrested for the crime. In this way the ghost destroys two lives with a single act.

Banshee (also Bean-Nighe)   The terrifying and deadly Banshee is known to both Ireland and Scotland and has haunted the nights in both countries for centuries. The Banshee is a "death omen," a creature of the night that appears to herald the coming of death. Though not a predator herself, the Banshee is always around when death—usually violent death—is imminent.

A more accurate name for the Banshee is the Bean-Nighe, which means "little washer by the ford," and refers to one of the many legends of the banshee that she is a tortured soul who died while giving birth. As a result her mind and soul went mad with grief and she is often seen washing bloody clothes by the banks of small remote streams, ostensibly washing away the bloody proof of her own demise.

The Banshee's cry is plaintive and both sad and frightening; but one thing the Banshee does not do is wail. The "wail of the banshee" is a literary device bearing no relation to the centuries of folklore.

The Banshee is seldom seen, but when she is, observers either see a spectral figure floating on the night winds, or a strange hag with glaring eyes, a sharp single front tooth, a single large nostril, pendulous breasts, and great webbed feet. She is horrible to behold and yet some intrepid adventurers have tried to find her because there is a legend that if someone were to suckle at the breast of a banshee they would be granted a single wish and would thereafter be protected by the creature.

Baobhan Sith (also Bobban Sith and Bean Si)   In Scotland the difference between a "vampire" and one of the "faerie folk" is often difficult to distinguish, and the Baobhan Sith—the White Women of the Highlands—are perfect examples. Different tales paint differing pictures of these monsters, but all agree that on first meeting they appear to be women of unimaginable beauty and utterly compelling sexual appeal. No man who beholds one remains unmoved, and most are so enchanted that they will do anything to follow and catch one. As with many of the faerie legends, the Baobhan Sith led them a merry dance, making them lose their way in the woods and driving them to the brink of madness as they flit just beyond reach. If the Baobhan Sith were merely faeries this would not be that bad, because even a lovestruck victim of enchantment can usually find his way home. But the Baobhan Sith are not faerie folk—they are murderous vampires and once they have amused themselves with their hapless followers, they turn and attack.

In many stories the Baobhan Sith are dressed in flowing white gowns, in others they wear gray cloaks over green dresses; and in both cases the long hems of their gowns hide the fact that their legs are hardly the alabaster legs of lovely young women but the hooved and hairy legs of demonic goats.

Some of the Baobhan Sith lure their victims over cliffs in the dark or into deadfalls hidden by ground mist, and then rush to the fallen bodies and feast on the flowing blood welling from wounds received in the fall. In other stories they allow the pursuers to catch up and then turn, taking them in embraces of unbreakable strength, holding them fast while they tear at their victim's throats.

In a few of the older tales of the Baobhan Sith, the creatures feasted not on blood but on life energy and even sexual potency, leaving a man withered and impotent, but alive and capable of feeling wretched about his diminished state.

In no tales are the Baobhan Sith kindly woodland faeries.

These creatures can be killed, however, as elusive and powerful as they are, though it takes a coordinated hunt by strong men with weapons and torches. These hunters generally are led by a seer who can sense the spiritual world as well as the physical. When they track the Baobhan Sith to her forest lair, the hunters form a ring around her and trap her, then one hunter enters the ring and stabs the Baobhan Sith with a pointed iron shaft or a steel sword. A scythe is also effective, but if the creature is not killed on the first swing, she is fast enough to attack the slayer before he can swing again.

The Baobhan Sith will boldly attack any traveler who goes forth on foot, but the creatures are unaccountably terrified of horses and will often flee from them. A pack of hunters on horses, therefore, have a decidedly higher chance of running this monster down.

Barbegazi In the mountains that connect Switzerland to France there is a strange race of beast-men called the Barbegazi, whose name means "frozen beards," and which are only seen in the depths of winter, and then only rarely. When standing still they appear to be men who have been frozen in ice or sculpted out of ice, but when they move it is clear that the ice merely coats their hair and beards, making it look like they are coverd in icicles. They have large flat feet, excellent for walking on snow, and though large they are quick and nimble.

The Barbegazi are generally kindly and will warn climbers of avalanches by uttering a hooting noise, and when they find a traveler suffering from the cold they will carry him to safety and build a fire. However, if a traveler attempts to follow a Barbegazi back to its lair, then the icy bearded fellow will just as likely toss him off the mountain.

Barghest (also spelled **Barguest)** The Hound of the Baskervilles that nearly killed Sherlock Holmes and Doctor Watson was not purely a literary invention of Sir Arthur Conan Doyle. Great spectral *Hellhounds* have long been a part of the folklore of Great Britain, and they appear as death omens. These monstrous hounds come out of the shadows and often chase victims down country lanes, or stand baying in the forest near a home where someone is doomed to die. The howl of the Barghest can be heard on the moors and in the fields in the dead of night.

In some tales, especially those in Yorkshire, these hellhounds actually chase down their prey and kill them with savage teeth, though when the bodies are found the marks have mysteriously vanished. In the West Country the hound's baying is enough to freeze the heart. In southern England the hound is more omen than predator, but is still counted as an evil creature in league with the powers of darkness.

Bas It is a conceit to believe that all of the powers of darkness are directed against humanity. According to many of the world's belief systems, supernatural predators have existed since the creation of the world. Even now not all supernatural predators hunt humans, as demonstrated by the Bas of Malaysia, who hunts livestock.

Among Malaysia's Chewong people there is a strong belief in the existence of a race of vampiric creatures called the Bas who feed almost exclusively on pigs, and when one has moved into the territory it can work its hungry way through a farmer's entire herd and then denude the forest of swine as well. These are hungry beasts who sometimes kill for the sheer pleasure of it even though they've already satisfied their hunger.

Malaysia espouses a number of variations on the Bas legend. The majority of them speak of it as a flesh-eater, but quite a few mention it as a kind of essential vampire that feeds off the *ruwai*, or life energy of its prey, causing a wasting sickness in the animals. In either case, it needs to feed often and it is very hard to stop.

However, if the Bas is denied its preferred food—or if it has already wiped out all of the pigs—it will very often turn to human flesh for sustenance.

Despite its voraciousness, the Bas is not a powerful monster. It attacks quietly and slyly, and shies away from confrontation. It can be chased away by loud noises and the clanging of bells, and because of this, many pig-herds place bells around the necks of their swine. Fire is also used to drive the creature from the vicinity, and smart farmers build campfires and even bonfires when a Bas is thought to be lurking.

There are tales of the Bas ranging back hundreds of years that claim that the Bas is a real monster; but more recently scholars and medical researchers in Malaysia have come to believe that the Bas is a kind of folkloric metaphor for a variety of ordinary communicable diseases, in much the same way as legends of the world's various nosferatu are thought to be the root of many vampire beliefs.[10]

This may, of course, be the truth, but in the deep jungles and remote villages of Malaysia they still clang their bells and build their fires high to ward off this ancient evil.

Bebarlang Vampires seem to haunt every corner of the Philippines and appear in a variety of ghastly forms. These Filipino predators also vary in their method of hunting and in the sustenance they steal from their prey, and vampires that feed on life essence rather than blood are by no means uncommon. One such essential vampire is the Bebarlang.

The Bebarlang is not a revenant or demon: It is a human being who has developed vast psychic powers and who has cultivated the difficult skill of astral projection to a very high degree. The Bebarlang mystic finds a protected shelter for his body and then enters a deep trance from which his spirit can rise and go forth, directed by sheer will. While stout walls and armed servants guard their bodies, the Bebarlang spirit-walkers go searching far and wide for the houses or villages of their enemies. Singly or in concert with others of their kind, the Bebarlang descend onto the village and settle like cloying blankets over their victims and begin feasting on the raw life essence of their prey.

A Bebarlang who has mastered even darker sorceries can actually enter into the sleeping mind of his victim and steal his secrets as well as his life force.

Only the most potent magical charms can prevent the attack of the invisible Bebarlang, and these charms must be specially made. The charm must contain essential elements of the wearer and generally include drops of blood,

10. Chapter Four explores many of the scientific theories behind the pervasive belief in vampires.

bits of hair, and fingernail pairings mixed with wax and mud taken from just outside the person's front door. These materials are fashioned into a small icon of a holy person or angel, then hung over one's bed; or they can be worn around the neck on a cord. This latter method is particularly favored by travelers.

It is very difficult to predict the attack of the Bebarlang, and death sometimes occurs in a single night—though more often the victim is gradually drained of life force and wastes away. Knowing this, the Filipinos who fear the coming of a Bebarlang have charms made in advance and wear them constantly.

Ben Varrey   The Ben Varrey is a murderous mermaid who preys on fishermen along the coastlines of the Isle of Man in the British Isles. Like most traditional mermaids, the Ben Varrey has the upper torso of a beautiful woman, the lower half of a scaly fish, and long golden hair in which water flowers are caught. Her laugh is enchanting and her voice so appealing as she swims close to a boat and whispers enticing promises to the fishermen that the men toss down their nets or rods and leap into the water; at which point the Ben Varrey drag them down into the frigid depths, wedge them between two rocks until they drown, and then eat them. Thoroughly charming.

Berserkir (also **Berserker** and **Berserkr)**   Throughout the Germanic countries there has always been a hazy line between what can be called a werewolf and what is merely a psychological condition in which a person *believes* himself to be a wolf. Nowhere is this distinction more uncertain than in the case of the Viking Berserkirs.

These Berserkirs were the fiercest of fighters, totally unflinching, absolutely committed to battlefield murder. They were extraordinarily strong, resistant to injury, and filled with such a battle rage that just the presence of them on the battlefield was often enough to make enemies break and run.

The Berserkirs covered themselves with animal skins (bear, wolf, etc.) and they fully believed that the spirits of these animals then entered into them and imbued them with animal cunning, power, and a predatory joy of the kill. These men were mentioned frequently in the epic sagas of Norway and Iceland.

While wrapped in their skins the Berserkirs believed that they could not be harmed by sword or fire. Only a wooden club, wielded with great force, could hurt them by smashing their bones or crushing their skulls. When they attacked they howled like wolves. This combative fury became known as the Berserkir (or Berserker) rage, an expression that still lingers in common usage today. The Berserkirs were capable of great savagery, and they often drank the blood of their enemies in order to acquire their power as well.

The Berserkirs believed that Odin—the king of the Norse gods—allowed them to become one with their animal spirits, and so when they fought it was with the belief that their chief god was very much on their side. This combination of intense psychological belief and religious fervor turned them into the deadliest kind of battlefield fanatic. Often Viking attack forces would place a dozen Berserkirs in the forefront of an advancing line to break the enemy formations, and this the Berserkirs did with a complete passion for battle and a fury unmatched by anything human or animal.

Were they truly possessed by the spirits of the great hunting animals, or merely religious fanatics? That's hard to say, but the enemies who looked into the eyes of the Berserkirs as they raced across the battlefield probably saw nothing human there.

⊰ SHAPE-SHIFTERS ⊱

In the excavated ruins of Catal Huyuk in Turkey (formerly Anatolia), cave paintings from 6000 BCE clearly show hunters wearing the skins and heads of animals, suggesting either a real or psychological link with animal predation methods.

Bhayangkara   One of the most ancient vampires in the world, the Bhayang-kara is also the least documented in the English language. Generally referred to as "the awful," the Bhayangkara is a terrible supernatural predator who preys on human and animal alike. Many Tibetan temples make blood offerings to appease the Bhayangkara, else it will ravage the entire village.

Bhuta (also **Bhuts, Bhut,** and **Vetala)**   It's a sad truth but in many cultures a person who is different—deformed, mentally unstable—is often feared because of these differences. Even in advanced cultures many people have an uncomfortable knee-jerk reaction to the deformed, recoiling by reflex as if the deformity is either catching or in some way a threat. In third-world countries, especially in preindustrial eras, deformity was not only considered alien, but also was suspected as being evidence of inner evil.

This prejudicial belief is seldom as sharply defined as with the legends of the Bhuta of India, where it was believed that anyone who was mentally or physically deformed was considered to be a vampire in the making. These unfortunate persons were widely believed to be fated to become a vampire after their death. This seems a pretty harsh celestial punishment for a life already lived in torment.

When these recently deceased persons reawaken as vampires they possess enormous powers, not the least of which is the ability to shape-shift into almost any flying creature, most commonly a bat, owl, or other winged night hunter. Some Bhuta even become fiery balls of light, like a malicious will-o'-the-wisp.

The Bhuta tends to stake a claim around the place where it had been buried or cremated, and eagerly attacks any living person who chances to pass there.

Bhuta are true nosferatu—plague carriers—and though death by disease is not their preferred tactic for killing, they do enjoy the pain and suffering created by the diseases they spread. Their true sustenance is of the most disgusting kind: they feed on the excrement and intestines of newly buried corpses.

Some Bhuta have the demonic power of possession and can take control of a human host and use that body to attack the living. When in their fleshly disguise they prefer to attack suckling babies, biting them to consume the mother's milk the infants had just ingested.

When not possessing a human host, the Bhuta always travel by flying and eschew touching the ground, which is sacred in Hindu beliefs. Sacred ground destroys the Bhuta's power.

Not everyone in India fears the Bhuta; some even worship them, or perhaps they pity them. In any case these devotees construct shrines called bhandara at which those faithful to the Bhuta can worship them; and in which the Bhuta themselves can rest and be protected. Because the Bhuta cannot touch the sacred earth, the bhandara are built on poles well above the dirt.

In some areas, especially those with a high percentage of young children who are still nursing, the bhandara are built not as shrines but as placatory platforms on which bowls of milk and other offerings are left for the Bhuta so the creatures will not attack the village.

In some parts of India the legend of the Bhuta is vastly different, though the two disparate creatures share the same name. The second kind of Bhuta is the vicious ghost of a man who has been violently murdered, executed, or died by suicide, all of which are deaths that leave the spirit unsettled and angry.

Like all Bhuta the spirit of vengeance Bhuta cannot touch the ground and travels by flying, usually in the form of a bird or insect. This Bhuta (also called a Bhut) can speak and has a distinctive and very nasal sound to its voice.

This Bhuta is generally neither appeased nor worshipped by bhandara shrines. Instead it is kept away by burning fresh turmeric in copper bowls. When camping or cooking outdoors, especially for families with little children, a pinch of turmeric tossed into the cookfire will drive off any Bhuta in the neighborhood.

A third species of Bhuta is the Airi and is the ghost of a man slain while hunting. This frustrated and angry ghost hunts for victims in the mountains and jungles, a vicious pack of ghostly dogs at his side. Just catching sight of the Airi can frighten a person to death, but some have survived it. In fact, their survival earned them great notoriety and, according to some tales, the Airi himself bestowed treasure on the survivor, being so impressed by courage of that degree in a human.

Like the Bhuta of the deformed, the Airi Bhuta is appeased by bhandara shrines, and in some remote spots in India temples have even been built to honor these deadly hunters.

Blood Dogs (also **Scots Hounds**) In Scotland and northern England there is a very old legend of massive hounds that haunt the sites of battles and lap up the blood of the fallen. These Blood Dogs coalesce out of morning mist on the day after a battle and then slink around the field, digging in the dirt to get at bloody seepage, and often feasting on the bodies of the unburied dead. Blood Dogs have gray bodies, dark red eyes, and hot breath that can scorch the earth.[11] Despite their hulking size the Blood Dogs leave no mark on the ground and their baying sounds like the wind.

The Scottish version of the story differs slightly from the English version in that the Blood Dogs only fed on English blood, and it is hinted that they are the ghosts of Bonny Prince Charlie's hunting hounds.

Bloody Mary Urban legends are the new folklore and they've spawned their full share of horrific monster tales. Perhaps the most chilling and enduring is that of "Bloody Mary."

The legend has is that if you light some candles and stand in front of a mirror and say "Bloody Mary!" thirteen times it will invoke her spirit. As her name implies Bloody Mary is not a friendly ghost. She is a demented spirit of vengeance, and depending on the version of the story you hear, she will either kill you, scratch out your eyes, drive you insane, or (worse yet) pull you through the mirror and into a Hell dimension where you'll be trapped forever in torment.

---

11. In some old stories the Blood Dogs appear as humans with dog faces.

Despite this unnerving tale being so widespread, no one seems to know how the legend got started. There are a number of regional variations. In the deep South the story has it that she was a woman wrongfully put to death for witchcraft; in the Heartland she's the ghost of a girl killed on her prom night. In the East, Mary is a murder victim whose desperate cries went unanswered and now she seeks vengeance on all the living.

In any case, and despite the fact that we all *know* that this is just a myth . . . will you stand in front of a candlelit mirror and chant her name thirteen times? (I know I won't.)

Blue-Cap or **Blue-Bonnet**   Not all creatures of the dark are evil, as in the case of the Blue-Cap, a creature known only to dwell in deep mines and that is willing to work alongside human miners. Of course the Blue-Cap expected to be paid for its labors, and gold would put a gleam in its eye as easily as in the eye of its mortal coworker. The mine foreman had to be precise in the sharing out of payment, because the Blue-Cap wanted only an exact payment for the day's work. If the payment was short, then the Blue-Cap would leave it—and the mine—and never return; however, the Blue-Cap was fair, and if the foreman left too much, the Blue-Cap would leave the change and take only what he felt was his due.

The Blue-Caps are very much like the dwarves of Tolkien's *Lord of the Ring:* very strong and industrious and possessing a supernatural gift for understanding rock and ore, and for manipulating it. Perhaps tales of the Blue-Cap gave Tolkien the idea for Gimli and his fellows.

When not engaged in physical labor the Blue-Cap moved about the mine as a ball of blue-white light that was cold to the touch.

Tales of the activities of the Blue-Cap vary wildly, and in some the creatures never assumed a form other than a will-o'-the-wisp ball of light, while in others the Blue-Cap turned into a sturdy troll-like creature that could scoop rock out of the wall with its bare hands.

In Cornwall there is a tale that a group of miners met a goblin down in a copper mine that had murdered several miners. The foreman appealed to the

Blue-Cap who went down alone into the mine. There was a great rumbling and shaking as the two supernatural creatures fought. In the end the Blue-Cap came out of the darkest hole, picking its teeth with the goblins shin bone.

Another Cornish tale relates how a sneaky miner stole the money the foreman had left for the Blue-Cap and the creature was filled with such rage that he stretched out his arms and pulled down all of the support timbers, burying the thief and a dozen other miners in a deadly collapse.

Blue Witches   The Blue Witches are little-known legends from ancient Ireland and Scotland who were sometimes spotted on battlefields during the early conflicts between the Celts and the invading Romans. These warrior demons took the form of towering naked blue-skinned women who scouted across the bloody fields looking for wounded Roman soldiers to kill. The Blue Witches carried magical swords of great antiquity, which they looted from the tombs of kings; and they would use these swords to lop off the heads of the invading Roman soldiers.

It is possible—perhaps likely—that the legends of the Blue Witches is an outgrowth of tales of some of the Celtic women warriors, such as Queen Boadicea, who would paint their skins blue and ride into battle side by side with the men. Even so, the stories grew in the telling, and these women are now regarded—fondly, by the Irish and Scots, less so by Italians of Roman descent—as demonic warriors of unstoppable power.

Blutsauger (also **Blautsauger)**   Though its name means "blood sucker," the Blutsauger of Austria, Germany, and Bosnia-Herzegovina is also a flesh-eating monster. The Blutsauger is in many ways the archetypal vampire, at least as far as perceptions go in modern Western culture: It is a revenant who has the distinctive pale skin, rotting flesh, and emaciated features of a living-dead corpse. The Blutsauger sleeps in its grave by day and rises at night to feed on the living; but unlike vampires in film the Blutsauger has no fear of the sun. Not that it willingly goes forth during the day, but it is by nature a night hunter.

A person can become a Blutsauger merely by eating the flesh of any animal that has been slaughtered by a wolf. Somehow the bite of a wolf—an ordinary *canis lupus,* not a werewolf—carries some kind of spiritual taint. If a person
eats such flesh and then later dies by any means including old age, it will rise
from the grave as a monster.

The Blutsauger is a nearly mindless monster in most legends—a walking
killing machine that is only clever enough to elude capture, but it by no means
benefits from its immortality by increasing in wisdom. It is likely that when it
rises from the grave it only possesses an intelligence level on a par with an animal and lives only for the hunt.

One striking difference between the vampires of fiction and film and this
mythic monster is that the Blutsauger does not need an invitation in order to
enter a house; rather the reverse is the case, and this monster can only be prevented from entering by daubing all doorways and windows with a thick paste
made from mashed garlic mixed with the attar of hawthorn flowers. Garlic, being a blood purifier, is harmful or fatal to most of the world's many species of
vampire, and will act as an unbreachable barrier to the Blutsauger. Hawthorn
has similar powers against evil.

Also, like the Alp from the same region, the Blutsauger will not attack a
sleeping person who has placed scissors beneath his pillow with the points facing toward the head of the bed.

It is safest and wisest to try and kill a Blutsauger while it is sleeping. This is
accomplished by teamwork with several people surrounding the coffin as it is
opened, and as soon as the lid is raised, baskets full of garlic are dumped into
the coffin. The blood-purifying powers of garlic act like a stun gun to keep the
monster immobile and therefore vulnerable. To insure that the creature cannot
rise, a thick stake of sharpened hawthorn is then driven through its abdomen,
effectively pinning the Blutsauger to the bottom of the coffin like a butterfly on
a display board. Neither garlic nor stake actually kills the vampire, but rather
renders it helpless long enough for the next part of the Ritual of Exorcism, the

beheading, to be performed. Once the head has been removed, its mouth is then stuffed with more fresh garlic, turned backward in the coffin so that its face is pointed toward Hell, then the coffin is sealed again and reburied.

In Bosnia the legend of the Blutsauger has a slightly different aspect than do the stories in Austria and Germany, particularly in the assertion that the creature has no skeleton but maintains its shape through supernatural will. The Bosnian Blutsauger is also covered in stiff, dark hair, but otherwise looks like a dead and decaying person.

The Blutsauger of Bosnia is also a theriomorph and can shape-shift into a rat, wolf, or large hunting dog.

This Blutsauger is far smarter and more deceptive, and one of its tricks is to dupe a person into eating a small piece of dirt from its grave. The second the dirt touches the victim's tongue a deadly transformation takes place: The person's bones begin to melt, his heart will shrivel into a cold lump in the chest, and the signature stiff hair will sprout everywhere so that he becomes a Blutsauger himself.

All species of Blutsauger share that same peculiarity of mind that affects vampires around the world: They have an obsessive need to count items that have been scattered on the ground. In this case, petals of the hawthorn flower scattered along the roads leading away from its grave or tomb will keep the monster occupied until sunlight, when, weak and frustrated, it will crawl back into its grave.

Known in Norway as Blodsugar, and Bloedzuiger in Holland.

Bogey Hobgoblins abound in British folklore and few are as vicious as the Bogey, a big, black, shambling creature that haunts the night and sometimes travel in packs, often taking the form of dogs. Whether called a Bogey, or the Bogey-man, Boogie-man, Bugbear, Bug-a-boo, or Bogey-beast, the creatures are deadly and love to torment their victims by scaring them as much as possible before actually killing them in creative ways. It is the Bogey's greatest de-

⊰ THE RITUAL OF ⊱ EXORCISM

Killing vampires requires more than nerve and a sharp stick. The process of destroying most species of vampires requires an exorcism of the demonic spirit that has entered into and reanimated the dead body. The Ritual of Exorcism varies from culture to culture, but most versions include the following steps:

- The grave of the suspected vampire is opened.
- A long stake is driven through the vampire's body, pinning it to the coffin or to the ground. This stake does not need to pierce the heart and ideally should be made of hawthorn or other rose wood. This does not kill the monster and will only hold it immobile for a few moments.
- The vampire's head is quickly cut off before the creature can free itself from the stake.
- Fresh garlic is stuffed into the vampire's mouth and sprinkled liberally throughout the coffin. Normally the garlic will break the bonds between spirit and flesh.
- The arms and legs of the corpse are bound to prevent movement.
- A corn, block of wood, or other object is used to prop open the vampire's mouth so that it cannot bite.
- Long needles are driven through the extremities of the vampire to further immobilize it.
- The coffin is resealed and buried again.
- If there is any doubt about whether all of this has succeeded, incineration is the most reliable backup plan.

light to actually scare a person to death, but failing that it will be very happy to lure a person into a fall, topple some chimney bricks down on a person's head, or otherwise cause a painful death.

Some Bogies love to hide in a fireplace and kick embers out onto the rug to cause fires. Others like to turn food bad or poison water. Some bring pestilence to the crops or disease to the livestock.

Boggart (also Boggleman)   Shades of Harry Potter! Boggarts are nasty poltergeists that like to play on the fears of whomever beholds them. In J. K. Rowling's wonderful Harry Potter[12] novels the Boggarts are visible and take on the form of whatever the viewer most fears, but in folklore the Boggart is nearly always invisible and frightens people by engaging in the kind of activity poltergeists are known for: throwing things around, moving objects, breaking things, pulling off the bedclothes, causing items in a closet to topple out unexpectedly.

The Boggart loves to wait for a quiet moment when things are still and then do something very loud and dramatic so the abruptness of the action has as much effect as the action itself.

Some Boggarts can manifest enough of a physical presence (invisible but felt) so that they can attack humans—kicking, slapping, shoving, biting, and even scratching them with unseen nails. A few Boggarts have managed to possess domesticated animals, causing strange and violent behavior.

Like demons, the Boggart can only be gotten rid of by exorcism, though in recent years, burning sage has also been known to work.

Boitatá   Duality is certainly nothing new in folklore, but with the Boitatá of Brazil it is taken to extremes in that there are two versions of this monster legend, and in each version it is a totally different kind of monster.

In one version the Boitatá is a great hulking creature that walks upright like a man but has the head of a bull, glaring crimson eyes, and flaring nostrils

---

12. Most notably in *Harry Potter and the Prisoner of Azkaban*.

BOITATA Sandro Castilli

from which it snorts fire. This version of the creature is the embodiment of an evil soul that is cast free after death. Not a true revenant, the Boitatá simply manifests its monstrous body so that it can continue to pursue wickedness in the physical world.

In the other version, the Boitatá appears in the form of a fiery snake of enormous size; it mainly preys on animals, killing them and eating just their eyes from which it drains life essence in order to stoke its inner fires. This version of the Boitatá began as a dying human who tried to cheat the Devil and was damned to spend eternity in the form of a serpent.

Bori   The Bori is a forest-dwelling vampire who appears in the folklore of the Hausa people of West Africa in various odd and hideous forms, most commonly that of a headless man with goat legs and cloven hooves. The Bori is a theriomorph who can take any form it chooses, though when trying to blend in to the natural jungle it often adopts the appearance of a python or other large snake. It can also take the form of monkeys, birds, and even swarms of insects.

The Bori is a trickster, and it delights in using a variety of ploys—plaintive calls, taking the appearance of a lost child, and so on, to lure the unsuspecting into a secluded spot in order to attack.

The Bori seldom kills outright. More often it drains off blood or life energy and leaves its victims dazed and dreamy, often incoherent.

In some of the regional tales of the Bori, it is a potentially helpful creature, as long as it is appeased with offerings of freshly killed fowl or bowls of fruit. If a person chances to learn the Bori's true name, then the creature is instantly enslaved and must do whatever that person wants. On the other hand, if the master of a Bori is careless enough to burn the creature by accidentally scattering sparks or touching it unthinkingly with a cigarette, the heat breaks the bond of enslavement and the Bori is free. The first thing a freed Bori will do is savagely attack its former master, and often the entire family of its master. An irate Bori is rather a bad thing to have in the house—no one and nothing is safe from its wrath.

When one is attacked by a Bori, the only reliable defense is a weapon made of iron—even a fire poker will do. Like so many supernatural creatures, the Bori cannot abide the touch of iron.

Many thousands of miles from West Africa, in Australia, there is another creature called a Bori. This being is an invisible disease-spreading monster. It is uncertain whether the creature exists to spread disease, or whether it is a vector, like a rat or mosquito, spreading disease as a side effect of its bite. In either case, the Australian Bori feeds on health and is very much feared.

Bouda   Unique among the world's theriomorphs is a were-hyena of Morocco called the Bouda. This creature, also found in Tanzania and Ethiopia, is a living vampire—a bloodsucker that has that nature while still alive, as opposed to one who becomes a monstrous predator after rising from the grave. The Bouda is also a deliberate theriomorph and uses sorcery to transform itself into animal form.

The Bouda is a hard creature to classify because its evil qualities are many and they overlap. For example, it is a living vampire, and a shape-shifter, a bloodsucker, and a flesh-eater. It is also a sorcerer, and it uses magic intentionally to orchestrate its attacks on its victims.

Most Boudas are blacksmiths by trade, and they labor in their forges to make amulets and charms of enchanted metals that will enhance their own inherent preternatural strengths, or to give them more precise control over their shape-shifting abilities.

When the Bouda is in animal form it looks like an ordinary hyena, except for a small charm worn on a chain or thong around its neck. This charm is the means by which the Bouda will then transform back into a human. Without the charm two things happen: first, the Bouda is unable to regain human form, and second it eventually becomes a true hyena, losing all of the human cunning it normal possesses even when in animal form.

Though fierce, the Bouda does not possess supernatural strength and has no powers of invulnerability, and can therefore be killed by any ordinary means either in human or animal shape.

⚔ CHARMS AND TALISMANS ⚔
AGAINST EVIL

Though the cross may not be a reliable defense against vampires (it was just a literary invention by Bram Stoker), there are many items used throughout the centuries and even into modern times as proofs against evil and misfortune:

ALL-SEEING EYE is a charm made to look like an eye surrounded by radiating beams of light, and has been used by scores of cultures, even appearing on the Great Seal of the United States, as a symbol of Freemasonry, where it represents the Great Architect of the Universe.

ARCANGEL ROOT (also known as Holy Ghost Root, Angelica Root, and Dong Quai) is used to protect women from harm, and valued as an aid to healing.

BLUESTONE is used in Vodoun for protection from evil and for gambler's luck and is a common ingredient in a Mojo Hand (a small bag of magical roots and items).

CAT'S EYE SHELLS are charms made from a Turban shell or Turbo (a mollusk), and used in Europe and the Middle East for protection against the Evil Eye.

CORNUTO (or Corno, or cornicello) is a small twisted horn worn around the neck on a chain. The horn may be made from red coral, gold, or silver and is worn as a protection against the Evil Eye.

DEVIL'S SHOESTRING is a species of Viburnum, usually *Viburnum alnifolium* (alder-leafed viburnum or hobblebush), and sometimes the related species *Viburnum opulus* (cramp-bark) or *Viburnum prunifolium* (black haw), all woodland plants of the honeysuckle family. The "strings" of Devil's Shoestrings are flexible roots and are used to "trip up the Devil" or "hobble" him so he can't get in a house.

EYE-IN-HAND combines the imagery of Greek and Turkish blue all-seeing eye charms with the downward-facing Arab and Israeli hamsa hand, and is a protective talisman in India and the southern Mediterranean region.

GLASS EYE is a common charm in Greece and Turkey; this is a blue glass eye, which "mirrors back" the blue of the Evil Eye and thus "confounds" it.

FOULED ANCHOR is carried to ensure safe travel and a safe return to the home of any traveler (on land or sea); but in Vodoun it also brings a straying lover home to his or her spouse.

GARLIC CHARM is a locket or small pouch filled with garlic and used throughout Europe to ward off witches and vampires.

HAMSA HAND (ARABIC) OR HAMESH HAND (HEBREW) is an ancient amulet for protection against the Evil Eye. The words "hamsa" and "hamesh" mean "five" and refer to the digits on the hand. An alternative Islamic name for this charm is the Hand of Fatima, in reference to the daughter of Mohammed. Another Jewish name for it is the Hand of Miriam, in reference to the sister of Moses and Aaron.

JOHN THE CONQUEROR ROOT is a plant root named after a black slave whose life (whether real or fictional is unknown) was an inspiration to slaves who wanted to rebel against their masters but could not do so openly. John, said to be the son of an African king, was in captivity, but he never became subservient, and his cleverness at tricking his master supplied many a story with a pointed moral. John the Conqueror is likely the embodiment of the trickster so commonly found in African moral folktales, or is an interpretation of the West African deity known variously as Eleggua, Legba, and Eshu. Having John the Conqueror root in one's Mojo hand (or protective pouch of herbs and charms) insured good luck and protection from evil.

MANO CORNUTO is an ancient Italian amulet against misfortune and ill will shaped like a hand gesture in which the index and little fingers are extended while the middle and ring fingers are curled into the palm.

OJO DE VENADO ("Deer's Eye charm" is a Mexican charm made from the seed of velvet bean (*Mucuna pruriens*) also known as Cowhage, and is a protection against any kind of spiritual evil.

Brahmaparush (also Brahmaparusha) The Brahmaparush vampire of India is such a gluttonous creature that it not only tears its victims heads off and drinks their blood, but it also consumes every ounce of flesh in an orgy of feasting. This ritualistic monster follows a very exact ceremony of slaughter. First it punches a hole in its victim's skull, then drinks the blood until there is not a single drop left in the body. Without even a pause to digest, the Brahmaparush then sucks out the entire brain, savoring this as a treat. Next, it rends the body limb from limb, devouring it entirely, bones and all. The only part of the body that it saves is the intestines, which it then winds around its own head like a grisly turban.

Killing a Brahmaparush is not easy. The creature is devious and strong and very elusive, and only a warrior who is pure in spirit can even attempt it. When one of these creatures is suspected in the vicinity, an outstanding warrior is selected to be the village champion, and he then undergoes a long ritual of physical and spiritual cleansing that takes ninety days. At the end of three months of ascetic living and constant prayer, the warrior must make a pilgrimage to nine shrines and in each he must pray for nine hours. Then he takes a sword that has been passed nine times through the smoke from blessed incense. Sword in hand, he is now ready to face the monster. If he is lucky he can dispatch the monster without taking too much damage himself; most often, though, even when victorious the champion is also wounded unto death.

Brownie (also **Bodach, Bwca, Fenodaree)**   Like the Blue-Cap, the Brownie is a benign creature who delights in helping humans, though Brownies are inclined more toward domestic chores than mining. Brownies become attached to a certain family and will work tirelessly at household tasks, eschewing payment because it is the work they truly love.

Brownies stand about three feet tall and are usually dressed in drab rags. Tough they love their work they often look sad because, as legend has it, they were created to ease Adam's burden after his eviction from Eden and it is by God's will that they serve without thought or want of payment.

⊰ HYPER-AESTHESIA ⊱

Many of the world's supernatural creatures have heightened senses far beyond human capabilities, a condition referred to as hyper-aesthesia. This allows them to sense prey more easily than the prey can sense them.

In the Harry Potter novels by J. K. Rowling,[13] the "house elves" fit the basic description and character of Brownies.

There is a more violent side to the Brownies than in the Harry Potter house elves, however, and in some Welsh tales, where the Brownies are called Bwca, they have been known to turn on their masters if they suspect that anyone in the household has become a servant of the Devil. Since Bwca, like English Brownies and the Cornish Pixie, are descendants of creatures appointed by Heaven to serve man, they have a strong sense of religious right and wrong. Old tales tell of Bwca slaughtering whole families after learning that the family had become dedicated to evil.

Bruja Mexico and other Hispanic lands are rife with tales of bizarre witch-vampires such as the dreaded Bruja. These creatures are essentially human, but over the long years of their studies into the blackest of magics they have lost something of their humanity and gained great unnatural powers. Most Bruja (masculine is Brujo) are theriomorphs and often assume the shapes of black hens, crows, flies, dogs, and other creatures so they can blend into the natural world during their hunts.

The Bruja are deeply addicted to the blood of innocent children, though in a pinch they'll take adult blood and even the blood of farm animals. The most treasured blood, however, is that of a child born within sight of a holy Catholic shrine because the taking of that blood is regarded as a slight against Heaven, which earns the Bruja the favor of the Devil.

In some villages the Bruja are not regarded as evil—or at least not as entirely evil—and are often consulted for cures and potions. A Bruja of one village may sell charms of protection to her neighbors to protect them against Brujas from other towns. Whether this is done out of some loyalty to her own people, out of spite for her rivals, or as an attempt to ingratiate herself is not known.

There are also charms against Bruja (and other evils) that can be made by

13. Beginning with *Harry Potter and the Sorcerer's Stone.*

anyone, though they are difficult to get right. The most powerful of these is made from blades of grass plucked at midnight, soaked in a virgin's tears, and then placed in a ceramic jar. The jar is placed in a shrine for an entire lunar month, then brought back home and buried beside the front door. A house protected by such a charm is permanently barred to the Bruja.

Another ward against the Bruja is the placing of scissors under pillows of sleeping children, or on nightstands. Bruja fear sharp objects and will hesitate to draw close. In many areas small cloves of garlic are sewn into the lining of clothes as an added protection.

The Bruja can also be foiled by a trick that is standard throughout much of the world—an appeal to the obsessive-compulsive nature of vampires. By scattering seeds, wheat, or rice in front of doors and windows, or at the foot of each bed, the Bruja will be compelled to stop and count each one—a process that will take all night. Though sunlight will not kill a Bruja, she fears being recognized in the light of day and will flee at the cockcrow.

Brukulaco (also **Bruculaco** and **Burculacas)** In the regions of Thessaly and Epirus in Greece there are old superstitions about the lingering spirits of those who have been excommunicated from the church and who are later buried there. These spirits, denied entry to Heaven, are forced to wander the Earth in rage and torment; and they generally take out their frustrations on their former neighbors and family.

From the graves of these damned individuals a creature called a Brukulaco rises—a beast that bears a superficial resemblance to a wolf-man—a hunched body with savage teeth, glaring eyes, and sharp claws—but which is not a shape-shifter. Its new body is created, Golem-like, from the mean things of the Earth—in this case excrement, mud, and slime.

The Brukulaco has a massive barrel chest that, when struck, booms like a bass drum. Its arms and legs are heavily muscled, and when it comes to life it smashes its way out of its tomb or grave and immediately begins seeking human prey.

The Brukulaco uses a deceptively plaintive cry to lure the curious into remote spots so it can attack. Sometimes this cry sounds like a lost child, an injured woman, or even a whimpering dog. It shapes the sound by instinct and intuition into whatever sounds most likely will draw its potential victim. Then, when that person comes to investigate, the Brukulaco strikes.

Aside from being a flesh-eating revenant, the Brukulaco is also a nosferatu and has been known to spread plague throughout rural Greece.

In the region of Thessaloniki there is a somewhat different version of the Brukulaco legend. There it is believed that when a person suffering from catalepsy lapses into a fit, his soul leaves the body and enters that of any nearby wolf. At once the wolf becomes a killer and will hunt down livestock and human alike.

The only sure way to destroy a Brukulaco is to cut off its head and burn both head and corpse. In the case of the Brukulaco from Milo, the severed head should be boiled first in a pot filled with clean water and fresh garlic and then placed in a coffin or shroud with the corpse and reburied.

Bruxsa (also spelled **Bruxa**)　Like its close cousin the Bruja of Spain and Mexico, the Bruxsa is a witch-vampire whose evil is a conscious choice rather than the result of a curse or an accident of birth.

By day the Bruxsa leads a normal life and takes the illusory form of a ravishingly beautiful woman. In this form she can marry, bear children, attend church, and essentially pass unnoticed among her prey; but at night the Bruxa's true nature emerges. The Bruxsa is a theriomorph, and as the sun sets she transforms into a bird and flies into the darkness to seek her unnatural amusements. The Bruxsa loves to torment lost travelers, leading them astray, confusing them to the point of despair, and then attacking them.

Her meal of choice, like that of many vampires, is the blood of children. In some of the more unnerving tales it is said that she actively seeks out virile

⊰ CATALEPSY ⊱

Catalepsy is a disorder of the nervous system that causes a kind of suspended animation. Symptoms include a loss of voluntary motion, rigidity in the muscles, and a decreased sensitivity to pain and heat. Someone suffering from catalepsy can sometimes see and hear, but cannot move. Their breathing, pulse, and other regulatory functions slow down to the extent that, to an untrained eye (such as a villager in the Middle Ages), it would seem as though they were deceased. Many people have been buried alive as a result of this condition, which may account for some reported cases of misdiagnosed vampirism. When the coffin of such a victim was opened, there would be clear evidence that the "corpse" had been awake post-burial. Signs of extreme agitation were often present, and even signs that the buried person had torn at its own skin and clothes and even tried to feed on itself. This condition can last from minutes to days.

men who can impregnate her so that she can feast on the blood of her own offspring.

The Bruxsa has vast sorcerous powers. Immortal and invulnerable, she can cast spells to bring about drought, spread sickness, cause destructive rain, and cause livestock to miscarry.

A Bruxsa cannot be killed by any ordinary means, but there are many charms and spells that will keep her out of the house. Like many monsters, she loathes garlic, and charms made from fresh garlic are often worn by children or hung above windows. A mash of garlic paste and holy water is sometimes spread around window and doorframes to keep children safe. Many of the better charms against these witch-vampires are made by traveling Gypsies who have no love for supernatural predators of any kind.

Buata The forests of the western Melanesia island of New Britain are said to be haunted by a monstrous creature that resembles an overgrown wild boar, but which has tusks as long as swords and eats people whole. This creature is said to be enormously strong and shockingly fast for its size.

Some accounts claim this monster, the Bhuta, can actually talk, but it has only a rudimentary intelligence and little reasoning powers beyond the need to hunt and hide.

A strikingly similar creature, the *Pugut*, has been reported in the more remote parts of the Philippines.

Bucca Great Britain has many more or less benign monsters that seem content to serve humans rather than hunt them. At least most of the time. This tradition also extends to monsters living in the waters surrounding the British Isles, and includes the great sea beast, the Bucca.

Once a powerful sea god, over the centuries the Bucca has fallen on hard times and is now a lesser creature on a par with a demon or goblin, which still makes it tough enough should it be crossed by an unwary sailor. On good days the Bucca helps fishermen by driving fish toward their nets or nudging a boat away from jagged rocks; but the Bucca's graces must be encouraged by sacrifices of fish or bread. The tradition among the coastal fishermen is to toss a piece of bread over their left shoulder during shipboard meals, and to spill a small splash of beer onto the deck of the boat during meals. Also, for every catch the Bucca helps the fishermen take the smart sailors leave behind one fish as a token. The Bucca does not need these offerings for nourishment, but it does seem to appreciate the courtesy.

In the waters of the Orkney Isles, the Bucca's reputation is a little less serene—perhaps as a result of not being placated by simple offerings of fish, bread or beer—and the sea beast has been known to rip the keel right out of a fishing boat and swallow the fishermen whole.

The upshot is that Orkney fishermen who want to be at peace with the creatures of the sea make very sure to offer a nice fish to the Bucca, and to toast it with good ale at each meal, whether at sea or back on land.

Budas There is a legend from the days of ancient Abyssinia of a type of lycanthrope that existed as a social sub-group rather than as cursed individuals. As the old stories tell it, a sect of ironworkers and potters had somehow acquired the power to become werewolves on a specific (and secret) single day of the year. This was apparently accomplished by some kind of jewelry they made (earrings in some stories, decorative belts in others).

These evil craftsmen used their powers to spread bad luck, sickness, and death wherever they could best serve their secret agendas.

In his book, *The Black Death and the Dancing Mania*, J. F. C. Hecker wrote this account:

> *The Abyssinian Zoomorphism is a no less important phenomenon, and shows itself in a manner quite peculiar. The blacksmiths and potters form among the Abyssinians a society or caste called in Tigre Tebbib, and in Amhara Buda, which is held in some degree of contempt, and excluded from the sacrament of the Lord's Supper, because it is believed that they can change themselves into hyenas and other beasts of prey, on which account they are feared by everybody, and regarded with horror. They artfully contrive to keep up this superstition, because by this separation they preserve a monopoly of their lucrative trades, and as in other respects they are good Christians (but few Jews or Mohammedans live among them), they seem to attach no great consequence to their excommunication. As a badge of distinction they wear a golden ear-ring, which is frequently found in the ears of Hyenas that are killed, without its having ever been discovered how they catch these animals, so as to*

decorate them with this strange ornament, and this removes in the
minds of the people all doubt as to the supernatural powers of the
smiths and potters. To the Budas is also ascribed the gift of enchant-
ment, especially that of the influence of the evil eye. They neverthe-
less live unmolested, and are not condemned to the flames by
fanatical priests, as the lycanthropes were in the Middle Ages.

The Buffalo God   The Shawnee of Kentucky had their own tales of a giant monster, whom they called the "father of all buffalo"—a beast that was so massive and fierce that it drove away all the other game.

The elders of the Delaware tribe told similar tales to Thomas Jefferson, which he recorded in his papers. In both stories the gods destroyed these giants with lightning bolts and left their bones as reminders of the gods' dominance.

Excavations of sites where these giants were known to hunt have yielded the bones of gigantic mammoths. One wonders what other monsters from prehistory may have lingered into the age of man long enough to have become the creatures of nightmare and legend. What's really spooky is that there were reports of mastodons and mammoths as late as 1828, many thousands of years beyond the point where scientists insist they became extinct.

Buggane   The Buggane is one of the many variations on the legend of the Boggart, particularly the version to be found on the Isle of Man. The Buggane has a beastlike body with a great fierce head, taloned hands, and sharp teeth. Like the Boggart, the Buggane is a shape-shifter and has been seen masquerading as an oversized calf, a horse, and or even a great hound.

The Buggane lives near waterfalls or ponds and is believed to be a water spirit who ventures onto land only to hunt.

Bunyip   If a fierce bellowing cry breaks the night in the remoter parts of Australia, it's best to run for cover because the Bunyip may be issuing its hunting call. This monster is somewhat like a hellhound and is often described as being as big as a moderate calf. It lives in the ponds and other spots where the waters are calm, and for the most part it leaves people alone; but if its home or its territory is disturbed, the Bunyip can turn quite spiteful and savage.

The name "Bunyip" comes from the Aboriginal word for "spirit" and the Bunyip is an immortal and supernatural creature. The creature appears in the Aborigine Dreamtime stories and has been described in a variety of different ways: from a feathered creature not unlike an otter to a beast with flippers and walrus tusks.

One eyewitness account from 1847[14] describes it this way:

> It was about as big as a six months' old calf, of a dark brown colour, a long neck, and long pointed head; it had large ears which pricked up when it perceived him (the herdsmen); had a thick mane of hair from the head down the neck, and two large tusks. He turned to run away, and this creature equally alarmed ran off too, and from a glance he took at it he describes it as having an awkward shambling gallop; the forequarters of the animal were very large in proportion to the hindquarters, and it had a large tail.

Scientists have tried to explain away the Bunyip for years, and the two most persistent theories are that it is either a poorly reported saltwater crocodile or a seal; while other scientists speculate that the creature resembles the Diprotodon, an animal the size of a rhinoceros that became extinct about 10,000 years ago.

Buruburu (also Zokuzokugami and Okubyohgami)   When walking through the moonlit forests of rural Japan one should always be cautious when encountering an old man or old woman who seems to be shaking in a fit of palsy, especially if the old crone has only one eye. This most common disguise belongs to the dreaded Buruburu, the Ghost of Fear.

The Buruburu does not directly attack a person, but as the traveler passes

---

14. George Hobler's account as it appeared in the *Sydney Morning Herald,* 1847.

by it sheds its mortal disguise and in spirit form attaches itself to the person's spine. The traveler feels a sudden chill, and goose bumps appear all over his skin—and he knows that he is carrying on his back the Buruburu. Instantly the traveler's heart seizes up and he dies of sheer terror.

The very name "Buruburu" comes from the sound one makes while shivering. The creature is the spirit of mortal terror and can strike at any time.

The legend of the Buruburu has appeared, in one form or another, in a number of folktales and in fiction, and is widely considered to be the inspiration for the 1959 horror film *The Tingler*, starring Vincent Price.

In some tales the Buruburu has the power to possess its victims without causing death, but it pollutes that person's life with unbearable fear, making them afraid of everything. Often these victims shut themselves inside their homes, fearing to come out, and live miserable and lonely lives. Suicides are common escapes for victims of Buruburu possession.

It is possible that the Buruburu feeds on fear—or of some essence created while a person is feeling great fear—which qualifies it as an essential vampire of the most potent kind.

Bushyasta (also **Buyasta)**   Some of the world's essential vampires are less obviously destructive than others, as demonstrated by Bushyasta. This Zoroastrian demon feeds on energy and efficiency rather than life force and leaves its victims lethargic and prone to sloth. The result of this lethargy is that its victims neglect their social and—more important to the demon—their religious duties.

Büxenwolf (also **Boxenwolf)**   German werewolves are among the world's most vicious, and the bloodthirsty Büxenwolf is no exception. This lycanthrope is a thinking monster who willingly enters into an unholy pact with the Devil in order to gain secret knowledge, wealth, and vast supernatural powers. Once the pact is sealed, a demonic messenger from Hell brings the potential Büxenwolf a magic girdle, and when the belt is worn the transformation from human to wolf is immediate. The Büxenwolf is a true werewolf, meaning that it turns into a wolf, not a half-human wolf-man.

In its wolf form, the Büxenwolf retains human intelligence but has the enhanced senses, speed, stamina, and instincts of the wolf. It is only as strong as an ordinary wolf, however, and can be killed by any normal weapon.

If a priest or monster hunter were to trap a Büxenwolf, there is a trick to making it reveal its true human name. A sliver of steel or iron (iron in the older tales, steel in the more modern ones) is held above the creature's head. The metal breaks the connection between the monster and Hell, and the creature must reveal its true name; after which the priest performs an ordinary exorcism for demonic possession.

C

Caddy (also **the Sea Hag)**   In 1920 a giant sea creature was spotted in the waters of Cadboro Bay, near Vancouver Island, British Columbia, and it has been seen frequently since. Described as a large serpentine beast forty to fifty feet in length, with a ridged or knobbed spine and flippers shaped like those of a humpback whale, though not as large. When first spotted, the creature was called "the Sea Hag," a nod to the legends of the *Old Hag* known to appear in the dreams and folklore of many nations; but over the years the creature has come to be called "Caddy" and, like many lake monsters, is fondly regarded as a kind of local mascot.

The description of Caddy bears a striking resemblance to Ogopogo, a cryptid known to haunt nearby Lake Okanagan, and may be of the same species or even the same creature.

Cailleac Bhuer (also **Black Annis, the Blue Hag,** and **the Stone Woman)**   Cailleac Bhuer is a one-eyed Scottish hag with blue skin who haunts the moors and rocky passes of the Scottish Highlands. Also known as Black Annis, she is relentlessly hungry and will attack any lone traveler. She brains her victim with a sharp rock and then drags the dazed and dying person back to her cave for a savage feast. Those few persons who claim to have spied the Cailleac Bhuer in her lair describe her as sitting on a pile of human bones.

When Cailleac Bhuer cannot find a human to kill, she will resort to slaughtering livestock, but man-flesh is by far her preference.

When spotted on the road, Cailleac Bhuer generally pretends to be a weak old crone, frail and bent under the weight of her years as she struggles along, leaning on a walking stick. She often has a crow, perhaps as a familiar, perched on her shoulder.

Callicantzaro (also **Kallikantzaros**)   Vampires of Greek folklore are often extraordinarily vicious and their creation is frequently linked to some unfortunate accident of birth. The Callicantzaros species of Greek vampire rises from the grave of a recently buried person who had originally been born in the Holy season between Christmas and New Year's Day (or, in some tales, between Christmas and the Epiphany, January 6th). Not all persons born during this time share the same fate, but anyone who has such a birthday must make sure to live a life free from sin and one that ends with proper last rites and exact attention to the sacred burial traditions.

The Callicantzaro (plural is Callicantzaros or Callicantzaroi) is a decidedly violent monster whose hunting and feeding habits include traits of both vampire and werewolf in that it will eat flesh as well as consume blood. However, it is a predator whose hunting calendar is limited to that same Holy period between Christmas and New Year. For the remainder of the year, the Callicantzaro is consigned to the Netherworld where it is trapped with other demons and creatures of darkness. In these long months the Callicantzaro suffers all of the tortures of the truly damned, and when the year cycles around so that it is free to hunt, the creature takes out its rage and frustration on the living.

The Callicantzaro has exceptionally long and strong fingers that end in talons sharp enough to cut through leather and even some light metals; they use these powerful claws to rip their victims to shreds.

When a Callicantzaro cannot get a live prey it will dig up the freshest of corpses and feed on them, marking it as a ghoul as well as a vampire-werewolf hybrid. Some scientists have postulated that the legend of the Callicantzaro is a way of explaining the rare and extreme aberrant psychological condition of necrophagism, where a person eats the body parts of someone who was recently murdered.

During the active part of its hunting cycle, the Callicantzaro hides in some dark place (a cave, tomb, or ruin) by day and then sneaks at sunset to attack anyone caught on the roads at night.

Stories are told of a male Callicantzaro who captured a living woman and dragged her down to the Netherworld with him, forcing her to bear his children. The offspring of this hellish rape are born as Callicantzaroi, though they are often more ghostly and less substantial.

To prevent all this, if a child is born during this Holy period, precautions have to be taken to prevent it from rising as a monster after death. The newborn is lowered feet-first into a fire, held just above the flames until the baby's toenails are singed black. The toenails must then be eaten by the family of the child to secure the reincarnation of the deceased. The ingestion of these clipping creates a kind of spiritual link between tainted child and untainted adult, and as the clippings are digested the spiritual link becomes too strong even for the pull of Hell.

Calling Ghosts A number of the world's predators use deception instead of a more direct approach to ensnare their prey. These creatures use various ploys to lure humans to them—usually by getting them to follow calls or apparitions to secluded spots—and then attack them. These creatures are often grouped together under the category of Calling Ghosts, though in truth not all of them are ghosts.

Sometimes the attacks are then direct and overwhelming, as in the case of

CALLING GHOST John West

the *Ilimu* of Kenya and the *Otgiruru* of Namibia; perhaps in those cases it suggests that the creature is physically more powerful than its prey but prefers not to be revealed to the general population.

Other Calling Ghosts use seduction as part of their strategy and exert magical powers that render the victim helpless, dreamy, groggy, or otherwise unable to resist. At this point the predators drain them of what essence it is they require. Many of the world's essential vampires fall in this category, including the *Leanhaun-Sidhe* of Ireland, the *Dames Blanches* (White Ladies) of France, and the *Langsuir* of Java.

Calling Ghosts often imitate the plaintive voice of a child in order to exploit the natural sympathies almost anyone would have for a child in distress; but these creatures also imitate children in order to entice living children to follow them. This is a common practice of creatures such as the *Moroi* of Romania, the *Vjestitiza* of Montenegro, the *Trazgos* of Spain, and the *Algul* of Iraq.

If you hear a strange call in the night . . . make sure you know who—and what—is calling before you venture out into the hungry dark.

Cambion   The half-human and thoroughly evil child of a succubus, conceived during a nocturnal rape of a man by a ghostly female essential vampire. The Cambion is a trickster and delights in driving people insane, ruining lives, and otherwise causing great misery.

Canchu (also **Pumapmicuc)**   Many of the world's supernatural predators—like those in nature—attack only the weak and infirm, but the Canchu of Pre-Columbian Peru preyed only on the very strongest warriors. This doesn't mean that the Canchu was particularly brave, however; it never attacked these warriors while the young men were awake and armed. It preferred to sneak into houses and tents during the night and feed, taking every last drop of the potent blood of the young and strong. Some Canchu used to take only a portion of their victim's blood, then allowed them time to regain health and vigor, and then attacked again.

There are newer legends of the Canchus with sightings as recent as 2002. In these tales the monsters, lacking a warrior class to prey upon, attack any reasonably healthy person who is unlucky enough to venture into the more remote areas of that mountainous land.

Ceasg   In the lakes and along the coasts of Scotland lives a very weird creature that has the upper torso of a gorgeous woman and the lower half of a giant salmon. If a Ceasg falls in love with a human she will transform into a fully human woman, and her children will always have a powerful attraction to the sea. When the Ceasg feels unloved, however, she will vent her spleen by luring fishermen to a watery death. She is also easily offended, attacking anyone whom she perceives has snubbed her or spoken ill of her. She is not above overturning boats,punching holes through hulls, and using a fisherman's net to ensnare a human and drag him screaming underwater.

Champp   In Lake Champlain, which touches on parts of New York, Vermont, and Quebec, an enduring legend tells of a powerful lake monster who has earned the rather tame nickname of "Champ." This is one of the few lake monsters apparently caught on film in what has been called among cryptozoologists "the Mansi photograph."[15] The photo shows a creature with a thick body and a long tapering neck reminiscent of a plesiosaur, which became extinct about 65 millions years ago.

The legend of Champ dates back to the Iroquois Indians who lived in that region, though in their tales the creature was a great horned monster. More recent sightings—and there still are sightings of Champ—do not describe horns of any kind.

Reports of the monster appear in newspapers beginning around 1873, when it was spotted by men laying a railroad track near the town of Dresden in New York. The workers claim to have seen the head of an "enormous serpent" rise up from the water and look at them. The men, wisely, fled. In August of that same year a small tourist ship was reported to have struck the creature and nearly capsized. The newspaper reports following the collision claim that passengers saw the creature on the surface of the water thirty or so yards from the ship.

As was his habit, the showman P. T. Barnum put up a $50,000 reward for the "hide of the great Champlain serpent to add to my mammoth World's Fair Show." He never had to pay out the reward.

15. A famous photo of Champ was taken on July 5, 1977, by Sandra Mansi.

Champ has never been a particularly aggressive monster and has become a kind of mascot for communities around Lake Champlain. There are Champ festivals, rides, collectibles, and hundreds of souvenirs.

Though the monster has never been reliably photographed (the negative to the Mansi picture was lost) or studied, the creature never seems to go away. Every now and then someone sees something large and presumably unnatural moving through the waters of that massive lake.

Chedipe   The folklore of India is glutted with tales of vampires, and a number of them are different types of vampire prostitutes. The Chedipe is a prime example since the name even means "prostitute."

In folklore and various old paintings, the Chedipe is depicted as an obscene slattern sitting astride a huge male tiger, often under a moonlit sky. When this powerful female vampire identifies a prey, it is seldom a single person but rather an entire household. She casts a sleeping spell over the house and while everyone is in an insensible trance she enters. There she selects the strongest male to be her victim and sets to feeding by sucking his blood out through bites she makes in his toes.

Often the Chedipe sexually assaults the man while he sleeps, thus polluting the sanctity of the household and weakening the marriage bond, tainting the bloodline, and sowing despair. It gives her great pleasure to devastate a family's love, trust, and marital purity, because the Chedipe also feeds on sorrow and misery, making her an essential vampire as well as a blood-drinker.

The Chedipe's bite is seldom mortal, but the vampire may return again and again, taking more blood before the body can replenish what has previously been stolen. The victim will soon become weak and begin to waste away, and if he does not seek out proper medical and spiritual treatment, he will die.

The surest way to defeat a Chedipe is to keep it from ever entering, which is accomplished by sanctifying the home with incense and holy icons. The incense must be renewed every hour, meaning someone has to stay awake all night. The presence of an awake person maintaining the rituals of sacred protection frighten off the Chedipe, causing her to seek out another household in the neighborhood and begin the ruin of another family.

Cherufe   In coastal South America, the nation of Chile is home to a monster so fierce and powerful that it lives in the lava of active volcanoes. The creature is said to venture forth and, using the furnace heat of its body, flash-fry an unsuspecting peasant, sometimes devouring the flesh and leaving nothing but charred bones, and other times leaving a whole corpse but feasting instead on life essence.

In ancient times virgin sacrifices were sometimes made to the Cherufe, a propitiation that appeared to have been successful for indefinite stretches of time. The monster became so used to the regular feedings that it would rumble the mountain to signal its hunger.

The people appealed to their gods, particularly the Sun God, who sent his two daughters to help the people. These daughters were no helpless princesses but rather fierce and powerful warriors who came armed with swords whose blades were as cold as outer space. With these blades they were able to weaken Cherufe and drive him back into the magma where he made his home.

The sisters stood guard on the mountain, their swords ready. Most of the time they were able to keep Cherufe confined, but being confined is not the same as being defeated. The sly and relentless Cherufe occasionally found ways of escaping his home to hunt mercilessly until the warrior sisters found him and chased him back.

The Cherufe could not be killed, only contained, and even today when the mountains rumble the people of the precipitous areas of Chile pray that the bold daughters of the Sun God are still standing vigilante at their posts.

Chiang-Shih (also **Kiang-Shi** and **Kuang-Shi)**   The vampires of China, the Chiang-shih, have a strange duality about them. In some ways they are a much closer match to the popular view of vampires held by the general public in Europe and America (which is largely based on cinematic elements and plot devices and not very heavily based on folklore); in other ways they are as unique and alien to the Western vampire paradigm as it is possible to get.

Similarities to both pop culture and folkloric elements of Western vampires include some of the ways in which this vampire is created and some of its strengths and weaknesses. The most common way of becoming a Chiang-shih is to die a violent death such as murder, hanging, drowning, suicide, or a death occurring during the commission of a crime. This leaves the soul unsettled and therefore bound to the Earthly plane, a concept often found in tales of vampirism in Europe. Also, the Chiang-shih fear sunlight (a rarity among the world's vampires), is repelled by garlic (an almost universal commonality), cannot cross running water, and can shape-shift into a wolf.

But there the similarities end.

In Taoist metaphysics a belief exists that a body houses two separate souls: one very strong and rational (called *hun*) and one weak and irrational (called *p'ai* or *p'o*). It is the lesser soul that inhabits the body first in its fetal stage and then again at death. Generally, at the moment of death both souls depart and move on; but sometimes the lesser soul does not want to leave the body and lingers, thus creating the aberrant and unnatural being called the Chiang-Shih.

The method of ambulation is the most strikingly unique quality of the Chiang-Shih. These vampires have great difficulty walking due to the pain and stiffness of being a decaying corpse, or (if they are recently dead) from rigor mortis. So they hop instead. In fact, a series of horror–comedy–martial arts movies have been made about the hopping vampires of China. Whereas hopping scenes in the movies are largely shot for laughs, the creatures of legend are no laughing matter. Chiang-Shih are vicious and sadistic and always hungry for blood. In addition, they are enormously strong and enjoy tearing their victims limb from limb.

The longer a Chiang-Shih lives the more powerful it becomes and eventually the rigor mortis wears off, allowing the monster more freedom of movement and—according to some legends—a great measure of both intelligence and malevolence. Some of these more powerful Chiang-Shih have been known to sexually assault female victims, favoring virgins or nuns because of the despair these kinds of women would endure because of the rape.

Whether advanced or newly risen, the Chiang-Shih is a very sadistic vampire, driven by pure bloodlust and heedless of any consequences. They act insanely because they are the manifestations of the irrational aspects of the soul.

A sub-species of Chiang-Shih are tall, emaciated, reanimated corpses with wild hair covering their bodies. This hair is either white, green, or a tangled mixture of both. This particular sub-species has savage talons, great fangs, flaring ruby eyes, and breath so fetid that they can kill with a single breath. This type also seems to be the most perilous because they can leap great distances and with enormous vigor, and some have even learned to fly. Providentially, this more dangerous species is also the most rare.

Another uncommon species of the Chiang-Shih is that of a ball of flickering light, which sometimes moves across the countryside as a frosty and bone-chilling mist.

Fortunately there are many ways to both fight and elude these lethal creatures. One quick way is to hold your breath if one draws near. The Chiang-Shih has very poor vision and relies on hearing and their sense of smell. They try and smell the breath of their victims, so if they cannot smell a person's breath, they cannot locate them and will pass by.

As with many other kinds of vampires worldwide, the Chiang-Shih is compelled to stop and count seeds or grains of rice left out for it. If enough is left out the vampire is forced to complete its chore even if it takes all night. Leaving a pile of rice, a mound of dried peas, or even tiny iron pellets on its grave ensures that it does not stray far once it has risen. If it is still counting the grains at dawn, the sunlight will destroy it.

Lightning is also fatal to the Chiang-Shih, but clearly hard to arrange. However, Taoist monks have developed numerous strategies against these creatures and are often called upon to combat them. Using chicken blood, these priests write powerful spells on small pieces of yellow paper. The trick then is to get close enough to the Chiang-Shih to affix these small paper charms to the monster's forehead. This task is easier said than done, considering the vampires are fast, strong, and have lethal breath. If it can be accomplished, however, the Chiang-Shih is instantly helpless and will remain immobile. The placing of these slips of paper is depicted in all of the "hopping vampire movies"—of which there are quite a few, ranging from comic to frightening—and often advanced kung-fu is required to get the job done. Folklore tells us that kung-fu may actually have been used by real priests and heroes in the centuries-long battle against this species of evil.

⇥ METAPHYSICS ⇥

Metaphysics is the overall category of all psychic research. The word comes from a conjunction of "meta," meaning "beyond" and "physics."

Children of Judas Throughout Serbia, Romania, and Bulgaria exists a cult of malicious red-haired vampires called the Children of Judas. It is widely believed in Christian folklore that Judas had red hair, and in many early (and not so early) Christian cultures red hair was seen as a clue to a person's lurking evil nature.

The Children of Judas have a unique killing style: With only a single bite they can drain their victims entirely of blood. Most of the world's vampires take some blood but rarely enough in a single feeding to cause death.[16] According to some very apocryphal bits of Christian folklore, the bite mark of the Children of Judas is supposed to resemble the Latin number thirty—

16. Repeated feedings are common in vampire folklore, resulting in a kind of wasting sickness leading ultimately to death.

xxx—apparently symbolic of the number of silver pieces Judas received for betraying Jesus.

Judas is sometimes portrayed in folklore as a vampiric character because of his part in the Last Supper during which he drank from Jesus' cup. This cup was symbolically held out to the Apostles as the blood of Christ. That very night Judas betrayed Jesus to the authorities, resulting in His arrest and crucifixion. Though Judas apparently repented of his crime and hung himself in remorse, he is widely considered by most Christians as the embodiment of evil and is forever damned. It should be noted that this is technically incorrect since Jesus was supposed to have taken on the sins of the world during His crucifixion, resulting in the New Covenant, which should have given every human being a clean soul at that moment. If so, then Judas was forgiven his sin. This point has been the center of an understandably heated debate for some centuries.

The crucifixion of Jesus as a result of Judas' betrayal is very likely the basis for the belief that crucifixes are anathema to vampires. However, this concept holds far more weight in fiction than it does in folklore. Another view is that this was added to the common belief largely because of Bram Stoker's *Dracula*. Stoker, being Irish Catholic, added quite a lot of Christian imagery to his story.[17]

Chimera   The ancient Greeks loved their monsters, and they had them in all sizes and shapes. One of the most savage was the fire-breathing predator called the Chimera, which was an amalgam of the whipping tail of a serpent, the head of a lion, and the body of a she-goat, though some depictions have the beast sporting heads of goat, lion, and dragon. The creature was the offspring of the deadly giant Typhon and the she-dragon Echidna; it killed indiscriminately from the moment of its birth.

The creature was raised by the king of Caria (in Asia Minor) who used the Chimera to terrorize the region of Lycia, forcing the locals to pay tribute just

---

17. Scholars of the subject should take time to visit the Rosenbach Museum in Philadelphia where all of Stoker's research notes are on permanent display. They are quite instructive.

to buy their own lives. The Chimera was a thoroughly murderous and destructive monster, reveling in butchery and capable of laying waste to entire towns. Iobates, the king of Lycia, began desperately casting around for a hero who was both tough and clever enough to defeat the monster, and by chance his son-in-law, Proetus, knew of a great warrior: Bellerophon. Proetus wrote a letter of introduction for Bellerophon and the deal was struck.[18] It was during this time that Bellerophon—with a bit of help from the goddess Minerva—was able to catch and tame the hippogriff,[19] Pegasus, and this gave him a chance to meet the monster on equal footing. The two fought on land and in the air, and ultimately Bellerophon defeated it by impaling it with a lead-tipped spear; but it was a near run thing.

Chindi   According to the Navajo, when a person dies all that is good in a person ends with physical life but all that is evil and corrupt lives on in the form of a spiteful ghost called a Chindi. The Navajo believe that if proper burial rituals are observed, the Chindi is released into the night winds and dispersed by the vastness of the sky. If the burial rituals are not done properly, the Chindi linger in the vicinity making mischief for its living relatives and causing sickness. If a person has been touched by Ghost Sickness, a complex ritual called a "sing" is needed to cleanse the people and drive away the evil ghost.

Chonchon   Few cultures in South America have survived unchanged since pre-Columbian days, but the Mapuche Indians managed it, partly by living in such remote and inaccessible areas and partly through a powerful cultural structure that fiercely resisted change. Their culture has lasted for 12,000 years and at the center of their society are the Machi: female spiritual leaders and healers who train for most of their lifetimes to become both healers and monster hunters.

The Machi use animal familiars as allies in their ongoing battle against a

---

18. Very likely Proetus suggested that Bellerophon visit Lycia because his wife was a bit too fond of the heroic young man.
19. Flying horse.

species of vulture-headed witch-vampires called the Chonchon. These monsters are part of a larger group of evil spirits called the Wekufe, and they are called into being by malicious witches called the Kalku, who are the diametric counterparts of the Machi.

The Chonchon swoops down on people as they walk through the jungles at night, knocks them to the ground, and savages their throats with wicked teeth in order to feed on human blood.

The Machi use their potent magic to bless spears and knives in order to make them effective against the Chonchon, but even so the best a warrior can do is drive one away temporarily. To kill one, however, the Machi must imbue her familiar with special magical powers, transforming it into a jungle snake or a great hunting bird. In those forms the familiars can slaughter the Chonchon.

Chordewa   The Chordewa, a monster from the folklore of the Oraons people of the hills of western Bengal, is a peculiar blend of witch and essential vampire. The Chordewa can create a second body for itself, always in the shape of a large black cat. Once this second body is prepared, the Chordewa astrally projects her soul and deposits it into the cat, leaving her own body somewhere secret and safe. This cat then enters a town or village and ingratiates itself with potential prey, acting very sociable, eating the victims' food, and even showing "fondness" by licking people on their lips. This lick, however, is a kiss of death. The cat slowly but surely drains the victim's life force, which is absorbed by the Chordewa. Some Chordewa legends hold that if the cat so much as licks a person's shadow, it is sufficient to doom that person to a swift and sure death. The victim will soon waste away and die while the creature becomes very much stronger.

While in cat form, the Chordewa can be identified by its peculiar mewing, which is like that of a child in distress. Few people can just ignore the sounds of a child calling out for help, and thus the Chordewa has as much prey as it needs.

Anyone wise enough to diagnose that a Chordewa is in the vicinity, and can then locate and identify the cat, has a chance, however slim, of destroying

THE AUFHOCKER by Ken Meyer

In German folklore there are tales of the *Aufhocker*, a savage hulking canine monster

BAOBHAN SITH by Lee Moyer

The Scottish "White Woman of the Highlands," the *baobhan sith*, is one of the world's many strange creatures that cross the line between vampire and fairie.

The Blues Witches by Andy Jones
The blue witches were female warrior demons who haunted the battlefields of ancient
Ireland and Scotland, searching for wounded Roman soldiers to kill.

CIHUATETEO by Jason Beam

The *cihuateteo* is a vampire-ghost of the Aztec people of old Mexico created when a woman dies in childbirth. Both she and her child rise again as immortal monsters.

THE GHUL by Jason Beam

The *ghul* is a fierce flesh-eating monster from Muslim folklore. She lurks in grave-yards or on battlefields, feasting on the flesh of the newly dead.

REVENANT by Robert Papp

Revenants are the undead: those brought back to unnatural life by demonic forces to

SIREN by Lee Moyer

Sirens appear in many forms in folklore, usually as incredibly beautiful women who

THE SHTRIGA by Ken Meyer

The shtriga *is a tremendously powerful and evil witch-vampire who preys on innocent children and often takes the form of night-hunting birds.*

the monster. Any injury visited on the cat will be reflected on the Chordewa's real and hidden body; and if the cat is slain, then the Chordewa herself will die.

Chorti   There are reports all over the world of hairy wildmen living in the remote places of the Earth, be that a forest, a snowy mountain, or a tropical jungle. In the sweltering forests of Mexico and the humid jungles of Guatemala, the Chorti is the Torrid Zone's species, and it is a ferocious example of the breed.

The Chorti is huge, standing at least seven feet tall (often much taller), with shoulders and arms packed with heavy muscle. Its arms are long and apelike, and its legs are bandy and strong. Physically it resembles the typical "bigfoot" kind of beast except in its armament: It has savage claws on both hands and feet that can tear bark from trees, crack stone, and slice a man's head off with a single swipe.

In some of the earlier tales of the Chorti (particularly those told by the Yaqui Indians of Mexico),[20] the creature's feet are turned backward pointing the way it has traveled. But this structural anomaly does not seem to affect the true Guatemalan variety.

Depending on the storyteller, the Chorti is either a benign woodland spirit that serves as a guardian of the woods or a malevolent predator that savages men and feeds on both flesh and blood. Interestingly, the stories of a hostile Chorti have cropped up most often since the beginning of the deforestation. This hostility suggests an angry reaction to the destruction of its natural habitat. Though footprints have been cast and claw marks on trees photographed (much like Bigfoot, the Yowie, and others) no body has ever been recovered.

Churel   Any pregnant Indian woman who is unlucky enough to die during the festival of Divali[21] is in even greater danger of returning to life as a Churel—a soul-

---

20. *The Supernaturals* by Williams and Hill. Aldus Books, 1965.
21. The Hindu Festival of Light.

less blood-sucking revenant. These Churel are repulsive vampires with lolling black tongues, coarse lips caked with rouge, and wild tangles of greasy hair. They have heavy pendulous breasts and their feet are twisted around backward.

Because they have died so unjustly—carrying new life—they are resentful and return to take out their antipathy on the living. The Churel primarily attacks young families—stalking children, pregnant women, and sometimes handsome young men. Their chosen prey represent things lost, and there they direct their rage.

Ideally, though, they prey on their own families, hating their living relatives for having let them die during pregnancy and a holy festival.

The rage of a Churel can never be satisfied, so the best method of defeating one is to prevent it from coming into existence, which is why such care is given to pregnant mothers. If the pregnant mother should die, the last recourse is to bury her with the utmost attention given to every detail of the burial ritual. One slip, one missed element of the complex death rituals, can ignite the anger of the departing soul, causing a new Churel to be born into the world.

Should this calamity occur, only a Hindu Pundit[22] can drive it out, using complex and often-repeated prayers, special incense, and offerings. This method is difficult and time consuming, and it does not destroy the Churel. At most it drives it away for a period of time, but the indestructible creature will generally return.

⊰ BURYING THE DEAD ⊱

The history of the supernatural clearly tells us that we have to take great care when burying the dead or they may come back angry and vengeful. Improper burial rites are tied to the creation of many species of vampires, such as the Callicantzaro of Greece, the Mrart of Australia, the

22. Priest.

Chindi of the Navajo, the Doppelsauger of Germany, the Langsuir of Malaysia, the Nelapsi of Czechoslovakia, the Tenatz of Bosnia, the Kathakano of Crete, and the Pret, Churel, and Gayal of India.

Burial customs take two forms: those that honor the dead and those that protect the living against the dead. Most folks are familiar with the former, but the latter procedures are even more crucial, especially in areas where vampirism has been known to flourish. Prophylactic steps include the following:

- Binding the limbs of a corpse so that it cannot move
- Blocking the movement of the jaw with a coin or piece of wood (to prevent the newly awakened vampire from feeding on itself to gain strength)
- Placing garlic in the coffin
- Driving long nails through the limbs of the dead to further immobilize it
- Putting the deceased's shoes on the wrong feet so that they will become confused when they try to walk
- Laying a sprig of holly on the throat of the corpse
- Filling the coffin with splinters of hawthorn or other rosewood

Of course procedures such as tightly sealing a coffin and burying the coffin at a sufficient depth are also useful to prevent the dead from troubling the living, but these last precautions speak more to the prevention of disease rather than preventing a monster from rising. It should be remembered, however, that many of the world's vampires are known to spread disease. Makes you wonder.

Cihuateteo (also **Civatateo)**   The Cihuateteo, of the Aztec people of old Mexico, is a revenant of a woman who died in childbirth. Unlike other similar vampires throughout the world,[23] however, the child of the Cihuateteo also becomes a vampire. After death both mother and child rise from the grave and begin attacking children, not for blood, but to infect them with a horrible wasting sickness. In rare cases the Cihuateteo and her child will drink their victims' blood, but most often they act as both nosferatu (spreading disease) and essential vampire (feeding off the resulting despair and anguish).

The Cihuateteo often dresses to imitate Tlazolteotl, the goddess of sorcery, lust, and evil; and this image was often enough to terrify pre-Columbian victims. In more modern times (and reports can be traced to as late as the mid-1800s), the Cihuateteo more often appeared as a normally dressed woman and child; but even so it was only holy relics of the ancient Aztec religion that were able to drive away these demons.

Craitnag   On the Isle of Man the old saw "let sleeping dogs lie" should perhaps be changed to "let sleeping bats hang." According to folklore, the Craitnag (Manx for "bat") is one of seven creatures believed to hibernate through the winter months (the others being *Cooag*,[24] "the Cuckoo"; *Cloghan-ny-cteigh*, "the Stone-chat"; *Gollan-geayee*, "the Swallow"; *Crammag*, "the Snail"; *Doallag*, "the Dormouse"; *Foillycan*, "the Butterfly"; *Shellan*, "the Bee"; *Jialgheer*, "the Lizard"; and *Cadlag*, "the sleeper," a mythical animal). Normally the Craitnag is a mild creature and there are accounts of people hand-taming them with food, especially when they rouse themselves naturally from their hibernation.

However, folktales tend to drift toward the worst-case scenario, and one story concerned a young fellow named Murdach who had a longstanding and very bitter rivalry with his brother, Doolish, both of whom loved the fair Blaanid.

Doolish (the tragic hero of the tale) was clever and good at crafts and of-

---

23. Such as the Kudlak of Croatia, the Babylonian Ekimmu, the Pontianak of Java, and the Langsuir of Malaysia.
24. Folklore of the Isle of Man, A. W. Moore, 1891.

ten made some beautiful item for Blaanid. Murdach was a clod who tried to impress her with rabbits he'd caught and killed, but their blood-streaked pelts made her ill. When Murdach brought her a brace of pheasants he'd shot, Blaanid shrieked in horror—pheasants were, apparently, her favorite bird, but only when alive.

At home, Murdach saw that Doolish had made a marvelous birdcage for Blaanid, fashioning it out of rare woods and carving it beautifully in the likeness of leaves and berries and butterflies. Doolish told his brother that he was going to go out and trap a live pheasant and present it to Blaanid as a betrothal gift on Christmas Eve.

Murdach knew that he had no chance now because he lacked the skill to make beautiful things. All he was good at was hunting and trapping. Then he had a wicked idea. He told his brother that he realized now that Doolish was the better man and best suited to marry Blaanid, and offered his help as a trapper to secure a perfect pheasant for the cage. Doolish, noble but dim, agreed, not suspecting that his brother's frustration would lead to a bad end.

They set off into the snow-covered forest early on Christmas Eve, Doolish going east and Murdach going west. Doolish, for all his skill with making things, was a babe in the woods and soon got lost. Murdach, wiser in woodcraft, went directly to a cave and very carefully removed a Craitnag from where it hung from the ceiling, deep in its winter sleep. He then brought it back home and put it in the beautiful cage. Afterward he caught a pheasant, then went out and found his brother wandering in the woods.

At home he told Doolish that he would put the pheasant into the cage, and when his brother was busy writing out a card to go with the gift, Murdach snapped the pheasant's neck and tossed it out the window. He closed the cage doors and threw a coverlet over it and handed it to Doolish, who never bothered to look inside.

When the young man presented the gift to Blaanid, she was delighted at the beauty of the cage and happily reached inside to caress the pheasant.

By this time all of the jostling had jarred the bat out of its sleep, making it very angry. When Blaanid reached inside, the Craitnag clamped its teeth around her questing fingers. She screamed and withdrew her hand, but her finger was torn. The Craitnag escaped from the cage and bit her on the breast and the earlobe, then flew out of the house. The cold of the frigid December night killed it and it fell to the snow.

Naturally the proposal did not go well, and Blaanid threw the hapless Doolish out of the house. Dejected and utterly unable to explain how the pheasant had turned into a bat, he went home and wailed his misery to his brother, who comforted him while hiding a smile. Murdach felt that he would now have no rivals for the affections of the lovely Blaanid.

That night the young Blaanid, taking to her bed in shock and distress after the attack of the bat, lay in a swoon. The window of her room opened and in flew the ghost of the dead Craitnag. It settled on her breast and once more began to feed.

Late on New Year's Eve, having gone a week without hearing from his beloved, Doolish lay sprawled on his bed, completely wasted by grief. There was a thump on the window, and when he turned he saw that a huge bat was tapping against the glass. Thinking that it was the same Craitnag that had bitten Blaanid, the young man snatched up a poker from the fireplace, threw open the window, and tried to clobber the creature. But it eluded him and swept into the room, diving at him to bite him now and again, or scratch him with its talons. Already Doolish was bleeding from a number of deep bites on his neck.

Doolish was helpless before the creature's rage and fled the room, screaming for Murdach to help him. The Craitnag chased him through the house and they came to Murdach's room. Doolish rushed inside with the Craitnag clinging to his back. Ever the hunter, Murdach snatched up a hunting knife and slashed the creature in two halves.

To their horror, as it fell to the ground the halves became the severed halves of Blaanid, who had succumbed to the Craitnag's bite and become a vampire.

In a flash Doolish put the pieces together and realized that it had to be Murdach the hunter who had replaced the pheasant with the Craitnag. He fell on his brother and tried to kill him, but after a fierce battle, Murdach escaped and fled into the cold night and was never heard from again.

Then, heartbroken, Doolish collapsed on the bloody corpse of his beloved Blaanid, and there he died.

To this day, say the folktales, you can still hear the rustle of great bat wings on the night air as Doolish, now in the form of a great Craitnag, goes hunting for his brother, seeking revenge.

Craqueuhhe   Like most European countries, France has had its share of vampires, and they exist in great variety, from seductresses who live in fens to

⊰ VAMPIRES IN THE ⊱ ANIMAL KINGDOM

Mother Nature is a bit strange at times and occasionally conjures up some particularly nasty creatures, including several kinds of vampire. Here are a few of her more gruesome creations:

VAMPIRE SQUID (*Vampyroteuthis infernalis*): This sea creature inhabits tropical and subtropical oceans of the world at depths ranging from 300 to 3,000 meters, staying in what is called the "oxygen minimum layer" of the ocean where almost no light penetrates. The vampire squid gets its name from its jet-black skin, winglike webbing between the arms, and glaring red eyes.

LEECH: Wormlike creatures with suckers on each end that can range in length from one centimeter to over twenty-five centimeters. Some leeches feed on decaying plant material; others prefer blood.   *(continued)*

MOSQUITO: Annoying and dangerous, there are 2,700 species of these little bloodsuckers around the world. They can attack at will, day or night, but their predation increases 500 percent on the nights of a full moon (science is still trying to determine why). They are finicky, too, and prefer children to adults and even blonds to brunettes. Females are the ones that bite and they can live from 3 to 100 days; whereas the male lives 10 to 20 days. Though a mosquito drinks only about 5-millionths of a liter, it can leave behind any number of diseases, from malaria to West Nile virus, and it is the creature responsible for the most human deaths worldwide!

TICK: These tiny arthropods prey on live animals and humans and burrow their head into their victim's flesh in order to feed on blood. Like the mosquito, the tick can also spread disease with its bite, particularly Lyme disease and Rocky Mountain spotted fever.

VAMPIRE BAT: Vampire bats need about two tablespoons of blood each day and will starve to death if they go two days without feeding. Despite the propaganda, bats rarely carry disease, and if they do they will most likely die from it before it becomes a threat to humans or livestock. Most states do not allow bats to be kept as pets. Responsible bat organizations, such as the Organization for Bat Conservation, strongly discourage taking wild bats as pets. Erecting a bat-house in your yard, however, helps keep down the local insect population . . . though vampire bats are generally not the species to attract.

super-destructive revenants capable of destroying whole towns. Of this latter category the fiercest and most savagely powerful of the French monsters is the Craqueuhhe.

The Craqueuhhe is a true revenant, animated from dead flesh and rising from the grave of a person who died unbaptized or unrepentant. The Craqueuhhe is a decaying corpse, though one possessing enormous physical strength. It has bloodless wax-white skin, sunken eyes, and greasy hair that is clotted with dirt and writhing with maggots. Its fingers are usually ripped and torn from having clawed its way out of its grave. When it rises it has the power to walk even if it was badly mangled during its human death. The site of one stalking along on twisted and broken legs is a true inspiration for nightmares.

The Craqueuhhe is both a blood-drinker and flesh-eater and when it attacks it will eat any part of a human it can find, stopping only when its belly is full and leaving grisly remains behind. The creature is thoroughly immune to pain, being truly dead, and even shooting it or lopping off its limbs won't kill it. As long as it can writhe along the ground it will try to hunt and kill.

There are only two things that will stop a Craqueuhhe: fire and beheading. However, the monster is remarkably fast and powerful, so accomplishing either requires bravery and great skill. Only skilled fighters protected by consecrated relics or a group of people with torches and sharpened staves are likely to bring it down and lay it to final rest. Once it has been defeated, even if it was beheaded, the reanimated flesh will cling obstinately to unnatural life. The Craqueuhhe must be incinerated in order to prevent it from rising again or tainting the soil of the entire graveyard, thereby creating a host of these hideous monsters.

The creature does not fit the usual image of the grave-risen vampire, but more closely resembles the flesh-eating ghouls in films such as *Night of the Living Dead* and its followers.

Cuegle   In the Cantabrian legends of northern Spain there is a story about a monster who walks upright like a man, but who has three eyes, a great horn on his forehead, arms without hands, and five rows of razor-sharp teeth. This beast, the Cuegle, is an omnivorous predator and will eat anything it can catch.

The Cuegle, however, is not an industrious killer and tends to look for prey that cannot elude its attack. Nestlings, helpless animal young, and human babies left untended in basinets are its preferred diet.

The Cuegle cannot be killed, but it can be driven off or discouraged by spreading holly or oak leaves around the house, particularly near or inside the cradle. Both of these plants are as toxic to this monster as garlic is to vampires.

Cuero (also El Bien Peinado)   Most of the world's giant sea monsters are either described as sauropods or some species of squid, but the Cuero of South America is a gigantic octopus. The Cuero differs from the typical member of the family *octopoda* in that it has clawed hands at the ends of its tentacles, and on its vast head it sports large ears that are, strangely, covered with a variety of eyes. These eyes, legend tells us, can be made larger or smaller at will. The larger eyes apparently allow it to see great distances, and the smaller eyes help it see inside dark places where prey might be hiding.

The creature's name comes from the appearance of its skin—the name means "cow hide"—and the Cuero does seem to have a leathery appearance. Its alternate name, El Bien Peinado, is also descriptive and means "the smooth-headed one," a reference to its bulbous and smooth octopoidal head.

This cryptid dwells in Lago Lacar, located in the southern Andes and from that home base it attacks animals—and sometimes unwary humans—on land as well as in the water. Strange tracks have been found near muddy beaches, and the torn remains of animal hides and broken bones have been found, indicating where the monster has made a kill.

Culebre   In the Cantabrian region of northern Spain, home of the vicious *Cuegle*, there is another and far more powerful supernatural predator: the Culebre. This beast is a rare species of man-eating dragon that has powerful

CUERO Sandro Castilli

leathery wings and a long, sinuous serpentine body reminiscent of Chinese dragons. However, whereas Chinese dragons are often spiritual and even sometimes benevolent, the Culebre is neither. It is a killing machine that breathes fire and sulfurous gas and delights in the hunt.

Like many dragons of European legend, the Culebre is attracted to things that shine, particularly gold and jewels, and over time will amass a vast horde of treasure. Though they are hard to find and even harder to kill, knights and adventurers of the Middle Ages would seek them out in hopes of slaying the beast and obtaining the fortune.

Dakhanavar (also Dashnavar) From Armenia come tales of the Dakhanavar, a wicked mountain spirit who attacks worn-out travelers who camp out of doors at night. The Dakhanavar lives in remote spots on or around Mount Ararat and lurks in trees or in the hollows of trees, watching the roads for potential victims. Once it has spotted its target, it follows that person until they stop for the night, waiting until its prey has fallen into an exhausted sleep. Then it creeps into the camp or tent and makes a small bite on the quarry's toe or on the sole of a foot, and begins to feed. If driven by great need the Dakhanavar will sometimes sneak into an inn or remote house to feed.

The Dakhanavar is ferociously territorial and will assault anyone who tries to make a map of its lands, or even count the hills and valleys in the region, correctly fearing that a thorough knowledge of the landscape would reveal all of its secret hiding places.

A popular legend tells of two clever travelers who bedded down with their feet tucked under each other's head. The Dakhanavar, vicious but not particularly bright, was confused and thought that it was seeing a large two-headed monster. Fearing that it was in the presence of an even more terrible predator than itself, it fled into the darkness and was never seen in that particular region again.

Even today some travelers in Armenia, particularly those going into the region of Mount Ararat, generally take precautions against evil beings such as the Dakhanavar. Often they put small cloves of raw garlic in various pockets, or mash it and rub the paste on their shoes. At night, if camping out of doors, these travelers build a large fire and toss garlic bulbs into the flames. The combination of garlic aroma and a blazing fire will drive almost all of the world's many species of vampires away.

⊰ GARLIC ⊱

Garlic (*Allium sativum*) is the one constant element in vampire folklore around the world. All vampires fear it. In the movies garlic merely annoys vampires and is used to prevent unwanted entry, but in folklore it has much stronger powers. When used in the Ritual of Exorcism (described earlier), garlic breaks the spiritual bond between reanimated bodies and the evil entities that inhabit them. Throughout the world garlic paste is used to smear doorways and window frames to prevent evil from entering. Garlic is a blood purifier, so perhaps that explains the mystery of why it is believed to repel creatures who desire to taint human blood with supernatural infection.

Hippocrates, the father of medicine, prescribed garlic for infections, animal bites, wounds, cancer, leprosy, and digestive disorders. Garlic also possesses the ability to inhibit the growth of parasites in the intestines, including amoebas that cause dysentery, which is useful in combating the various vampires who spread disease.

Around the world there are other superstitions associated with garlic, both good and bad. Here are just a few:

- In Europe during the Middle Ages (and later) it was believed that to dream about garlic, especially about garlic in the house, was a sign that good luck was coming.
- To dream of eating garlic was a sure sign that one would discover something hidden that will prove to be of great value. *(continued)*

- In ancient Rome, soldiers ate garlic to strengthen their resolve and make them more courageous.
- In Egypt, slaves were given a diet heavy in garlic in order to make them stronger and therefore able to work harder.
- Theophrastus tells us that the ancient Greeks placed garlic atop piles of stones at crossroads as an offering to placate Hecate.
- A Muslim legend, however, claims that garlic is not so savory and that when Satan stepped from the Garden of Eden, garlic blossomed from where his left foot stepped, and onion from where his right trod.
- In Europe marathon runners sometimes eat a clove of garlic in the belief that it will prevent anyone from getting ahead of them.
- Tibetan monks are forbidden to enter a monastery if they have eaten garlic. This probably stems from the belief in that region of the world that garlic is an aphrodisiac, which does not help monks retain their detached calm.

Dames Blanches (White Ladies of Fau) In the Jura lake region in eastern France there are tales of the White Ladies of Fau, gorgeous female spirits who live in the forests. At first hearing these stories sound like fairy tales about beautiful princesses waiting for their Prince Charmings, but the White Ladies have no place in stories for children. These beings are actually monstrous predators who use their physical charms and magical allure to ensnare young men and bring the willing lads to quiet and remote places, where they attack them, feasting on both blood and flesh.

WHITE LADY OF FAU
Jason Beam

The most famous of the White Ladies was named Melusina, about whom many stories have been written. The legend of Melusina became very popular during the Middle Ages, mainly in France, but her stories also reach well into Germany. Most of these tales were collected by the scholar Jean d'Arras in the fifteenth century and published in two volumes, *Chronique de Melusine* and *Le Livre de Melusine en Fracoys,* the latter of which was published posthumously. Research by d'Arras drew heavily on earlier investigations by William de Portenach, but sadly, de Portenach's writings were lost. Fortunately both works by d'Arras still exist.

These writings, and the many other tales of Melusina, disagree as to the exact nature of the creature. In some stories Melusina is variously a tragic heroine suffering under a terrible curse (and therefore her demonic nature is not her fault); in others she is a monster trying to pass as a human; and in still others she is a demon living among humans in order to sew discord. In each legend, however, there is one constant: Melusina always requests that her lover respect her wish that one day a month she could be sequestered away where no one could see her. In folklore, as in real life, such promises seldom last, and each doomed lover invariably spies on her—usually because he could not bear to be parted from her for even a single night, or for some equally romantic drivel. In these tales, when someone does spy on Melusina in her hiding place, the creature is invariably seen as she is in the process of a physical transformation. In the nicer stories Melusina would be bathing in a tub with her mermaid's tail flopping over the rim like Daryl Hannah in the film *Splash*; but in other tales she would be in a hidden forest pool feasting on human flesh.

It makes an interesting study to read the various stories and listen to the poems and songs of Melusina,[25] to see how often she appears in the literature of Germany and France, and to see how disparate are the tales and descriptions of this White Lady of Fau.

Dearg-Dul (also known as Dearg-Due)   Throughout the islands of the United Kingdom, particularly Ireland and the Isle of Man, there are countless tales of ghosts, spirits, and faerie folk; but these two islands are also the home of the deadly Dearg-Dul. This ancient vampire's name, "red blood sucker," reveals its nature. The creature also spread to the Orkney Isles and other places around Great Britain, but it is in and around Ireland that it has claimed most of its many victims.

Legends disagree as to whether the Dearg-Dul is a revenant or a kind of

25. Professor D. L. Ashliman of the University of Pittsburgh maintains an excellent website with many of the songs, stories, ballads, and poems of Melusina: www.pitt.edu/~dash/melusina.html#contents.

eternal faerie. Certainly the Dearg-Dul does not appear as moldering corpse, though it does sleep in graves.

The Dearg-Dul is not a hideous monster, and in fact most stories agree that both the male and female Dearg-Dul appear as beautiful and sexually appealing figures whose charismatic aura is utterly compelling. They use their irresistible charms to lure potential victims to trysting places—where they attack and kill them. The Dearg-Dul are immensely strong, but they can also cast spells that can lull the victim into a stupor, making resistance impossible.

The Celtic druids have battled these creatures for a thousand years and have devised a number of clever ways of defeating them. The most common way is to locate the grave of a suspected Dearg-Dul and then erect a heavy cairn of stones over it, sealing the stones with prayers and placing sprigs of holly between the rocks. Even with their unnatural strength, the Dearg-Dul cannot dislodge thousands of pounds of rock, and the holly saps their strength. Trapped in their graves, the vampires will eventually degenerate into dust.

The Isle of Man offers another take on the Dearg-Dul legend, one with a far more romantic—and still predatory—element. Like her Irish cousins, the Dearg-Due of the Isle of Man is a beautiful female vampire faerie. She makes an unholy pact with a mortal man to provide him with creative inspiration in exchange for his eternal love. However, to the Dearg-Due "love" means "life essence," revealing this member of the species to be a kind of essential vampire. The Dearg-Due holds her mate imprisoned in an underwater palace from which he cannot escape, and though he may be inspired to write great songs or works of literature, no one will ever read them. Over time the Dearg-Due drains her constant lover of all energy and vitality, and when he is dead, she casts him off with not so much as a tear of farewell and begins the hunt for a new "eternal love."

In some tales, both in the Isle of Man and in Ireland, the Dearg-Dul is also a blood-drinker of a sort, and in these stories she holds her victim captive, drains every ounce of his blood, boils it in a crimson cauldron in which she brews her special magic, and makes potions for herself that imbue her with her eternal and ageless beauty.

Demons   Demons appear in the spiritual beliefs of nearly every culture on Earth and throughout history. The term is used generally to describe any supernatural being whose antipathy for humans defines their nature. The Bible and other great religious books mention these creatures frequently, and in the vast amount of religious folklore and mythology that builds up around any religion the number and variety of these creatures seems limitless.

The existence of demons is so widely accepted that they often seem to be just another part of the spiritual landscape, an accepted reality. Luckily most people don't encounter demons and therefore the belief that they exist is "safe," and they regard demons as counterpoints to angels, a part of the cosmic balance.

There is no one specific kind of demon. The demons of each culture are different in ways too diverse to explain in one listing. Scattered throughout this book, however, are individual entries for specific demons (or demonic creatures).

Dila   One of the strangest of the Filipino monsters is the Dila who is actually nothing more than a spectral tongue. The Dila flows through the Earth and then when it comes under a house it rises up the floorboards and seeks out a sleeping person and then begins licking the exposed flesh. The person begins to sicken and if the Dila comes back several nights in a row, the person will die.

This suggests that the Dila is one of the world's many essential vampires, feeding either on life energy or, perhaps, health.

Djien   Among the Seneca Indians of the northeastern United States there is a great predatory monster spider as big as a man and as fierce as a demon. This gigantic arachnid, called Djien, keeps its heart buried in a secret place underground, which means that in battle it cannot receive a mortal wound.

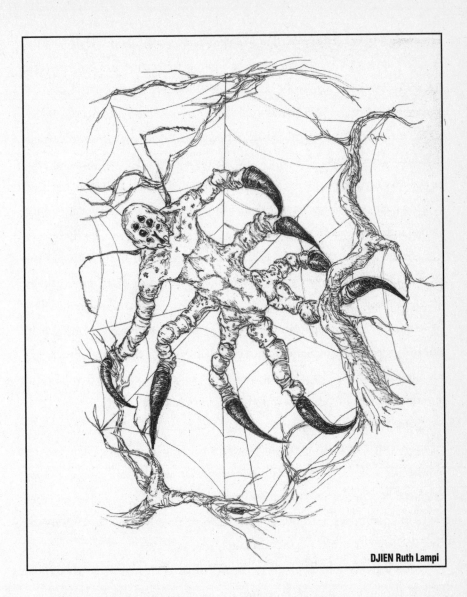

DJIEN Ruth Lampi

When the Djien attacked people it did so with a reckless abandon, and if it were injured, even hacked and disfigured, it could retreat to a safe place, recover its heart, and instantly regenerate into a whole creature once more.

However the heroic and wise Seneca warrior Othegwenhda, who was part human and part spirit according to the legend, discovered the secret of the Djien and took a tree limb and stabbed down through the earth hard enough to piece the creature's heart.

Doppelgänger The word "Doppelgänger," often misused in conversation and writing, is a German term meaning "double walker" or "double goer," and refers to a kind of shadow self that is bonded to every human. This other self is sometimes benign but often is quite nasty, and the Doppelgänger is the basis for the phrase "evil twin." In the Doppelgänger a person's less savory qualities are exalted. Most often the Doppelgänger is invisible and lacks any real power, but certain people have the misfortune of having a shadow self who has, through some mischance of fate, a spell, or other spiritual calamity, gained independence of action.

Once a Doppelgänger has become empowered it can either influence the mortal self into doing evil or corrupt misdeeds or can separate itself (usually while the mortal body is asleep) and roam free to cause all manner of mischief.

Generally the only person who can see a Doppelgänger is its mortal half, and even then it is rare. Sometimes one's shadow, seen out of the corner, will be capering instead of behaving normally; or a reflection in a mirror will be doing something quite different from what it should be doing.

Some folktales tell of people who have managed to open a line of communication, either verbally, telepathically, or through diary writing, allowing the mortal half and the Doppelgänger to become familiar. In rare cases the Doppelgänger has been benign and has offered advice, insights, and encouragement. In other tales the Doppelgänger whispers directly into a person's mind, driving them to distraction and ultimately into madness.

Some legends hold that a person sees their Doppelgänger only when their own death is imminent, but sometimes it appears to warn of impending ill fortune. Whether this warning is meant to help a person avert disaster or as a way of mocking them for a fate they can't escape is not quite clear.

The bottom line is that many people in Germany and surrounding countries believe in the existence of the Doppelgänger, but few can agree on the nature of the being. Some speculate that it is the desire of the Doppelgänger not to be understood, to remain enigmatic and therefore something to feel uneasy about. After all, it is disquieting to think that there is a shadowy spiritual reverse of ourselves constantly observing us and possibly whispering dark thoughts in our most secret ears.

Doppelsauger   There are many characteristics that allow folklorists to group and sub-group the world's many supernatural predators. For example, some vampires shed their skin and become floating fireballs, some tend to bite only toes or feet, and some prey exclusively on children. One very common sub-group is the vampires who deliberately place their bites on the breasts of women, either to drain blood or milk—and sometimes both. The *Alp* of Germany is one, the *Nora* of Hungary is another, but perhaps the most deeply breast-fixated is the Doppelsauger of Hanoverian legend. This creature not only feeds off the breasts of its female victims, but in a pinch will eat its own breasts.

Folklore tells us that the Doppelsauger is created when a mother has permitted a child who has already been weaned to breast-feed again, hence the name Doppelsauger, which means "double-sucker." If that child were to die it would be condemned to return to haunt the living as a Doppelsauger. Even if the child grows up, grows old, and dies naturally he is still fated to be a monster.

In the grave it begins its transformation from human corpse to undead monster, awakening in the coffin with an unnatural hunger. Often it will tear at its own breast for sustenance so that it has the power to fight its way out of coffin and grave. Once it has gained the strength and risen, it will seek out its family and begin to haunt them, coming by night to feed on the breasts—flesh, milk (if any), and blood—of the people it once loved. Although the Doppelsauger characteristically attacks only its own relatives, it will attack anyone when pressed by great hunger.

Various preventive strategies are available to the family of a deceased person who is likely to become a Doppelsauger. The key thing is to ensure that it cannot begin eating itself while in the grave. Denied this initial and entirely unwholesome meal, the Doppelsauger will lack the vigor necessary to escape its grave. Thick wooden blocks are put in place to prevent the corpse's jaws from working, and often a metal coin is wedged upright between its teeth, or a semicircular wooden board is placed under its chin to make it impossible for the corpse to bite at itself. Also, thick linen bandages are wound around the body to keep the creature from using its hands, and great care is taken to make sure that any cloth from the shroud or burial garments does not come into close contact with the mouth. If it can get cloth between its teeth (and if the teeth are not properly blocked), the creature can use chewing motions to gradually tug and shred the bindings out of place thus freeing its hands.

Should the Doppelsauger rise, it can be killed by beheading, a bullet to the brain, or by burning. No other method will work, though garlic has been known to repel the creature, and garlic bulbs are often placed in the coffin as an added precaution to keep the creature weak and reduce the likelihood that it will have the strength to tear through shroud and coffin.

Drakul   Despite the fact that the real person on whom Bram Stoker based Dracula was not a vampire, there is still some relation to actual vampire lore in the tale—even though it takes great license in its presentation of vampire powers and defenses. Aside from basing Count Dracula on Vlad Tepes, the infamous Prince of the Eastern European nation of Wallachia, many of the qualities Stoker assigned to his fictional vampires can be found in the legends of the Moldavian creature called the Drakul. The name can he translated as both "devil" and "dragon," and is actually used as a common, and rather harsh, expletive. Fighting words, in any country, but more so in Moldavia.

When referring strictly to a creature of the night, the term "Drakul" refers to a pale-skinned, hollow-eyed blood-drinking revenant similar in many ways to the vampires of popular film. Similar in many ways to the *Vampiro* of Moravia, the Drakul is a dead body brought to a semblance of life through demonic possession. The demon inhabits the corpse while it rests in the grave, and once ensconced there it reanimates the dead flesh, reactivates the memories the corpse had when it was alive, and then rises to harass the living. The demon

TOMB OF VLAD THE IMPALER
Kimberly Zagoren

uses these purloined memories to select prey and often terrorizes the family of the deceased.

Like the fictional Dracula, the Drakul cannot be separated for long from its coffin or it will disintegrate, but unlike the famous Count, the Drakul carries its coffin around on its head.

Since the Drakul must sleep by day in its coffin, the most direct way to kill it is to dig it up, tip it out of the coffin, and then steal the coffin. Once stolen, the coffin is burned using torches made from thorn bushes. As the coffin burns to cinders so the Drakul will turn to dust.

This method sounds far easier than it actually is, because unlike movie vampires, the Drakul is not in a helpless trance while it sleeps. It can wake up, it does not fear sunlight, and will fight to prevent its coffin from being stolen. The Drakul is both vicious and very fast, and it's powerful enough to tear a strong man's arms right out of his sockets. To bring one down, it's best to bring along the traditional angry mob with torches and pitchforks to surround it while a dozen doughty men with long stakes and axes rush in to end its existence.

Draugr   The Draugr are strange creatures found in Norway and the surrounding regions. Not typical revenants, they in fact share some qualities with dragons in that they collect treasure and guard it jealously.

The Draugr is a demonic spirit that enters the grave of a fallen Viking and inhabits its flesh so that the corpse rises to hunt and kill. As Vikings are often buried along with stores of great wealth, the Draugr will protect its own horde, attacking and killing anyone who tries to take so much as a silver penny, and will also rob other graves in order to gather even greater wealth.

Occasionally the Draugr leaves its grave in the dead of night—when it deems it safe to leave its treasure unprotected for a short time—and attacks sleeping humans, tearing its victims apart, feeding on their flesh and blood, and taking the bones back to its den to chew on at leisure.

The Draugr has the power to control the weather and can summon thick fogs to shroud the region so that it can safely leave its cairn and go hunting, or conjure storms to hamper pursuit from relatives of its prey. The Draugr is also a shape-shifter and can transform into a hunting bird or a great gray wolf, which it does mostly to allow it to travel quickly and without arousing suspicion.

If hunters do manage to track it back to its lair, the Draugr has little difficulty protecting its fortune as it possesses fantastic supernatural strength and is immune to any weapon. Swords will shatter on its breast, spears will

DRAUGR George Martzukous

snap in two, and war hammers will splinter. No weapon made by human hands can harm the Draugr, and yet it is not invincible. Only a hero—a true hero, whose heart is pure and who is in good standing with the gods of Valhalla—can stand up to the Draugr with any hope of victory, let alone survival. Even then the hero must fight empty-handed because the monster can only be overcome with wrestling alone: bare hands and a noble heart are the only weapons that can defeat this monster.

Duppy   The care, appeasement, and management of supernatural beings are dicey problems, not to be undertaken lightly, and never to be taken for granted. A single mistake or break in ritual can take a demon who is enslaved and set him loose to do unimaginable harm.

Such is the case with the Duppy, a ghostly being found in the West Indies. The Duppy itself is the distilled evil that seeps like vapor from a corpse after death, which generally lingers around the grave. This energy can be summoned by a variety of rituals and then takes on a somewhat corporeal form. Once invoked, the Duppy can be used as a bound servant to attack one's enemies, learn secrets, and generally act as a weapon. But if control over the monster is lost, then it will turn and destroy everything of beauty or value in its former master's life before finally murdering the unfortunate master in the most grisly of ways.

Sometimes a Duppy is invoked by accident—playing cards near a recent grave is enough; or sometimes it is deliberately brought forth by someone who just wishes to see how much mischief the creature will cause. Pouring rum and a few silver coins into a grave is the easiest way to bring it to life.

During night hours the Duppy is impossible to kill. The best that can be hoped for is to keep it occupied—scattering tobacco seeds outside the house will keep it busy for hours. The trick is to keep it occupied so that the rising sun shines on it, which weakens the monster considerably. During daylight hours it is virtually powerless.

Dwende   In the Philippines, just as in many places around the world, there are supernatural creatures who are potentially evil, but are not always so. The Dwende, for example, are small impish creatures who live mostly in rural areas and generally ignore humans altogether; however, sometimes these beings do come into contact with men and that contact can either be wholesome or decidedly unwholesome.

The Dwende (their name comes from the Spanish word for "dwarf") can be appeased and cajoled through offerings of food left for them on the floor by a door. If the Dwende like the food and accept the offering, then they can be quite helpful to have around. They bring good luck and are excellent at finding items that have been lost. The Dwende sometimes become so accustomed to being with a family—as long as the food is properly and frequently offered—that they even protect the house from other creatures—natural and unnatural—who try to enter.

However, if a Dwende is intentionally given bad or spoiled food, or if it has been given food in the past but the offerings have stopped, or if some other offense is given (or perceived), then the Dwende shows its other face. An offended Dwende brings bad luck to the house, and can act like a poltergeist—throwing things around, damaging crockery, stopping up the drains, tipping over the trash, and even bringing in sickness to the house.

Dwylla the Huntress Elf (also Shim'ragh, Green Linn) Irish folktales are often intertwined with superstition. One such story tells of a beautiful girl named Dwylla who was born to a mortal woman who had been raped by an elf sorcerer. Dwylla, who is known as Shim'ragh and Green Linn in different parts of Ireland, was raised as a normal girl but knew that she was not human. Perhaps it was the pointed ears, the ability to see in the dark, or the fact that she could understand the language of birds. On her sixteenth birthday she overheard her mother telling her aunt about how she had been raped by the elf wizard.

Upon hearing this, Dwylla—who had secretly romanticized her heritage as something marvelous and special—went totally mad. She fled into the woods, stole weapons from farms, and began hunting for her father, desiring his death above all other things. She never found him, but along the way she killed scores of other elves, either because they wouldn't tell her how to find her father, or just because they were elves. In some tales her parentage is reversed and it is an elf maiden raped by a human nobleman who gives birth to the half-breed. In those versions of the tale it is humans that she hunts.

DWYLLA
Andy Jones

In some of the paintings of Dwylla she is depicted riding a unicorn; in others she is portrayed as a very fierce and murderous huntress.

Eigi Einhamr   Shape-shifting takes many forms in folklore. A person may acquire the talent as part of a study of magic, as the result of a curse, or it might be a natural quality of a supernatural being. In Norway and Iceland the process involved simply putting on an animal skin and then desiring to become one with that animal. The people who did this were known as Eigi Einhamr, which means "not one-skinned," a phrase that certainly describes this cult of were-animals who could easily change from man to animal and then back to man.

The Eigi Einhamr were deliberate shape-shifters and they appear all throughout the history and folktales of that region of the world. In the great Ynglinga Saga of Odin the process is described as follows: "He could change his appearance. There his body lay as sleeping or dead. But he became a bird or a beast, a fish or a serpent, and at a moment's notice could go into distant lands on his own business or on that of others."

Like most of the more powerful shape-shifters around the world, the Eigi Einhamr retained their human intelligence when they were in animal form. These creatures were different, however, from many of the other shape-shifters in that they were not necessarily evil. They were fearsome to their enemies, of course, but the power to shape-shift was believed by them to be a gift from Odin, the king of the Norse gods and something of a clever theriomorph himself. In the ancient Norse epic of the Ere-Dwellers, the relationship between human shape-shifter and god was clearly described:[26]

> (Thrand) "was said to be not of one shape while he was heathen,"
> & etc.—ok var kallathr eigi einhamr. The meaning of this is, that
> Thrand had the power of changing his shape as occasion served,
> which power was believed to be the special gift of Odin, the first and
> greatest of shape or skin-changers: "Odin changed shapes; lay then
> the body, as if asleep or dead, while he himself was a fowl, or a four-
> footed beast, or fish, or snake, and went in a moment into far-away
> countries on his own or other folks' errands."

El Dientudo   In the dense forests surrounding Buenos Aires, there are tales of a monster whose name means "Big Teeth," which should give some idea of its favored method of attack. This Argentinean creature, called El Dientudo, is

---

26. *The Story of the Ere-Dwellers,* chapter LXI, "Snorri Sends for Thrand the Strider."

a flesh-eating predator that looks humanoid in shape but which is completely covered in thick dark hair, stands over seven feet tall, and has a stench about it like rotting meat.

El Dientudo is sighted fairly often, though no artifacts of it have ever been found and there are no reliable theories as to its origins or nature. The only signs of this cryptid are some eyewitness accounts of it dragging people off into the woods and occasional discoveries of broken bone and blood-stained clothes.

Ellefolk (also **Elleman, Ellewoman**) In the region surrounding the moors of Denmark tales abound of small creatures who appear, at first glance, like harmless little gnomes, but who are in fact very dangerous and more akin to elves.

The female of the species, known as the Ellewoman, is beautiful and seductive if seen from the front. This is just a sham, for seen from behind she is hollowed-out and sports a bovine tail. Being hollow she is naturally heartless—both literally and figuratively—and she uses her disguise of beauty to attract willing young men. Once they see her she begins to strum the strings of an exotic instrument very like a harp, and the sound is thoroughly entrancing. Any man who breaks free from her allure and spurns her is cursed with sickness.

The Elleman is even more dangerous. He appears in the form of an ancient, weathered old man with flat cap pulled low over his brow. He sets traps by appearing to either be ill and in need of assistance, or he lays sunbathing in places where people are likely to stumble upon him. In either case, when someone encounters the spiteful little creature he focuses his ill will upon them and will send sickness to them and to their entire village.

The very nature of the Elleman is so toxic that if an animal comes to graze on a hill where one of these creatures has either spat or relieved himself, the animal will quickly develop a fatal illness. If a cow eats such tainted grass, the sickness will be passed on through her milk and anyone—calf or human—who drinks it will become deathly ill.

On the other hand, the Ellefolk do respond to courtesy—or at least are flattered enough by it to give the appearance of being gracious—which means a farmer can ask their permission for his animals to graze, and if such permission is given then no sickness will result.

Ellyon   In the United Kingdom live a variety of helpful household spirits. One such species is the Ellyon of Wales, which are tiny fairie folk who delight in cooking and cleaning. For the most part they prefer to remain invisible—coming out when everyone is asleep—and they chatter among themselves in thin, reedy voices, speaking in their own exotic language. They make their own meals from a yellow fungus that grows on the roots of trees, which they call "faerie butter" and on toadstools and pollen.

In rare cases where someone has been able to spy on them, the Ellyon tend to go about their work like something out of a Disney film: singing, laughing, and dancing. If they discover they are being spied upon, however, the Ellyon will vanish and never return.

Only in Welsh stories of the latter part of the nineteenth century is there a dark tint to this happy picture. In those tales the Ellyon are only benign when left alone, but when seen they become angered and react like poltergeists, throwing things around and generally trashing the house, sometimes even using pieces of broken crockery to jab and slash at the person unlucky enough to have seen them.

Eloko   Among the Nkundo people of Zaire dwell vicious flesh-eating dwarves called the Eloko. These creatures are revenants and vengeance ghosts both, created from the spirit of a person who died under unfortunate circumstances and cannot spiritually "move on" until they've settled the score with whomever was responsible for their death.

No matter what the person looked like prior to their death, the Eloko rise from the grave as ugly dwarves whose bodies are covered with coarse grass instead of hair, and its garments are made of leaves. The Eloko have razor-sharp claws, snouts like dogs, sharp teeth, and eyes that flicker with tiny flames. One fearsome peculiarity of the Eloko is that its snout, normally the size of a small dog's, is hinged like a snake's and can yawn wide enough to consume a fully grown human being!

While hunting, the Eloko carries with it a set of small enchanted bells and with its garments of leaves and grassy hair it blends easily in with the foliage. As a traveler walks by the Eloko rings its enchanted bells, which has the immediate effect of lulling any human into a stupor. Once it has the person helpless the Eloko settles down to its feast of human flesh.

The Nkundo witch doctors have devised a number of protective charms and fetishes for use against the Eloko, but all these do is prevent immediate attack only when the Eloko is suspected of being in the area. The unwary can still fall prey to the magic bells.

To kill an Eloko requires muscle and fighting skill. A warrior, armed with steel weapons as well as the fetishes, can stand up to the monsters. Like many species of vampire, the Eloko is usually stopped by using a spear like a stake to pin it to the ground so that its head can be cut off. Once beheaded the body and head are buried separately, thus breaking the curse and freeing the village from this supernatural killer.

Empusa (also Mormolykiai; plural Empusae)   Travelers have always been easy prey for hungry monsters, and this is as common today as it was in ancient Greece. Waiting in the shadowy passes and in the darkness by the sides of the road was the bloodthirsty Empusae.

These were horrific creatures with human bodies and donkey faces, but despite the seemingly comical appearance they were dreadful demons in the service of Hecate, goddess of the Crossroads and one of the most powerful goddesses in all of the ancient religions. In some tales they have one leg of brass and the other is like a donkey's; and it is suggested that this strange appearance is nothing but a projection to hide their true faces, which are rumored to have been to horrible to bear.

These monsters have been written about in scores of stories, histories, and plays for thousands of years, but the most famous and important account was that by Philostratus in his *Life of Apollonius of Tyana*.[27] He wrote of the handsome youth Menippus, who was enticed by an Empusa disguised as a Phoenician woman. Apollonius confronted the Empusa, and the Empusa revealed itself and admitted to fattening up Menippus so that she might devour him.

The young hero's solution to the attack is, to say the least, unique: "For they were traveling by bright moonlight, when the figure of an empusa or hobgoblin appeared to them, that changed from one form into another, and sometimes it vanished into nothing. And Apollonius realized what it was, and himself heaped abuse on the hobgoblin and instructed his party to do the same, saying that this was the right remedy for such a visitation. And the phantasm fled away, shrieking even as ghosts do."

The Empusa may be the only monster driven off by harsh language.

Eng Banka   Hellhounds and werewolves aren't the only supernatural members of the canine family. Malaysian folklore reports of an essential vampire called the Eng Banka that is a fierce doglike creature that hunts by night and steals a person's soul. The creature feeds on the soul and as it digests this spiritual energy, the victim quickly wastes away and dies.

Though the Eng Banka is fast and intelligent, it is no more invulnerable than an ordinary dog and can be killed by any conventional means. However, the corpse of an Eng Banka must be tossed into a fire and burned completely, and the ashes scattered, otherwise it will rise again and take a new body in order to return to the hunt.

Because the Eng Banka appears in a doglike form, many Malaysians fear dogs that they don't know, and often wear talismans to protect them against this kind of evil.

27. *Life of Apollonius of Tyana, Book II*, by Flavius Philostratus (c.170–c.245 CE), translated by F. C. Conybeare.

Engkanto   In the Phillippines there are two different legends of the super-natural monster called the Engkanto; in one the creature is fairly benign and in the other it is decidedly vicious.

The less hostile—relatively speaking—of the two is the Engkanto who dwells within lunok trees.[28] As long as the tree is left unharmed, the Engkanto is content to live and let live; but if someone is unwise enough to cut down the lunok, then the enraged Engkanto will curse that person with a disease that causes a raging fever and bloating of the stomach. Most often these symptoms are not fatal, but it is in the power of a particularly angry Engkanto to kill in this fashion.

The other Engkanto are more closely associated with demons and are be-lieved to be fallen angels doomed to live half in Hell and half on Earth, and constantly feeling the pain of being split between dimensions. Though this is a far more dramatic story, it occurs far less often in the folklore of the Philip-pines.

There are a lot of ways to detect the presence of the Engkanto. If a dog howls for no apparent reason, it's usually a sign that the creature is near. Hens cackling also indicate the presence of the Engkanto. In the latter case, tossing a handful of salt both quiets the birds and drives off the spirit.

The Engkanto is a very touchy creature, and even pointing at the lunok tree, or laughing while looking in its direction, is enough to give offense. If a lunok tree stands near a stream or pool, anyone planning to take a bath there should first bow to the tree and ask the pardon of the spirits within, otherwise illness is sure to ensue. When unsure if an Engkanto is in the area, a passerby should say, "Tabi-tabi po," which alerts the spirits to the presence of a nearby human. They don't mind people passing by, but they do not like to be startled.

Erestun (also known as **Xloptuny**)   In Russia, a person at the brink of death—through illness, accident, or violence—is doubly at risk of calamity.

28. Known in Tagalog as the Balete, the lunok is a member of the ficus family.

Aside from being in danger of death, the dying person is also at great risk of being possesed by an Erestun. In these cases it is not a demon who inhabits the weakened body, but the spirit of an evil sorcerer—one who has either learned to split his soul into separate but functional halves, or one who through some great misfortune has lost his mortal body.

If the Erestun detects a dying person, he enters in while in an invisible astral form and takes over the body, causing the body to make what appears to be a miraculous recovery. Though the body appears to be healthy once more, this is not the case, for in order to maintain control of the pirated body the Erestun needs to feed on fresh human blood.

Using the memories of the hijacked body, the Erestun begins to prey on the friends and family of its host, attacking them and draining them. Sometimes the Erestun takes only a little blood, leaving the victim alive but weakened; but if need is great, the Erestun drains all of the blood and life out of its victim. It is usually excesses of this kind that lead to its being discovered.

There are only two known cures for possession by an Erestun, both equally difficult. Either the possessing spirit can be driven out by exorcism, a tricky business since this is not true demonic possession and the standard rites of exorcism will not easily work; or the Erestun and its host can be staked, beheaded, and burned. Sadly, the victim host of the Erestun is generally not saved, even by exorcism, making that unfortunate the vampire's final victim.

Eretiku (also known as **Eretnik, Elatomsk, Eretitsa,** and **Eretnitsa)**
There is a female version of the Russian Erestun called the Eretiku, and though these two monsters share some similarities, they are also different in several significant ways.

The Eretiku takes its name from the root word *heretic,* and the creature is a deliberate religious blasphemer who delights in her practice of dark magic. In the Russia of a few hundred years ago it was widely believed that all heretics are damned to become some sort of vampire or pernicious ghost after death,

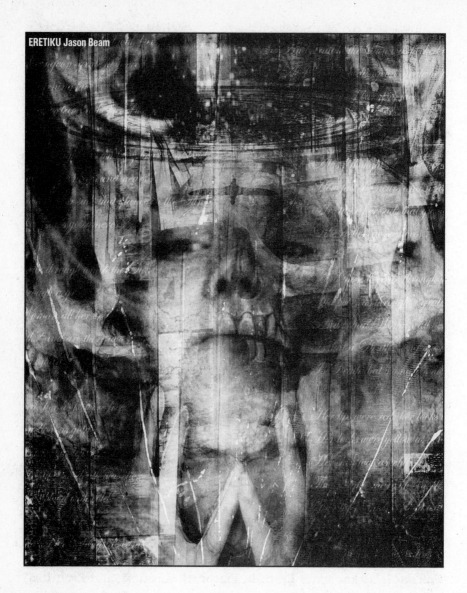

ERETIKU Jason Beam

a belief that has led to some shockingly savage punishments for suspect heretics.

The Eretiku is a woman who sold her soul to the Devil while alive and af-ter death returns from the grave to prey on the living. The Eretiku assumes the disguise of an old crone[29] and over time will seek out others of her ilk and with

29. The Eretiku is not part of the standard folklore of the *Old Hag*.

them will establish a coven that meets in the dark shadows of a deep forest ravine.

The Eretiku causes a wasting sickness, not through any bite but with the power of its stare. To look into the eyes of this creature is enough to develop a disease that will eat away at vitality, health, and sanity. It is for this reason that the Russians take particular care to ensure that the eyes of the newly dead are kept closed.

Some Eretiku—those lacking a cohesive spiritual force—cannot manifest new bodies and only become a kind of poltergeist, called a "doorknocker." These ghosts sleep in graves and at night rise and visit alehouses, public bath-houses, and other places. They make disgusting and disruptive noises.

Estrie   No creature in Hebrew folklore is dreaded more than the witch-vampire called the Estrie, a shape-shifting creature with an insatiable thirst for the blood of children. What could be more frightening than a nearly unstoppable monster who delights in murdering children?

When hunting, the Estrie will assume a variety of animal forms—birds, dogs, insects, even snakes—but it can also change its appearance to mimic other humans. Its choice of shape or face is entirely based on its judgment of what will most likely attract and deceive its prey. It might be a family dog for one victim and then a smiling grandmother to someone else. In either case, when the Estrie gets is prey alone it reverts to its true and utterly demonic shape. No living person has ever seen that face; those who have seen it became her victims.

Aside from terror and grief over the creature's murderous attacks, there is a secondary harm done to families or villages: faith is eroded, because all of the evidence points to trusted persons or otherwise harmless animals. Few people ever realize that a shape-shifter has been hunting among them, and many an innocent person was put to death for murders the Estrie committed while wearing their face. Luckily, destroying an Estrie does not involve the use of special magical weapons; ordinary guns, knives, and clubs will work, and fire is always useful. Should a human wound an Estrie, the creature will perish unless it somehow contrives to steal salt and bread from the house of its enemy. Consuming these things will restore the Estrie to health, and by the next evening it will be able to hunt again.

Fachan   In the highlands of Scotland survives a strange old tale of a bizarre creature called the Fachan who seeks out and ruthlessly attacks travelers walking alone through the mountains. The Fachan is very tall—at least a head taller than a tall man—and stands on a single powerful leg with which it can leap faster than a man can run. From the center of its chest sprouts a thickly muscled arm ending in a hand with an unbreakable grip. If the Fachan grabs hold of any part of its victim there is no escape. The Fachan also has a single, glaring eye with which the creature can entrance its victims, leaving them helpless to attack. The intense stare of the Fachan can also cause a strong man's heart to burst in his chest.

The only way to defeat a Fachan is to escape it. Though it can leap very fast, it is not as agile as a man, and a fleet-footed fellow who can dart around boulders and down crooked paths can sometimes elude it.

El Fantasma Malo   Poltergeists are common throughout the world, but El Salvador is home to a particularly nasty variety that plagues people living in rural areas: El Fantasma Malo—the Evil Ghost.

El Fantasma Malo generally are ghosts of persons who have built houses and then died in them, unable to either leave the dwelling they labored so hard to construct or unable to yield ownership to anyone else, even after death. In some cases El Fantasma Malo acts like a typical poltergeist, yanking blankets off of sleeping people, throwing things around the house, moving furniture, hiding things; but some accounts report the creatures doing far more than that.

One story tells of the ghost hovering like a thick mist over sleeping children and making it hard for them to breathe. The next day the children were ill and it was only after a blessing by a priest that they began to recover their strength.

A similar tale, recounted by Ernesto Gonzalez, a Salvadoran immigrant of my acquaintance, tells of El Fantasma Malo actually inhaling the breath of a sleeping baby and taking with it some of the child's life force. The child soon sickened and died.

A belief in El Fantasma Malo may be one of the many ways in which undereducated and superstitious people in rural areas try to explain away tragedies like sudden infant death syndrome (SIDS).

The most recent report of El Fantasma Malo was posted on the website, Ghostvillage (which tracks and reports ghostly sightings), where a twenty-eight-year-old Salvadoran man identified as "Elio" told of how a malicious poltergeist disturbed his sleep by breathing on him like a dog, touched him, sprayed water on him, and scared his farm animals.[30]

Farkaskoldus A number of supernatural predators boast of being part vampire and part something else. Often it is a ghost or a witch who makes up the other half of a vampire hybrid, but in Hungary the grisly creature in question is a cross between a vampire and a werewolf.

In essence the Farkaskoldus is a werewolf who feasts on blood rather than flesh. It is also a kind of vengeance ghost, a being that rises from its grave to seek revenge for some grievous wrong. Most of the Farkaskoldus of folklore are shepherds who had been abused or unfairly treated in life, and then after death rose as bloodsucking werewolves.

In most of the legends once the Farkaskoldus has gotten whatever measure of justice it—or some spiritual arbiter—deems appropriate, the monstrous spirit leaves the body of the risen shepherd and the empty corpse shambles

---

30. Courtesy of Jeff Belanger of www.Ghostvillage.com.

WEREWOLF Lee Moyer

back to its grave never again to disturb the world of the living. In a number of other tales, however, the Farkaskoldus is less easily appeased and continues to kill even after it has hunted down and killed its own oppressor.

The Farkaskoldus can be killed by ordinary weapons, but it is easily angered and always dangerous. Few men could stand up to one in single combat. The smartest and most effective method for dispatching the monster is to approach it while accompanied by a large group of heavily armed comrades.

Torches, long stakes, guns, a pack of hunting dogs, and many knives would be good ways to start a Farkaskoldus hunt.

Féar Gortagh Also known as fairy grass, the Féar Gortagh ("hungry grass") is an old Irish legend about a predatory force that is vegetable rather than animal. It is a patch of grass where someone has died violently, and the taint of unnatural death somehow imbues the grass with a pernicious quality that curses anyone who walks upon it with a hunger so insatiable that the person will literally eat himself to death. The legend is very old but during the great nineteenth-century famine of Ireland it was revived and embellished.

A similar legend, that of the Féar Gortach ("hungry man") tells of an old tramp who wanders lonely roads begging for food. Anyone who passes him by without even a token show of generosity is likewise cursed with the fatal hunger. However, anyone who shows kindness to the old man is granted good luck and great health.

Fetch A Fetch is a Scottish version of the *Doppelgänger* legend, and refers to a person's "other self"—composed of all of the negative qualities and unnatural urges that lead to aberrant or sinful behavior. This Fetch is usually suppressed with the human psyche, kept in check by sanity, an acknowledgment of societal laws, and religious faith; but sometimes a person becomes so dis-

⚔ ANCIENT WEREWOLVES ⚔

The Epic of Gilgamesh (a real historical king of Uruk in Babylonia c. 2000 BCE) makes mention of a lycanthrope (werewolf) in the character of Enkidu, a wild-man created by the sky god Anu. Enkidu and Gilgamesh are initially adversaries, but after the great hero defeats the werewolf they become great friends and share many epic adventures together.

turbed and unbalanced that this darker self breaks free and emerges to become a separate being, one that is capable of doing great harm.

Sometimes the Fetch remains intangible and invisible and just whispers in the ear of its better half, encouraging his twin self to do unspeakable things. Since, from that person's point of view, these urges are coming from within the good half, he begins to believe that he is going insane, and sometimes actually does.

A Fetch may also manifest itself outside the host body and act something like a poltergeist, causing damage and even attacking other people. Since the Fetch, when manifesting in physical form, looks just like its true half, the good aspect is often blamed for the crimes.

Feu Follet (also **Fifollet)**   In rural Louisiana lives a legend of a murderous fiery spirit called the Feu Follet who flits through the air as a will-o'-the-wisp and preys on victims for their sexual energy. The Feu Follet is actually the ghost of a sinner who was condemned to remain on Earth until it had completed its penance, but instead it has rebelled against humanity, against God, and even against its own salvation by choosing to continue on after death as a wicked being.

The Feu Follet divides its appetites between two particular types of meals: children, from whom it takes breath and the essence of vitality; and healthy adults, from whom it takes sexual energy.

Unlike many essential vampires, the Feu Follet does not hunt within one gender, but will switch back and forth to whomever it favors at the moment. In this way it is like both the Incubus (who attacks women) and the Succubus (who attacks men).

Only among the Cajuns in southern Louisiana is it called the Feu Follet; elsewhere in the state it is just referred to as a will-o'-the-wisp.

Forso   It is very likely that there are many categories of supernatural predators that have not been classified, and even more likely that many of the known categories have sub-groupings. Evidence supporting this theory is demonstrated in the Forso, a ghostly being from New Guinea and the islands off the northern coast of Australia.

The Forso ostensibly fits into the category of essential vampire in that instead of blood these types of monsters feed on less tangible things such as sexual potency, life force, and emotion; but the Forso twists the paradigm a bit more. What it feeds on is disappointment. The Forso is capable of causing bad luck and calamity and does so—not out of spite as is often thought—but because the depression and despair caused by ill fortune is a powerful energy. It is that energy which sustains the Forso and it siphons it out of a person through their aura.

The Forso is also a true ghost in that it is the spiritual remains of a person who has died. It is formless and invisible, rising from the grave as a presence rather than as a reanimated corpse. The Forso seldom strays far from where it was buried and lingers to harass the people of its former village.

Prayers and charms can be used to try to dissuade the Forso, but these work well only if the Forso, in life, had strong religious beliefs. Since the Forso is generally created during the death of a less than savory person, many Forso cannot be controlled through prayers.

Oddly the Forso is not considered an evil being by the people of these islands. In their view the Forso is simply a spirit who is bored and lonely and more or less "acts out" in order to get attention.

The best way to keep a Forso placated enough not to cast spells of bad luck is to regularly visit its grave and treat it like one of the honored dead, or to bring the bones of the dead into the house, thus including it in the family again.

— Chapter Two —

LIVE FAST, DIE YOUNG, AND HAVE A GOOD-LOOKING CORPSE

(The Vampire Paradigm in Fiction and Film)

LET US DIE YOUNG OR LET US LIVE FOREVER.
— *"Forever Young"*
by Marian Gold/Frank Mertens/Bernhard Lloyd; recorded by Laura Branigan

WHY WE FEAR VAMPIRES IS OBVIOUS. They bite. They attack, tear, rend, sip, sup, and slurp. They don't regard us as beings of the same species. We're food, in the same way that chickens and salmon are our sustenance.

So, if these beings are predators, and we *know* that they bear us ill will . . . why are we then so utterly fascinated by them? Over the last few centuries we've adored vampires so much they are now considered tragic figures, misunderstood, lonely, honorable, and deeply romantic. We have propagandized the vampire into a figure of compelling sexual charisma, which is totally at odds with their nature as presented in folklore.

Why? The answers are as complex as the human psyche, and as deep as our own dark desires.

The simplest answer is that we fear death. The one incontrovertible truth is that we are all going to die. Everyone we know, everyone we love—all doomed. Youth, no matter how powerful and perfect, will wither and fade. Vitality, it

FEMALE VAMPIRES Jason Beam

turns out, is on loan, and when the lease runs out even the strongest will crumble into dust.

The vampire, however, is immortal. Unchanging and eternally powerful.

This makes an incredibly seductive image: eternally young and incredibly powerful. It suggests a personal power greater than time, than death. Godlike.

How many people, given a chance at immortality, would not accept? Many would. Perhaps most. Even if it meant becoming a predator with decidedly unfriendly tastes.

When the vampire left folklore and entered fiction its paradigm went through a drastic change. This was largely because writers wanted to explore a specific aspect of its vampiric nature: immortality. Vampires became characters in stories, or rather in stories the vampires became "people." Writers often used vampirism as a way of exploring the pros and cons of immortality. In order to do that they had to create characters that were three dimensional, with pasts, personalities, and shades of good as well as bad.

This was totally at odds with the vampires of myth, which were generally regarded as plain evil. This new paradigm got its start in 1819 in John Polidori's classic short story, "The Vampyre," which featured the elegant and refined Lord Ruthven, a bold departure from the folkloric image of the decaying and often mindless revenant. Polidori's story was adapted into a play in 1820, *The Vampire or the Bride of the Isles,* by J. R. Planche.

As the nineteenth century wore on we were given a variety of vampire stories. Some gave a nod to folklore by giving us unpleasant monsters, but most continued to romanticize the vampire. Among the notable works are Johann Ludwig Tieck's 1823 novelette *Wake Not the Dead,* a story of vampirism and shape-shifting in which the monster bride ultimate turns into a man-eating serpent; Alexandre Dumas of *Three Musketeers* fame published *Les Mille et un Fantomes* (published in English as *The Pale Lady*), which sets the adventure in the Carpathian Mountains and deals with a Polish noblewoman involved with two brothers, one of whom is an unsavory vampire. And in 1860 *The Mysterious Stranger* was published by an anonymous author, in which the villain is a vampire count from the same region of the world. It's pretty clear that these last two stories, which introduced us to the Carpathians as a center for vampire activity and vampires who were noblemen—significantly a count in the 1860 story—that Bram Stoker mined these early tales for the creation of Count Dracula, a vampire story set in the Carpathians. This is one of the clearest examples of how the vampire image in the popular view is drawn from layer upon layer of fiction far more than from folklore. Jules Verne even added to this new archetype with his *Castle of the Carpathians* (1892) five years before *Dracula* was published. Stoker, by the way, had originally planned to set his novel in Styria (part of Austria), but was influenced into a location change, largely because of his readings of earlier vampire fiction and some delving into folklore.

In 1836, French author Theophile Gauthier published the short story, "La Morte Amoreuse," later translated into English as "Clarimonde."[31] It told the story of a Catholic priest who fell in love with a female vampire. In the story the vampire is presented as beautiful and compelling—in essence faithful to the concept of many of the world's seductress vampires—but the story had a lovely and ethereal air, far removed from the violent and bloody resolution of affairs with folkloric French seductress vampires like the *Green Ogresses* or the *White Ladies of Fau*. Literary license compelled Theophile to focus on the romance and skip all that rending and feasting.

Beginning in 1845 James Malcolm Rymer[32] gave us the first vampire soap-opera-cum-cliffhanger in book form with *Varney the Vampire or the Feast of Blood,* which was presented in 109 weekly installments as Penny Dreadfuls, eight-page booklets that sold for a penny (and which were also called Penny Bloods and Blood and Thunders). This story was lurid and not very well written, but it was exciting and it kept the readers interested for two years. Though Varney was no romantic hero, the story was not based on folklore and contained very little of value to someone interested in vampire history. It makes an amusing read, though, if you have lots of time and fairly low standards for amusement.

Perhaps the first truly three-dimensional vampire character was the titular Carmilla in the 1871 novella of that name by Joseph Sheridan Le Fanu. Seduction is again a major thematic element, though in this case it is the seduction of a female victim by a female vampire. This gave birth to a popular sub-genre of vampire fiction: homoerotic vampirism, which still has legs today in Anne Rice novels and similar works.

Oddly, in the 1897 landmark novel *Dracula* by Bram Stoker, the Count is

---

31. Among other titles.
32. Or Thomas Preskett Prest. Opinions differ as to which man actually penned the series. My money is on Rymer.

not really portrayed as a romantic figure, and he isn't all that charming; but just about every play, film, TV show, and pastiche novel about good ol' Vlad has painted him as the definitive tragically romantic figure. Bela Lugosi was the first who gave him the charm and the sexual charisma. Christopher Lee dialed that up even further in heaving-bosom Hammer films. It was the Frank Langella Broadway production—later made into the decent 1979 film—and the Gary Oldman interpretation in *Bram Stoker's Dracula* (1992) that really went all out to show Dracula as misunderstood, tragic, romantic, and sexy; a far cry from a lumbering, reanimated corpse with rotting skin.

In the vast canon of vampire literature *Dracula* is not the most thrilling read—a comment that is sure to earn me hate mail. The storytelling method, using diary pages and journal entries, is dated now and defeats mood and pace; and if it were to be released today the most frequent comment it would probably receive is that its plot is so good that it saves the whole book. However, no one can argue that the novel stands as the benchmark for vampire literature: All vampire storytelling that followed its release is measured against it. The effect of that one novel on popular culture cannot be calculated and we can see it in everything from cinema to the vast Halloween industry to children's education. Probably more than half of the children of the Baby Boomers learned their numbers from the Count on *Sesame Street*.

A handful of other, lesser-known nineteenth-century vampire novelettes are also worth digging up for any scholar of the subject, and these include *Last Lords of Gardonal* (1867) by William Gilbert; *A Mystery of the Campagna* (1887) by Anne Crawford; *A Kiss of Judas* (1893) by X. L. (pseudonym of Julian Osgood Field); *Good Lady Ducayne* (1896) by Mary Elizabeth Braddon; and *The Stone Chamber* (1899) by H. B. Marriott-Watson. And there were a few particularly interesting short stories of the same era: "The Last Lords of Gardonal" (1867) by William Gilbert; "Ken's Mystery" (1888) by Julian Hawthorne; "Let Loose" (1890) by Mary Cholmondeley; "The Last of the Vampires" (1892) by Phil Robinson; "The True Story of a Vampire" (1894) by Count Eric Stenbock; and "Will"

(1899) by Vincent O'Sullivan. Most of these stories are anthologized from time to time.

In the twentieth century and into the twenty-first enough vampire fiction has been recorded to fill up a fair-size library, and these books vary from the folklorically accurate to the wildly divergent. One of the few early novels to touch on the concepts of both psychic and essential vampirism was Henry Carew's 1925 book, *Vampire of the Andes,* which gave us very nasty vampires who were involved with unsavory occult practices and who drained their victims of blood, life essence, and even creativity.

The urge to romanticize the vampire ruled twentieth-century fiction, however, in both the novel and short-story formats. As early as 1911 writers like F. Marion Crawford were inserting romantic vampires into stories, such as his "For the Blood is the Life," just for the quixotic effect, even if the story would have been better off without that element. Other writers have managed to craft far more effective stories that blend romance and vampirism in ways that are both stylistically and literarily pleasing. Notable among these are the romantic histories of Chelsea Quinn Yarbro in which her principal character, Le Comte de Saint-Germain, is both romantic and heroic. Outstanding novels in that series include *The Palace* (1979), *Path of the Eclipse* (1981), and *Tempting Fate* (1982). Amanda Ashley has also turned out several strong vampire romances, notably *Night's Kiss* (2005) and *Midnight Embrace* (2002). Other notable authors of vampire romances include Shannon Drake (*When Darkness Falls*), Christine Freehan (*Dark Secret, Dark Destiny, Dark Melody*), Linda Lael Miller (*Tonight and Always, Forever and the Night*), Debbie Raleigh (*My Lord Immortality, My Lord Eternity*), and Karen Harbough (*The Vampire Viscount and the Devil's Bargain, Night Fires*) and others.

The cinematic vampire, especially in the second half of the twentieth century, was also presented as romantic or even overtly sexual beings. Films like *Tales of a Vampire* (1992), *Romance of the Vampires* (1994), and most of the most recent Dracula films, as well as TV shows such as *Dark Shadows, Buffy the Vam-*

pire Slayer, Angel, Forever Knight, and others romanticized the undead, often creating story lines in which humans and vampires were ciphers for the Montagues and Capulets in supernatural takes on Romeo and Juliet.

The connection between vampirism and sexuality has been further explored in great detail in the literary sub-genre of vampire erotica in which hundreds of short stories and scores of novels have been published. Likewise vampire erotic in film is a growing sub-genre that got its real start in the late 1960s, gained steam in the '70s, and exploded during the video and DVD era. Classics of this genre include several takes on the Carmilla story line including Roger Vadim's *Blood and Roses* (1961), Roy Ward Baker's *The Vampire Lovers* (1970), Vincente Aranda's *The Blood-Splattered Bride* (1972), José Ramón Larraz's *Vampyres* (1974), and Jesus Franco's *Vampyros Lesbos* (1970), which together became the models for softcore lesbianism in genre films. And the erotica naturally morphed (or perhaps descended, depending on your sensibilities) into the stronger almost-but-not-quite-explicit semi-porn of films like *Vampire Seduction* (1998), *Vampire Obsessions* (2002), and *Vampire Vixens* (2003). Vampirism even took a bite out of the porn industry with such "classics" as 1980s *Dracula Exotica,* and then huffed and puffed along with titles like *Vampirass, Bite: The First Blood, Intercourse with the Vampire,* and *Dracula Sucks.* And this genre spawned several spin-off sub-genres: gay vampire porn, and lesbian vampire porn, as well as S&M vampire films, in which romance takes a beating in favor of shock. In these aspects of the genre folklore is not even a fragment of the storytelling equation.

In the fiction of the twentieth century, vampires took off in all directions, warping the paradigm and eventually just knocking hell out of it, and generally relying on stronger storytelling elements than is typically found in the films. Colin Wilson, for example, blasted them into space in his 1976 novel *The Space Vampires,* filmed in 1985 as *Lifeforce,* in which vampirism is seen as the result of an alien invasion. Richard Matheson, in his powerhouse 1954 novel *I Am Legend,* conceived of vampirism as a plague; and science notwithstanding, created a thoroughly unnerving book that was a clear influence on such films as George Romero's 1968 cinema classic *Night of the Living Dead*. Sadly, two attempts to put *I Am Legend* to film—*The Last Man on Earth* starring Vincent Price (1964) and *The Omega Man* with Charlton Heston (1971)—were both sad disappointments. Each missed the gravitas and pathos of the novel, and both totally glossed over the powerful social commentary Matheson so eloquently explored.

Vampire fiction with a link to folklore got a nice jolt of CPR in 1975 with Stephen King's marvelous *Salem's Lot*, which brought back the idea that vampires are pretty unpleasant critters with no visibly redeeming characteristics. There is nothing at all charming or romantic about Barlow, the uber-vamp in that novel. He is charismatic, sure, but it's clear to the reader that it is just another tool he uses in order to destroy.

In 1981, Robert McCammon took a hearty swipe at the vampire tale with his novel *They Thirst*, again choosing to present the vampires as bad guys—this time with a major vampire mastermind and a whole gang of vampire bikers. A year later George R. R. Martin took a stand right on the middle ground and released one of the first books that presented both good and bad vampires at war with one another—something that has been copied and (pardon the pun) vamped ever since. His novel, *Fevre Dream*, presented a reformed vampire, Joshua York, prowling the Mississippi in a riverboat (from which the novel gets its name) looking for others of his kind. York has figured a way for vampires to feed without preying on humans and is actively trying to stop the predation. Naturally this leads to violence and bloodshed, but that's just good storytelling.

In 1976 Anne Rice released her first book about ultra-civilized vampires, *Interview with the Vampire*, which was a huge hit that not only spawned a number of sequels and a couple of movies, but launched an enormous, global cult following. Though her vampires are bloodthirsty predators, they are refined, erudite, and capable of creating their own complex society. They are also capable of changing their dietary habits so that not all of them feed on humans. Though the novels explore the arguments of right and wrong, the vampires are still a far cry from the decaying undead of folklore.

The TV series *Buffy the Vampire Slayer* and, to a somewhat lesser degree, *Angel* nicely explored issues of immortality, and also reworked the idea of good vampire vs. evil vampire. However these shows went a step further and through series' creator Joss Whedon's considerable storytelling skills, gave a nod to folklore and looked at one of the rarest aspects of the vampire legend: the redeemed vampire. In folklore there is a kind of vampire called the "Stregoni Benefici," a creature that had been evil and was eventually tamed and converted back to faith by a priest, after which the vampire became a kind of toothy hitman for the church, targeting other vampires. Whedon's characters, Angel and Spike, were presented as different takes on the reformed vampire concept, and for that and other reasons both series are worth a look. The reformed vampire fighting for good was also the central theme of *Forever Knight*, which, like Buffy and Angel, developed a strong cult fan base.

Looking back over the last century and a half of vampire fiction, and particularly the twentieth century, it becomes quite clear that the popular image of the vampire is not one of fear and disgust, but of a powerful appeal. It is the appeal of eternal youth, and of perpetual health. Of a life removed from the necessary crudities of human existence. Of power. Of acceptance, either through inclusion in a secret society of vampires or through charismatic attraction. It is the appeal of never having to fear death.

It is the lure of immortality.

Truly, if offered, how many of us could reject immortality without even a moment or two spent in consideration? No more worries about money, disease, job security, stress, weight gain, taxes, politics, bills, dating, or anything else. Beauty and health would be perfect and unchanging. That is surely tempting. Since the vampires of folklore are too nasty and ugly and mean, and most of them just kill without any benefit of immortality, it isn't so hard to understand why fiction writers and filmmakers have taken the core theme of the myth—immortality—and re-imagined it into an ideal solution. If the great masses were not hungry for such an illusion those books and movies would never have sold so well. It is what we all want. To live forever and look good.

Ask yourself . . . if all it took was a bite on the neck and a moment of pain, would you yield to it if it meant that you would life forever?

Forever young?

Chapter Three
VAMPIRES AND MONSTERS
G–M

G

Gaki (also Ga-ki) The Gaki is one of Japan's many predatory ghosts that haunt the rural countryside of those ancient islands. The Gaki lures its victims by calling out with lonely wails that sound like an injured child or the desperate cry of someone lost. Instead of finding a child in distress, any goodhearted person coming to investigate the cries, sadly, encounters a powerful vampiric beast with sharp teeth and a thirst for human blood.

The Gaki is a revenant, risen from the grave of a sinner and condemned to eternal torment as a monster whose unholy thirst can never be assuaged. It kills and kills, hoping to satisfy its need for blood, but as soon as it finishes feeding it is immediately and maddeningly thirsty again.

Variations of the legend describe the Gaki as looking like a starvation victim, with a distended stomach and a throat that is nearly closed from dehydration. In the tales the Gaki is unable to swallow more than a few drops at a time and can therefore not take in enough nourishment to keep itself satisfied. In similar tales the Gaki craves ordinary food and is often surrounded by it, but when the creature brings food to its lips it turns into hot coals or blood. In these tales the Gaki is not a blood-drinker at all and kills out of sheer frustrated rage.

The Gaki is a theriomorph and can take any form it wants, using trickery in form as well as voice, to trap its prey.

Conventional weapons are useless against the Gaki, but it can be driven off by prayers and rituals performed by Buddhist monks or Shinto priests. Scrolls stamped with the image of the Buddha and placed around the household will keep the Gaki from entering.

Garkain　None of the world's hairy hominids are known to be as fresh as spring flowers, but by far the worst offender for supernatural stench is the Garkain, a monster who frequently appears in the folktales of the Aboriginal people of the Northern Territories of Australia. The creature's reek is so overwhelming that if it approaches a victim quickly enough the odor knocks the prey into a dazed stupor, thus rendering the person totally vulnerable to attack.

The Garkain lives in out-of-the-way areas, inhabiting caves and other inaccessible places, though they venture into swamps and forests in order to hunt. Some Garkain are believed to inhabit the Liverpool River region. Wherever they live, when on the hunt the Garkains lurk in the trees waiting for isolated travelers. When a solitary wanderer walks by, the Garkain leap down out of a high tree limb and attack, feasting on the flesh of its victims.

Though the Garkain can be killed by everyday weapons, getting near enough to deliver a killing blow is difficult because of the beast's poisonous stench.

In recent myths the Garkains have been described as being more clearly supernatural and are often described as huge bat-like humanoids, as big as a man but with massive black wings, and a human upper body topped with the canine-looking head of a fruit bat.

Gashadokuro　Starving to death is a horrible fate, but in many cultures the pain and torment do not end when the body succumbs. A prime example is the case of the Gashadokuro, the specter of hunger and death.

The Gashadokuro—whose name literally means "starving skeleton"—is created when a person dies of starvation and from the grave of the poor wretch rises a towering and ghastly apparition: a skeletal giant fifteen times as tall as the corpse! This monstrous creature is sometimes invisible and sometimes walks so quietly and towers so high that it is shrouded by darkness and clouds. Usually the only warning a person has is a ringing in the ears, and often by the time they hear that alarm it's too late!

The Gashadokuro delights in killing, and its favorite method of dispatching the living is to reach down with a bony hand and snatch a person right off the ground and then bite the hapless victim's head off. It then feasts on the spray of blood erupting from the stump of the neck.

The Gashadokuro cannot be destroyed, but Shinto charms can deflect its attentions. The best course, though, is to hurry home whenever you hear a ringing in the ears on a dark and cloudy night.

⚔ APPARITIONS ⚔

The appearance of a dead being (human or animal) after death. Types of apparitions include:

APPARITIONS OF THE DEAD: By far the most common kind of apparition is that of a dead person that is often a blood relative of the beholder. Though others have reported seeing images of the dead in countless cases of hauntings, it is most common to see a dead (often recently dead) relative.

BALEFUL APPARITIONS: Frightening manifestations of creatures whose (apparent) intent is to cause fear or injury describe this anomaly. Several types of vampires are actually ghosts and only manifest a physical form.

PRIVATE APPARITIONS: These figures appear only when

the beholder is alone, and include a variety of encounters with divine beings, such as the many appearances of the Virgin Mary (at Lourdes, for example).

CRISIS APPARITION: Dramatic visions that appear during moments of danger or catastrophe are known as crisis apparitions. They can range from images that lure a person into danger to apparitions that appear to warn someone away from threat. In medieval times these apparitions would often appear to simply *mark* the importance of an event, such as the death of a king or the eve of a great battle.

DEATHBED APPARITIONS: Most of these apparitions, arriving at the moment of death, often take the form of celestial beings, spirit guides, or deceased friends/family who have come to lead the spirit of the dying person to Heaven. In some cases the deathbed apparition is less friendly and appears to usher the spirit to a darker fate.

Gayal (also **Ut)**   Improperly performed burial rituals often lead to supernatural consequences of the worst possible kind, and in these cases the dead who are not correctly interred do not lie quiet, as with the case of India's Gayal. This creature rises to take out its resentment on the members of its family in retribution for their religious negligence.

The Gayal is a rare vampire that attacks victims of its own gender, and therefore preys exclusively on the men of its own family. When he has exhausted that list of potential targets, he preys on the male members of other families in the area.

Ghaddar   In the deserts that border Yemen, Tihamah, and the upper parts of Egypt there is a sadistic female demon called the Ghaddar who is one of the more vicious species of seductress vampire. The Ghaddar appears in the form of a gorgeous woman of such intensely compelling sexuality that almost any man seeing her is captivated and must follow her. She leads her victims to remote spots and then batters the man half to death, tortures him for hours or even days, and then satisfies her unnatural hunger by devouring the poor fellow's genitals. Sadly, the victim is often alive when this feast takes place, though he seldom lives beyond that moment.

Only a man devout in his Islamic beliefs has the moral fiber necessary to break free of the Ghaddar's sexual magic.

⊰ GHOSTS ⊱

"Ghost" is a general term for the spirit of a dead person who lingers on the Earthly plane. Ghosts vary greatly in content and degree of consciousness, from apparitions that are little more than a spiritual snapshot of a face or figure to beings that have conscious control over their actions. Ghosts may be:

- Neutral (those that do nothing but appear)
- Benign (those that interact with humans but do not seek to do harm)
- Harbingers (ghosts who appear to either warn of coming disaster or who simply appear at times of disaster)
- Vengeful (ghosts who try to right a wrong, often in violent ways)
- Pernicious (ghosts who deliberately try to harm humans)

And there are many dozens of sub-groups of these. In folklore many supernatural monsters are actually ghosts who have manifested physical bodies in order to do harm.

Ghul   The Ghul is an evil creature from Muslim folklore who haunts the desert, generally staking out a hunting ground near graveyards, deserted oases, or in places where a battle has taken place. The Ghul is generally (though not always) a female monster, and she lurks around any place touched by death, preferably recent death.

Mostly the Ghul acts as a scavenging grave robber and digs up the bodies of the recently dead in order to feast on rotting human flesh. However some Ghul are more predatory and will shape-shift from their ordinary forms—that of decaying corpses—into the likeness of a prostitute. Thus transformed the Ghul lures men to secluded spots and lulls them to sleep with magic, and then either smashes their heads with rocks or cuts their throat before feeding on the still-warm flesh.

If a battle has occurred in her domain, the Ghul may take the form of a nurse or a water-bearer and pretend to seek out the injured in order to provide succor. Dying men will call out to her, but it will be she, not they, who takes a drink.

Ghuls are often created when a prostitute has died and, having shunned the rules of Islam while alive, is denied paradise and must live out eternity as a living dead monster. In such cases the Ghul can he exorcised by a holy man who visits the area and offers prayers to Allah for seven days on her behalf.

The Ghul is frequently mentioned in literature, including a number of references in *The Thousand and One Nights*, though in these stories the Ghul is as often male as female, as seen in this entry from Sir Richard Burton's translation of *The Seventh Voyage of Sinbad* (*The Book of the Thousand Nights and a Night*, vol. 6, 1885):

> *It was not long before I discovered them to be a tribe of Magician*
> *cannibals whose King was a Ghul. All who came to their country or*
> *whoso they caught in their valleys or on their roads they brought to*
> *this King and fed them upon that food and anointed them with that*

oil, whereupon their stomachs dilated that they might eat largely,
whilst their reason fled and they lost the power of thought and be-
came idiots. Then they stuffed them with coconut oil and the afore-
said food till they became fat and gross, when they slaughtered them
by cutting their throats and roasted them for the King's eating, but
as for the savages themselves, they ate human flesh raw.

Gierach   The Gierach of Prussia, a rare form of essential vampire, kills with the power of pronouncement. It climbs to the top of a house or church steeple and calls out the name of its victim. Only the intended victim can hear his or her name being spoken by the monster, but once the Gierach has spoken, the victim will die. Anyone else who hears the cry only hears it as the call of a raven, owl, or crow. It is for this reason that many people from that region of the world believe that owls, in particular, are evil.

Gjakpirë   The Albanian Gjakpirë is a revenant who relies on trickery rather than direct attack to manage its kills. Its most common tactic is to lie by the side of a road, pretending to be an injured traveler, waiting for a Good Samaritan to come along and offer aid. Once the well-intentioned person was within reach, the Gjakpirë would stab him in the groin or throat with a sharp stick, then wait for the victim to become weak with blood loss before attacking and lapping up the blood.

The Gjakpirës travel by night, often shape-shifting into a night-hunting bird, but it always changes back into its true form, that of a decaying human corpse, before returning to its grave to sleep.

Gloucester Sea Serpent (also the Great New England Sea Serpent)
A sixty-plus foot sea monster frequently reported in and around Gloucester Bay, Massachusetts, with sightings going back as far as 1817. Most lake monsters and sea serpents fall into two categories: those that look like aquatic dinosaurs and those that look like giant serpents. This one has been uniformly described as a gigantic undulating serpent.

SEA SERPENT
(Public Domain)

Though ferocious in appearance, this aquatic cryptid does not seem interested in attacking humans . . . but fishermen and recreational boaters in the region wisely do not try to provoke it when it pokes its massive head out of the water.

Goblin   There are wandering spirits of evil haunting the rural French countryside and invading country homes: the legendary Goblin. These creatures are small in size but vast in malicious intent and supernatural power.

The natural habitat of the Goblin is a deserted grotto or swamp, but like magpies drawn to shiny objects, a Goblin will be irresistibly drawn to a family that has beautiful children and a cellar full of good wine. Goblins covet both.

In olden times families often welcomed Goblins into the household because they promised to do chores around the house, and generally lived up to their claims. Stories abound of families that had long and harmonious associations with these creatures; but there are even more tales telling of how the house Goblin turned on the family that had taken it in.

The problem stems from the fact that it is not the Goblin's forté to be well behaved. They are mischievous by nature and as often happens, nature will out. When the Goblin's impish side begins to emerge the creature will act out in much the same way as a *Poltergeist*—banging pots and making noises in the night, disturbing sleep, hiding things, moving furniture.

Sometimes Goblins become more violent and nip and bite members of the family as they sleep. If a family attempts to evict them, the Goblin's spite sometimes becomes so great that it will leave—but will do so in the middle of the night, taking with it the most beautiful child of the family! The Goblin will then flee to its former grotto and enslave the child, forcing it to serve the Goblin until death.

In a few quaint folktales one odd method of eviction is purported to be very effective: flaxseed is thrown on the kitchen floor every night, and after a few days the Goblin will tire of picking up all the seeds and leave of its own accord. But this seems like a charming fairy tale sort of resolution and not one that would work against a creature with the intelligence, diligence, and spite of the goblin.

Goblin Scarecrow   In rural Pennsylvania, beginning in the mid-1950s and persisting to this day, there are legends of a demonic scarecrow with the grinning head of a jack-o'-lantern that haunts the farmlands. This creature, dressed in rags and wearing a pumpkin-head whose features can actually move and whose mouth can bite, does not have a body filled just with straw, but its mass is made up of tens of thousands of insects that are held together in the

GOBLIN SCARECROW
Jonathan Maberry

shape of a man by sheer demonic force of will. The creature was first spotted in Potter County by deer hunters. The creature chased them, howling like a banshee. One of the hunters shot at it but the bullet just passed through it and the "wound" dripped with worms and beetles instead of blood.

Since then it has been seen in Bucks, Berks, Cambria, Westmoreland, Mc-Kean, Tioga, and Elk counties. One report, from a hiker in Sullivan County, claimed that the creature chased him with a scythe. In two separate accounts, one person from Union and the other from neighboring Northumberland County swore that the creature just stood and screamed for a while before giving chase. No origin or details has ever been uncovered to explain this ghastly apparition.[33]

Grant   When strolling about in the English countryside at night, take note if you see what looks to be a yearling foal capering around on its hind legs. This bizarre creature, known as a Grant, is a harbinger of danger, and if it appears, then it is certain that your house is on fire.

Some folktales suggest that harm only comes if a person sees the Grant, and that managing to avoid it—by hearing its hooves clatter as it dances—is a way to avoid the touch of misfortune.

Gray Ladies   Another of England's many recurring ghost legends is that of the Gray Ladies, who appear as women dressed in either gray, black, brown, or white and who are likely the spirits of women who were either murdered during love affairs gone terribly wrong, or who committed suicide after affairs ended unhappily.

Though generally not dangerous, some stories reveal that a Gray Lady visits a person while they sleep and whispers her tragic story in the sleeper's ear, and that these whisperings are so crushingly sad that the sleeper sometimes wakes, leaves the house still in nightclothes, and looks for the handiest cliff from which to leap.

There are many houses in England purported to be the homes of Gray Ladies, a belief often played up to great success by tourist organizations.

The Green Ogresses   France has a variety of evil siren-like seductress vampires, most of who live in or near bodies of water. Though they superficially share some of the faerie-like qualities of the watery Naiads, these monsters are neither helpful nor benevolent. The Green Ogresses, for example, appear as beautiful women whose sexual appeal is too potent for any but the most wholesome of souls to resist; and since totally wholesome souls are fairly thin

---

33. The legend of the Goblin Scarecrow inspired a character in my novel, *Ghost Road Blues,* Pinnacle Books, 2006.

GRAY LADY Joe Zierman

on the ground, most persons who are unlucky enough to encounter a Green Ogress will generally succumb to her enchantment.

The Green Ogresses are seductive but they are not sexual; their sexual charisma lasts only until the men are lured into lakes or streams, at which point the Ogresses attack with rapacious hunger, slaughtering their victims with great violence and feeding on flesh and blood both. (See also *Dames Blanches*.)

Gremlin A bit of latter-day folklore that came into being during the war years of the mid-twentieth century when British soldiers would routinely blame machine failure and other mishaps on invisible imps called Gremlins; though sometimes these unseen little beings were considered helpful as well, depending on their mood, or perhaps on the mood of the storyteller. This new bit of mythology is a natural outgrowth of older tales of sometimes helpful, sometimes hurtful sprites of the past, such as *Brownies, Kobolds,* Kul, and Anchanchu.

Grindylow   For most people the Grindylow is a character out of fiction, appearing in the book *Harry Potter and the Goblet of Fire* by J. K. Rowling; but the creatures have actually been part of the folklore of Yorkshire, England, for many centuries.

The Grindylow is a nasty marsh imp, similar in some respects to the *Kappa* of Japan. It lives in swamps and stagnant ponds and waits for travelers, especially children, to wander too close to the water's edge, then it leaps up and drags them down into the water. Once it has its victim, the Grindylow either strangles them with its long spatulate fingers or holds them down until they drown, and at the moment the person dies—when the Grindylow feels the last pulse—it immediately starts to feast, delighting in warm human flesh.

Grisi Siknis   Plagues spread by supernatural means are not just confined to legends of the dark ages. As recently as 2003 in Nicaragua an epidemic called Grisi Siknis, "Plague of Madness," swept the country, and the government had to appeal for help, not from medical science, but from sorcerers living among the native tribes.[34]

The authorities of the Regional Autonomous Council of the Northern Nicaraguan Caribbean sent out an appeal to native shamen from among the Miskito Indians to cure a wave of dangerous irrational behavior that struck the town of Raiti, which is north of Managua. Raiti was the second town struck with the plague, following an earlier outbreak in nearby Kikrin in 2002. About sixty citizens were overcome with the madness and were found wander-

---

34. According to *El Universal* (newspaper—Mexico City), Monday, November 24, 2003.

GRINDYLOW Mardiy Byrd

ing naked in the streets, carrying machetes and other knives, eyes wild and murderous and apparently unable to recognize anyone, not even members of their own families. Most of the victims were women.

There was speculation that someone had somehow introduced a poison or drug into the town's water supply, though no toxicological tests have so far been able to prove it.

After conventional medicines and therapies were attempted—and found ineffective—the authorities then turned to a blend of natural and spiritual healing practiced by the shamen.

Among the Miskito natives it is believed that an evil presence has settled in the region and was using its supernatural powers to drive the people mad in order to feed off of the discharge of intense negative emotions. If so, then the as-yet unnamed creature would be a new species of essential vampire.

Though the source of the malady has not been determined either by medical or tribal science, the shamen have been successful in restoring most of the afflicted persons to health. Once restored they have no memory at all of what they had been doing while in the heat of madness.

Gwyllion   There are hundreds, perhaps thousands, of different supernatural tricksters in the collective folklore of humankind, ranging from minor pests, to the Coyote of Navajo myth to the Father of Lies. Among this group of beings is a subcategory of faeries or demons that delight in luring travelers astray for no reason other than malice. Another theory worth considering is that these "misleading tricksters" are a kind of essential vampire or psychic vampire, and that they feed off the fear and despair that lost travelers experience.

One such creature is the Gwyllion of Wales, a haglike being whose name is derived from the Welsh word "gwyll," meaning darkness and gloom. The Gwyllion are female demons who haunt remote mountain areas. Eyewitnesses describe them as old crones dressed in clothes the color of wood ash with aprons the color of bone. The Gwyllion wear strange four-pointed oblong hats and sometimes carry black iron pots, presumably for the mixing of magic potions. Their eyes are very dark and sometimes glint with red lights, in much the same way a rat's eyes show red in certain light.

The creatures walk along mountain roads or forest paths and when they see a human traveler they cry out in a plaintive voice. Gwyllions are apparently incapable of human speech and the only sound they can make has been described as the way a crow would sound if it was trying to speak in a human tongue.

The Gwyllion preys mostly on the kindness of any traveler who stops to offer aid, and while making her plaintive call she hurries away. Thinking that the Gwyllion is an old woman, possibly deaf, possibly senile, and apparently frightened or disoriented, the well-wishing traveler hurries after her in an attempt to catch her before she can come to harm; but before the traveler realizes it he has become lost in the dark. It is a particular trick of the Gwyllion to lead travelers into deadfalls or over the sides of cliffs in the fashion of a will-o'-the-wisp.

In a number of folktales the Gwyllion have come down into the villages that border the mountains, and in such cases a strange bond or agreement has been struck with the hags. Sometimes—especially if a storm is raging or when it is very cold—the Gwyllion will enter a house to get warm. The creature does not attack anyone, but just huddles by the fire until just before dawn, when she creeps back out and vanishes into the darkness. If everyone in the house leaves the Gwyllion alone, or better yet offers it food and drink, then the night will pass peacefully; if the Gwyllion is disturbed, a curse of horrible misfortune will descend on the house bringing bad luck, blighted crops, ruined finances, and sickness.

The only way to successfully eject a Gwyllion without incurring bad luck is to pull out a very large knife and hold it in the air where the creature can see it. The Gwyllion are terrified of knives and will flee instantly. When trying to appease the Gwyllion, however, all knives in the household should be kept out of sight.

Wise travelers in the mountains of Wales seldom go walking without a good knife easy to hand, and for this reason folks who spend the night out of doors in campsites often take to recreational whittling in order to keep the knife in plain view.

Hai-Uri   Like the Ga-Gorib, the Hai-Uri is another strange monster from the legends of the Khoikhoi[35] of southwestern Africa. The Hai-Uri is a trans-

35. Literally "real people," a division of the Khoisan ethnic group of southwestern Africa, closely related to the Bushmen.

dimensional being, meaning that half of it appears in our world, and the other half is visible only in the spirit world. The half that appears in our dimension has only one leg, one arm, and one half of a torso. On that single leg it can run as fast as a gazelle and leap over bushes and trees, much like the *Tikdoshe* of Zulu legend.

The Hai-Uri is a flesh-eating predator who chases humans and then clubs them down with its power fist or jumps on them with its single leg, striking them hard enough to break bones. Once it has knocked down its prey it eats most or all of the victim—flesh, blood, and bone.

Hamrammr   Like the *Berserkirs,* the Hamrammr of the Norse legends were powerful warriors who, upon donning the skins of animals, took on the qualities and sometimes even the form of those creatures. Unlike most shapeshifters, the Hamrammr has the potential for nearly limitless power because its strength grows with each enemy it kills or animal it eats. If it has killed and eaten a dozen wolves, then it will have the physical strength of a dozen wolves. Eventually a Hamrammr can become so strong that no man, animal, or weapon can kill it.

However, this drive to acquire power is often the downfall of the Hamrammr, and long before it has managed to attain invulnerability it often becomes so convinced of its power that it will attack recklessly. Overestimating oneself while at the same time underestimating one's enemy is seldom a formula for success.

Even so, the Hamrammr spoken of in *The Saga of the Volsungs*[36] were dreadful and powerful and their presence alone was sometimes enough to frighten their enemies from the battlefield.

Hantu   Among the Malays the word "Hantu" is a general term meaning "ghost," but within that culture there are many dozens of Hantu, some help-

---

36. An oral account of the Norsemen, created during the period between 1200 and 1270 in the Codex Regins (Book of Kings).

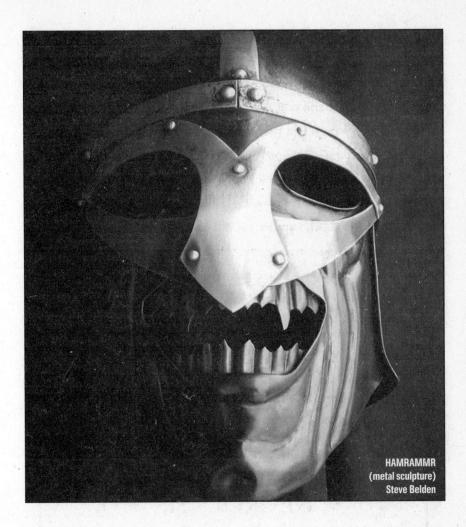

HAMRAMMR
(metal sculpture)
Steve Belden

ful and some decidedly harmful. These ghosts are similar in many regards to the demons of Shinto belief in that they possess great magical powers and are not necessarily the spirits of the dead.

Among the more common Malaysian ghosts are Hantu Rimba (deep-forest ghost), Hantu Belian (the tiger ghost), Hantu Ribut (the storm ghost), and the dreaded Hantu Kubor (the ghost of death and graves).

Haugbui   There is a monster from Scandinavian legend called the Haugbui, whose name means "mound dweller." Similar to the *Draugr,* the Haugbui was a revenant who rose from the grave and collected treasure, but unlike that more formidable creature, the Haugbui was not an invincible engine of destruction and could be killed by fire or by a band of warriors armed to the teeth. Though mortal, the Haubui was nevertheless ferocious, and killing it still required courage and skill at arms.

For villagers who found that a Haugbui had risen, the thought of confronting and battling it were out of the question. It was far easier to appease the monster by sacrificing and offering to it the first milk from a cow that had calved or the first jug of ale brewed in the household. These offerings would placate the Haugbui, who apparently did not need to hunt and feed as frequently as most revenants, and who seemed content—upon being appeased—to stay in his mound and count his treasure. If the creature became very hungry and showed some signs of being restless, the villagers would even go as far as sacrificing a cow to it.

When angered, however, Haugbui could do great harm, both physically and by using *trollskap,* a form of powerful black sorcery that could spread sickness and cause bad luck persistent enough to follow a family for generations. Well aware of this creature's poisonous nature, farmers even nowadays regularly make offerings to the local Haugbui.

⊰ NECROLYSIS ⊱

Necrolysis is the separation or exfoliation of necrotic tissue, often lending a temporarily ruddy appearance to dead flesh. It is presumed that this is the medical basis for the reports of disinterred corpses having a ruddy or healthy appearance.

Hayopan The *Asuangs* of the Philippines are dreadful creatures, even when they are in retirement. Their hunger for human flesh is just as strong as when they were active, but in their declining years they take a more roundabout course to obtain it. These "retired" Asuangs are known as Hayopans, and they generally settle down in swampy areas or near rivers because they want to be around crocodiles, who act like hunting dogs for them. The crocodiles are familiars for the Hayopans, and they do the hunting and killing, then bring back the choicest bits of meat for their masters.

Some folklorists have suggested that the Hayopan are really not so much "retired" as simply smarter, using their animal familiars to do the killings and thereby leaving no clues at all to the presence of a supernatural monster in the vicinity.

Hedammu   Coastal traders in the region of ancient Mesopotamia often kept close inshore to stay out of the deep-water hunting grounds of the Hedammu, a powerful sea serpent. The Hedammu was powerful enough to drag an entire ship below the surface and would eat every sailor aboard, then attack the next ship it could find without pause, forever trying to satisfy its insatiable hunger.

Hellhounds (also **Devil's Dandy Dogs, Gabriel Hounds, Night Hounds, Yeth Hounds,** and **Wish Hounds)**   Gigantic predatory black hounds appear in folktales all across Europe, and have chilled the blood of travelers for centuries. These Hellhounds are known by many names and are often described as hulking beasts with fiery eyes and scorching breath who hunt at night for humans to attack. When they hunt, it isn't just for food: To fall to a Hellhound is to lose your soul to eternal damnation for they are servants of the Devil himself.

The Hellhounds love to chase their prey for miles, making a sick game of it in the way a cat plays with a mouse, and only makes the kill when the victim is too exhausted to run a step farther. Then the Hellhound settles down to a meal of fresh meat and hot blood. The only thing it does not consume is the immortal soul of its victim, and this the beast carries back to its master in Hell.

The creatures can be thwarted, however. If a person can elude them long enough for the first cock of morning to crow, then the Hellhound will slink away, hungry and frustrated.

Hide   Not all lake monsters look like giant snakes or dinosaurs, as seen with the Hide, a beast that has long troubled the waters off Lake Lacar in Argentina. The Hide is as round as a turtle but its body is flat and flexible, like a manta ray. This bulky killer is regarded by the locals as the embodiment of evil and destructive forces, and unlike Nessie or Champ, the Hide is an omnivorous predator who goes after any prey it can catch.

His-Hsue-Keui   A general term in China for vampires. The name translates as "suck-blood demon."

Hodag (also the Black Hodag)   In West Virginia, Wisconsin, and neighboring states there is an enduring legend of a minotaur-like creature called the Hodag, a creature with the head of a bull but having a man's face; short, stout legs ending in fighting claws; the humped back of a dinosaur; and a serpentine tail ending in a tip as sharp as an arrowhead.

The Hodag feeds mostly on the creatures it finds around the marshes—turtles, snakes, muskrats, and so on—but it has been known to kill and eat a human over the years, either because the opportunity was there or perhaps for a little variety in its diet.

One of the most potent weapons of Hodag creature is its unbearably rank stench, a smell so powerful that it can make a strong man swoon. Generally woodsmen lucky enough to smell the monster from a distance will scamper off in the opposite direction at first sniff.

Late in the nineteenth century, a forester named Eugene Shepherd smelled the Hodag near the headwaters of Rice Creek in Oneida County, Wisconsin. With two companions he tracked the creature to a cave where it had apparently made its home. Shepherd and his companions blocked up the cave with stones so that only a narrow slit was left, and through this they passed a long stick around whose tip they had tied a rag soaked in chloroform. The Hodag passed out and the men then unblocked the cave, let it air out, and then with rags tied around their noses and mouths because of the creature's stench, bound it and transported it back to town, where it was put on public display . . . for a fee.

Sadly the pictures of this rare cryptid seem to have mysteriously vanished over the years.

Human Vampires of Malawi   Vampire legends and even vampire hunting are not entirely a thing of the past, as clearly shown by the violence that has occurred in the tiny southern African nation of Malawi during the early twenty-first century. The widespread belief that vampires were at work within the country has led to at least one death and a number of other murderous attacks.

The trouble springs from a misunderstanding as to the practices of certain individuals who have been taking blood from the Malawi people—namely government officials and Red Cross workers, as well as other international health researchers, who have been collecting blood samples for research purposes to combat the spread of HIV and other deadly diseases.

Naturally, as rumors will, the story grew into something fantastical and out of all proportion to the truth, and suddenly people were claiming to one another that they knew of whole villages that had been attacked by vampires and that wholesale slaughter was going on. One man was actually stoned to death in the village of Thyolo because he was suspected of being a vampire; three Roman Catholic priests were savagely beaten and nearly lynched[37] in the same town because the people thought they, too, were revenants; and an aid group in a nearby town attempting to drill water wells was attacked and their equipment destroyed.

When people were asked to show proof that there had been vampire attacks, villagers showed marks on their arms where aid workers had drawn blood.

Making matters worse, rumors abounded that the government of the des-

37. CNN.com/world December 24, 2002.

perately poor nation had made some agreements to sell blood to research organizations in return for food and other kinds of aid. The United Nations World Food Program estimates that more than three million people in Malawi need emergency food. Officially, Malawian president Bakili Muluzi consistently dismissed allegations of government collaboration with international aid organizations to take blood from famished villagers in exchange for food. President Muluzi accused opposition politicians of spreading the vampire stories to try to undermine his government.

Though the attacks and fears have calmed down a bit lately, largely due to a major information campaign by the government, in the villages the fears of vampires are still so great that people sleep with drums next to them in case they need to rouse the whole town to fight off a monstrous bloodsucker.

Igosha   Poltergeists and nasty household spirits come in a lot of shapes and sizes, but one of the oddest is the Igosha of Russia, who appears as a creature with no legs or hands. At first glance this would not seem to present a picture of a particularly threatening beast, but the Igosha is very cruel and possesses some telekinetic ability—not uncommon for a poltergeist—and can hurl things around the room with destructive force. It is particularly good at tossing cutlery.

Most often the Igosha is created when a child dies before it is christened, which to some religions means that its soul is lost forever to a tormented purgatory. The Igosha, enraged for being allowed to die without the protection of a baptism, takes its rage out on its family, or any other family it takes a fancy to. It cannot die, cannot tire, and cannot pass on to the Other Side, and so whiles away eternity by being supremely annoying.

The Igosha can be appeased, however, by acknowledging its presence in a nice loud voice, setting a place for it at table, and even laying out a hat and gloves in the wintertime. Once placated, the Igosha becomes far more docile.

Ikiryoh   The Ikiryoh is a Japanese essential vampire that is the physical manifestation of the evil thoughts and feelings cultivated within a wicked person's soul. If the person is sufficiently corrupt, then this collective evil will leave the body and become a monstrous predator that can only be driven off by recitation of Buddhist sutras.[38]

Ilimu   One of the most frightening and yet fascinating theriomorphic species found anywhere in the world is the Ilimu of Kenya. It is also the most comprehensively and reliably documented monster in the annals of folklore.

The Ilimu has two different approaches to hunting humans. In the majority of the legends it is a demonic force that inhabits animals, and once the possession has taken hold, it transforms itself into the likeness of a human. In that guise it infiltrates a village and lives among the people, playing the role of human with supernatural cunning and subtlety, but all the while selecting its prey. The method by which the Ilimu accomplishes the transformation smacks of a link between the spirit world and the hard science of genetics. For the Ilimu to take on the shape of a human it has to first obtain a specimen of tissue—hair, blood, nail pairings—and then absorbs the pattern data stored in the cells so that it can then metamorphose into an exact replica of that person. Once it has assumed the person's form, the Ilimu often murders the original and then takes his place, ingratiating itself into the community.

In human form the Ilimu has all of the intelligence and memories of the murdered "donor"; but it also keeps the feral hunting qualities of the animal it has possessed. The Ilimu plays the part very well and is often affable and charismatic enough to be invited into a home, often to share a holiday feast. Once the doors have closed and the feast begun—the Ilimu reveals its true self and slaughters the entire family.

Some less bold Ilimu lure victims to a secluded spot, ostensibly to reveal a secret or to fulfill a promised tryst, and then attack and kill. Many Ilimu pick

38. A brief statement of a principle or tenet of Buddhist philosophy.

a human form that looks frail or harmless, so the finger of suspicion is rarely pointed in the right direction. It takes a wise village medicine man or witch doctor to first diagnose the possession and then track it to its source. A shaman who knows the right magic can cast a spell that will transform the Ilimu back to its animal form, which makes killing it easier (both from a hunting standpoint and psychologically); or will cast the demon spirit out of the possessed creature thereby rendering it harmless.

The second hunting tactic favored by the Ilimu is to stay in the form of whichever animal it has possessed, but make the animal act with the deliberate tactical cunning of a human. Because the animal is not acting according to its nature, the hunters can have difficulty predicting its movements, making hunting the creature extremely difficult. Often the Ilimu set traps and will hunt them in turn!

In 1898, two lions were suspected of being Ilimu, and were responsible for the deaths of nearly 130 people involved in the building of a bridge across the Kenya's Tsavo River as part of the Uganda Railway project. The lions hunted together using deceptive tactics and trickery uncommon to animals, and over the course of their two-month reign of terror everyone—even the Europeans supervising the construction—came to believe there was something supernatural about them.

Big game hunters were brought in to bag the lions, but they failed and many of them died. Ultimately it was the railroad's chief engineer, Lt. Col. John Henry Patterson who finally brought the lions down. A century later, in April of 1998, a cave was discovered in the region that scientists believe contained bones of the creature's victims.

The incident was made into a movie in 1996, *The Ghost and the Darkness,* starring Michael Douglas and Val Kilmer as Patterson. These lions, now dead and stuffed, are on display at the Field Museum in Chicago.[39]

---

39. Website: www.fieldmuseum.org, address: 1400 S. Lake Shore Drive, Chicago, IL 60605-2496; phone: (312) 922-9410.

Imandwa   The Imandwa is a general name in Bantu for a ghost, generally one of an ancestor, who wants to be properly remembered and honored by its living relations. If mentioned in song, stories, prayers, or genial reminiscences, the Imandwa will seldom make itself known, though often it tries to exert some influence on the good fortune of those who honor it. If, however, the Imandwa is improperly honored, or completely ignored, it sometimes turns into a spiteful poltergeist.

Imap Imassoursua   Like the *Hide* of Argentina, the Imap Imassoursua is a gigantic octopoidal water monster who is believed to be the very embodiment of evil and ill will.

Imfene   In South Africa there is a legend of a great race of baboons that are so powerful and vicious, they attack cattle and slaughter humans for both food and sport. Unlike regular baboons, which may attack in defense, the Imfene are supernaturally intelligent and vicious. Some tales suggest that these creatures are, in fact, theriomorphs—witches who transform from human shape into predatory apes.

Other tales tell of witches using Imfene as mounts, riding them through the forests in search of prey.

Despite their size, unnatural intelligence, and strength, the Imfene can be killed by guns or other commonplace weapons. Of course, that means getting relatively close to them, and they are known to be cunning and to set traps for those that hunt them.

Impundulu and **Ishologu**   The Impundulu of South Africa appear in a variety of frightening folktales, in each they are rather different creatures. In the most commonly recounted tales the Impundulu is a kind of familiar handed down from mother to daughter in witch families. The creature is sometimes a slave and sometimes a companion to the witches, but as it is bound by spells the former condition seems to be dominant.

No records tell of what the Impundulu's true form is, but it often takes on the appearance of a handsome and charismatic young man, full of sexual appeal and virility. The specific form it takes is drawn from the minds of its victims and it, in essence, becomes the ideal male of the victim's deepest desires.

This façade of masculine beauty is only a sham, however—an enchantment used as a predator's trick to gain the confidence of a woman and to entice her into lowering her defenses. It is then, when the Impundulu has seduced her and drawn her off to some secret and secluded place, that the monster reveals its true face and its true nature. No one has ever received such a revelation and survived to describe it.

These seducer vampires flourish throughout the Cape region of southern Africa[40] and are often used to attack the enemies of their mistress, or family members of someone for whom the witch bears animosity. When not specifically targeted at an individual, the Impundulu will sustain itself by preying on livestock of anyone the mistress dislikes. If the dislike is strong enough the Impundulu may slaughter whole families and herds even without being directed to do so.

The Impundulu have an insatiable appetite for blood, and no single act of slaughter can assuage their hunger. Indeed the creature's nature is more defined by the act of killing than by the food they seek. In many cases, even with the most bloodthirsty vampire, there is at least a reason for the killing in the need for the sustaining qualities of blood; but the Impundulu doesn't need to kill as often as it does. It enjoys it. It is a glutton for murder and butchery.

If a witch does not keep the Impundulu under tight control, then the creature will go on killing without remorse or restraint. This monster has been blamed for the wholesale slaughter of entire families not to mention whole villages.

The Impundulu is also a nosferatu and habitually spreads diseases so virulent that they can devastate an entire region. A wasting sickness very similar

40. Robert Ross, *A Concise History of South Africa (Cambridge Concise Histories)*, Cambridge University Press, 1999.

to what is often called Mad Cow Disease (*Spongiform encephalopathy*) is the most common infection spread by the Impundulu; though it has also been known to spread *iphika,* a malady that prevents animals from breeding. A third disease, which has no Latin or English name, is characterized by a sharp and very intense pain in the head or chest, and followed by almost instant death. Among the tribespeople this is called being "taken by the bird of heaven."

Like many demonic spirits—of which this is almost certainly one—the Impundulu is difficult to keep under control. If the witch-mistress does not permit her slave to feed frequently, then the intensity of its bloodlust can become overwhelming and it will shatter the binding spell with which it is controlled. At that point the witch—and her family—are as vulnerable to the creature as are any other humans.

The Impundulu can itself be killed, however, and fire is its greatest bane. Folktales often recount how the villagers, fed up by the wholesale slaughter, have stormed the house of the witch and burned it to the ground, destroying the witch and the Impundulu together.

The Impundulu shares some characteristics with the Incubus of Europe, in that it is driven by sexual hunger as well as bloodlust. There are stories telling of Impundulu who have used their seductive powers even on their witch mistresses: seducing them and feeding off of their life force during sexual encounters. Considering how wily the creature is known to be, perhaps this seduction is done less for the sexual gratification than as an attempt to weaken the witch's power and control, and thereby weakening her binding spells.

Some witches, though, apparently enjoy the contest of wills enough to deliberately take on an Impundulu as a lover, forming a strange and unholy relationship that might last throughout her lifetime. Legend has it that this is why female witches seldom married.

The Impundulu are also known for inspiring madness in humans, even when it has not directly fed on them. When a person is under the spell of an

Impundulu they often have the insane desire to cut themselves and smear their blood all over their skin, a process that apparently drives them into a sexual frenzy. This form of psychosis is known as *haematodipsia*.

Unless destroyed by fire, Impundulu are immortal and handed down like family heirlooms from mother to daughter. If a witch dies without preparing the proper spells of transference, or if she has not yet had a daughter, or if her daughter is not old enough to have been properly trained as a witch, then the family's spell over the Impundulu is broken and the creature is freed. These ownerless vampires are called Ishologu, and are greatly feared because there are few ways to track them.

An Ishologu can be killed by fire but it has to be trapped and contained long enough for the fire to sap its unnatural strength. This place must be situated so that the attempt does not set fire to the whole region.

Then there is a second species of Impundulu, which is quite different from the first, though no less vicious. This Impundulu, which is also called Intaka Yezulu ("bird of the sky"), takes the form of a large white bird with scarlet legs and a bright red beak. When it flies through a cloudy sky its droppings become forked lightning and the beating of its wings creates the thunder itself.

Like the other species of Impundulu this creature can transform into the form of a handsome man, and in that disguise it seduces women and then murders them for their blood. In some cases, however, the bite of this Impundulu turns the victim into a witch!

The Impundulu has many servants, such as eagles, owls, and hammerhead sharks, and these creatures carry news to it and also scout for prey that might satisfy the Impundulu. Just the nearby presence of the Intaka Yezulu species of Impundulu can cause women to miscarry and can cause hemorrhages of all kinds.

Like the slave Impundulu, this bird-creature can be destroyed by fire, and in some rare cases, can be driven off by magic charms.

⊰ HAEMOTODIPSIA ⊱

A sexual compulsion to drink blood; this is sometimes manifested as sexual satisfaction attained through bathing in blood or smearing it over one's face and body. This mental disorder is widely regarded as being one of the root causes of the widespread belief in vampires. Also known as *hematomania*, this condition is rare but has seen several historical and modern examples, including Elizabeth Bathory, the Marquis de Sade, and Gilles de Rais.

Incubus (plural **Incubi;** also **Buhlgeist)** The Incubus is an essential vampire as well as a sexual vampire that embodies male sexuality in a raw and destructive way. The Incubus, which appears under many names in cultures throughout history, visits women as they sleep and uses supernatural charisma to induce the woman into intercourse, during which it feeds on the release of life essence. The victim is visited night after night, and following each visit she is weaker and sicklier, until finally her system gives out and she dies.

The name "Incubus" is derived from a Middle English term that itself is derived from Medieval Latin, and means "nightmare."

If the sexual assault of the Incubus results in a pregnancy, and the woman survives the encounter, the child is often destined to become a sorcerer with evil and destructive tendencies.

Intulo Among the Zulu of the South African province of KwaZulu Natal, there are ancient legends of a predatory monster that walks upright like a man but is actually some kind of lizard, as if a human and an alligator had conceived an unholy offspring.

In the creation myths of the Zulu, the people and the animals of the Earth were all created by the Great One to be immortal, but then the Creator changed his mind and decided that everything that lives should eventually die, and he sent Intulo to be the messenger of death to the whole world.

Nowadays the Intulo is somewhat akin to the *Bogeyman* and there are still some tall-tale sightings of it in the most rural areas.

Jaracacas   Theriomorphs around the world take many forms: wolf, bat, crow, moth, even cat; but in the torrid Brazilian jungles the vampire known as the Jaracacas slinks around as a snake. The Jaracacas preys on new mothers who are still breast-feeding. It waits until the woman and her child are asleep and then slithers in, insinuating itself between the dozing baby and its mother and then bites the breast to first drink up all the milk and then suck up blood. If the child cries or protests, the Jaracacas pushes its tail into the baby's mouth to silence it. This method of stifling the child's cries has also been known to suffocate a baby. Some of the Jaracacas are insatiable and devour the breasts themselves, much like the evil *Doppelsauger* of Germanic legend.

Many Brazilian families keep fierce dogs or large cats as protection against this sneaky monster.

Jersey Devil   The Jersey Devil is one of the most enduring of American legends, with thousands of sightings dating back more than two and a half centuries and more occurring every year. Stories of the Devil's origins vary dramatically, but there are two versions of the story that are told most often.

In the first version, a woman called Mrs. Shrouds[41] of Leeds Point, New Jersey, had twelve children. She was so frustrated by her hard life she swore that if God wouldn't help her provide for a dozen hungry kids, if she ever got pregnant again that child would be fathered by the Devil himself. That is, apparently, one of those things a person shouldn't say, because she certainly got

---

41. In some versions of the tale she is called Mother Leeds or Abigail Leeds.

JERSEY DEVIL Sandro Castilli

pregnant again and shortly after she gave birth the child transformed into a misshapen monstrosity with goat-like legs, a human torso, bat wings, and an elongated snout variously described as similar to that of a wolf, horse, fox, or crocodile. When Mrs. Shrouds tried to suckle the infant, it spread its wings and escaped up the chimney.

In the second most common version a young girl from Leeds Point supposedly fell in love with a British soldier during the Revolutionary War. The local townsfolk felt that she had betrayed her country and subsequently laid a curse on her that any child that came from that union would be a devil. This too, ended badly.

Since the birth of the Jersey Devil is has been spotted by politicians, digni-
taries, forest rangers, police officers, and thousands of travelers. Even Joseph
Bonaparte (brother of Napoleon) saw it while living in exile in America. In the
nineteenth century, a naval officer, Commodore Stephen Decatur, who was engaged in artillery testing at the Hanover Iron Works in Hanover, New Jersey,
fired at and hit it, but the creature flew away, apparently uninjured. The commodore claimed that the creature he saw was at least nine feet long from head
to tail.

Jigarkhwar   The Sind region of southwest India is the hunting ground of
the Jigarkhwar, a terrible vampire-sorceress who kills with a lethal stare. Once
she spots her prey, she fixes them with her charismatic glare, transfixing the
hapless person. While the victims linger there unable to move even a finger, the
Jigarkhwar magically removes their liver. The victims do not immediately die,
though they are deathly ill and will die unless this attack can be reversed.

The feeding ritual of the Jigarkhwar does not end here, however. Once she
has taken the liver she leaves her victim in stasis and then retires to her hidden
lair. There she takes a pomegranate seed, which has been prepared in advance
with magic spells, and throws it onto her cooking fire. In the heat of the fire
the seed expands, and once it reaches the proper size, she removes it from the
flames, allows it to cool, and eats it. Only after the vampire has eaten the
pomegranate seed will her victim finally die. Then, her digestive system prepared by the magic seed, the Jigarkhwar settles down to eat the stolen liver.

There is, however, some small ray of hope for the victim of the Jigarkhwar.
Since he cannot die until the pomegranate seed has been cooked and eaten,
there is time for some other intrepid and courageous person to track the Jigarkhwar to her lair and steal her supply of magical pomegranate seeds. If this
can be accomplished and one of the seeds forced down the throat of the ensorcelled victim, the spell is broken and the seed will instantly grow into a healthy
new liver.

A deviation on this tale argues that the Jigarkhwar uses enchantment to turn her victim's liver into a pomegranate seed while it is still in his body. He then vomits up the seed, which she then takes, cooks, and eats, leaving the intrepid helper with the task of stealing that specific seed back and returning it to the victim before he dies. In those stories the victim seldom survives.

If the rescuer has the nerve and the wits, he can also attack the Jigarkhwar with a hot piece of iron, brand her on both sides of her head, pour salt over her eyes, and then imprison the sorceress in an underground chamber for forty days. If this is accomplished, then at the end of the forty days the Jigarkhwar becomes human again, is cleansed of its evil nature, and can return to ordinary society.

Some reformed Jigarkhwar have been known to launch into a career of locating and subduing others of her kind, making her one of that rare breed of reformed vampires who become vampire hunters.

Kakli Besar   The hairy wildmen of the world vary between the timid *Sasquatch* to the savage *Shampe,* but one of the most pervasively evil species of hominid is the Kakli Besar of Malaysia. Nearly nine feet tall, this creature has gigantic four-toed feet that are at least eighteen inches long and claws that can slice through bone as easily as through flesh.

The tribespeople of the Johor[42] region believe that the Kakli Besar is not an unknown species of animal, nor an offshoot of human evolution—beliefs shared by many cultures that have a hominid in their legends. The people of that part of Malaysia believe that the Kakli Besar is the deliberate creation of demonic forces and was put on Earth to hunt and harass man.

Nor is this a creature of ancient myth, but a monster that has intruded into the lives of modern man, taking human victims when it can, or slaughtering livestock when it is denied its preferred meal.

---

42. Johor is the third largest (19,984 sq km) and one of the most developed states in Peninsular Malaysia. It is situated at the southern tip of the peninsula, just across the Straits of Johor from Singapore.

KAKLI BESAR Sandro Castilli

The creature does not fear man at all, but both fire and smoke repel it. As a result, those eating out of doors at night build big smoky fires and then huddle close to the blaze, hoping that the Kakli Besar will be dissuaded from attacking. Like many natural animals, the Kakli Besar does not like the sounds of clanging metal and will retreat from noise of banging pots, gongs, or other metallic din.

In 1995, a massive monster-hunting expedition was launched through the Tanjung Piai forests of Johor to try to bag one of these beasts. Although scores of law enforcement officers, forest guides, and armed civilians scoured the woods for days, hoping to capture one of these monsters so that more could be learned about them, none of the creatures were caught or killed.

Kakundakári   Another of Africa's shaggy beastmen, and very probably the same species as the *Agogwe* of Tanzania and the *Sehité* of the Ivory Coast.

Unlike either, however, the Kakundakári[43] does not seem to be a predator, or at least not one that hunts humans. In all other ways he is similar: the same muscular body that is about four feet tall and bearing both human and simian characteristics. The creature is bipedal and covered in rust-colored shaggy hair.

Kamaitachi   In Japan there is a small predatory creature called a Kamaitachi (kama means "sickle" and itachi means "weasel") who travel in small packs of three and work in concert to bring down their prey, slash him, and then for no reason anyone has ever understood, heal the wound they've just inflicted.

The Kamaitachi, or Sickle Weasels, get their name from the belief that they actually carry sickles with them. Their method of attack is to have one Kamaitachi attack at an angle to knock a person down; the second moves in before the body has even properly landed and slashes with its sickle; and then the third comes along and magically seals the wound before more than a few drops of blood have escaped.

It is fairly common to easily dismiss stories like this, but there have been so many reported cases—and in very modern times—that Japanese scientists have begun speculating as to whether there is something behind the story. Certainly there have been cases documented of people being knocked down and cut—usually by some invisible force—and then noticing that despite the severity of the cut the wound has bled very little and closed unusually fast. These attacks happen most often in swamps, which has led scientists to speculate if some kind of swamp vapor, rising in a viscous bubble and then popping with great energy, has caused the fall. If so, being in a swamp, a cut during

---

43. *Field Guide to the Sasquatch (Sasquatch Field Guide Series)*, by David George Gordon, Sasquatch Books, 1992.

a fall is fairly common. The hard part to understand is why the wounds heal so quickly.

Some cases report that persons thus attacked have become deathly ill and have even died. A number of the persons attacked in this manner claim to have seen three weasels running quickly away through the brush following the attack; and most folks have sworn that one or all of the weasels were carrying tiny sickles.

Kappa   Stroll by a pond or stream in rural Japan, especially while walking alone, and you might come face to face with the fierce and tenacious water demon known as the Kappa. The Kappa is one of the many supernatural beings of Japanese folklore called the Yôkai, and it is one of the nastiest and most dangerous of the lot.

This malicious water sprite is a nasty blend of life-sucking essential vampire and flesh-eater whose favorite morsel is a fresh human liver. A petulant and moody creature, the Kappa may sometimes take just a nip of flesh and at other times make a banquet out of a passing traveler.

The Kappa is amphibious and lives in pools of swampy, murky water. It isn't large—no bigger than a preteen boy, but it is enormously strong and a skillful fighter. The creature has greenish-yellow skin, a wide froglike mouth, great bulbous eyes, large webbed feet, and a hard protective shell on its back like a snapping turtle. The Kappa must maintain contact with the water, and when it leaves the pond it carries water in a bowl on its head. If the water is spilled the Kappa will lose its strength.

The Kappa's preferred method of attack is to wait for a traveler or, ideally, a fisherman, to come near the edge of the pond. The Kappa then lunges out of the water and pulls the victim in. The Kappa is adept at wrestling and enjoys holding its victim under water until the poor unfortunate drowns, at which point the Kappa will suck out the departing life force.

In some of the more playful versions of the legend the Kappa comes to the edge of the pond and challenges passersby to a game of finger wrestling, but

KAPPA Kelly Everaert

then grabs the person with both hands and yanks him into the water. In other tales the Kappa comes out of the water and challenges travelers to a wrestling match and then employs a fighting method that is a blend of Sumo wrestling and jujutsu to overcome even much larger opponents. The Kappa possesses supernatural strength and quickness and generally wins these impromptu matches.

Kappa have even been known to grab horses and oxen and pull them into lakes to drown.

There have been tales of Kappa being defeated, but usually this is through trickery and not skill. The best trick is to play on the knowledge that the

Kappa, for some unknown reason, is respectful of etiquette and will always return a bow. If a person bows very low the Kappa is obliged to return the bow, and a low bow will cause the water in its head bowl to spill out.

One very famous folktale tells of a Kappa who attempted to drag a strong young horse into the water. The horse reared and bolted and the Kappa's arm got caught in the reins; as the horse ran away it tore the Kappa's arm off. In agony the Kappa tried to retrieve the arm and followed the horse all the way back to the farm; but the farmer saw what had happened and took the arm. The Kappa begged for its return, but the farmer said that he'd return it only if the Kappa agreed never to harm anyone in the village again—and to tell others of its kind to likewise leave the villagers in peace. The Kappa reluctantly agreed and even used a webbed handprint to sign a contract stating his promise. According to legend there is a small rural temple in which the signed contract is on display.

In the days of the Samurai there were several legends of encounters between warriors and kappa. The great swordsman Mifune was said to have encountered a Kappa in the late seventeenth century and when challenged to a wrestling match defeated the Kappa using jujutsu and atemi-waza (precise strikes to nerve centers). The Kappa was so impressed by Mifune's skill that he said he would grant safe passage to any soldier of his retinue.

In a number of tales, wandering Samurai defeated Kappa and in return were given gifts of knowledge, particularly of healing arts such as bone-setting, the preparation of poultices, and formulae for herbal medicines. The Kappa, although he dislikes being beaten, is generous in defeat and apparently a good sport.

Likewise Muso, the great founder of the stick-fighting art of jo-jutsu (not to be confused with jujutsu) was said in have encountered a Kappa and used his jo fighting stick to roundly thrash the Kappa and batter it so badly that it crawled into the deepest part of the swamp and was not seen for a whole century.

Today, for those who follow the Shinto religion, the Kappo is still considered part of the metaphysical world and is often placated by offerings of melons, cucumbers, and eggplants. Most commonly a cucumber is inscribed with the name of a child or loved one and the Kappa—who dotes on cucumbers—will accept the offering and leave the named person alone.

Kapre   Most of the world's many hominids have been described as being covered in coarse brown or orange-brown hair like that of an orangutan; but the Kapre of Philippine legend has thick, shaggy black hair. Unlike other apparent hominids, the Kapre is also much smarter and is capable of using a brand of very dark magic.

One of the most common spells it casts—and one that shows a great degree of magical power—is to make a bed and its sleeping occupant disappear from the bedroom and reappear tucked into the crotch of a great tree limb high above the ground. Banana trees are the most common places for the Kapre to transport its victims, and there it falls on the sleeper, tears him to pieces, and eats everything except the bones and the bedclothes. Because of the Kapre's preference for those trees, it is sometimes called "an mutya ng saging," or "the Banana Fairy," a nickname that belies its bestial nature.

The Kapre can also put on human clothes and, despite its hirsute appearance, can blend in with people well enough to spend evenings smoking, drinking, and gambling.

In more recent Filipino legends, the Kapre has had a character makeover and is now seen as a relatively harmless amiable oaf who smokes cigars the size of a man's leg and who guards a jar of gold. If a person is smart enough to trick the Kapre out of its tree, then that clever fellow can steal the gold.

Kathakano   Ask anyone in the Greek island of Crete and they'll tell you that you should never trust a smiling stranger because there is a strong chance that the stranger will turn out to be a Kathakano. This grinning creature is a revenant blood-drinker who loiters around roadside pubs and pretends to be a friendly stranger or happy drunk; but as a wanderer comes closer to the

Kathakano its true nature is revealed and the smile gets bigger and bigger, revealing a huge mouth filled with row upon row of enormous teeth. The Kathakano spits blood at its victims in the same way that some snakes spit venom, and the blood is toxic and acidic enough to cause instant and agonizing blindness. While its victim is reeling in blind misery, the Kathakano leaps on him and begins biting with those terrible teeth.

As with many Eastern European vampires, the Kathakano returns to its grave at night and is helpless while sleeping. Though sunlight will not kill it, the creature has little physical strength during the daylight hours, which allows vampire hunters a chance to dig it up and perform the appropriate ritual of exorcism. The most effective method of disposal is to drive a thick stake through each shoulder and each thigh, thus pinning it down into the coffin. The head should immediately be struck off by a heavy knife or sword that has been cleaned with rainwater and then wrapped in a blouse once worn by a virgin no older than fifteen. This symbol of purity begins the process of driving out the evil spirit that has inhabited the dead body. The head is then placed in a large cooking pot that has been filled with a mixture of one part vinegar and two parts water from melted snow. The head is left to boil for one hour, the time kept according to the chimes of a church clock tower or, in the absence of that, a priest's pocket watch. Once the head has cooked for an hour, it is removed from the pot and returned to the grave, where it is placed face-down in the coffin and liberally sprinkled with diced fresh garlic before being reburied.

A Kathakano that somehow manages to rise again is a clear indication that some part of the ritual was improperly performed. In such cases the grave is dug up the next day, only this time the monster and its coffin are burned to cinders, and the ashes are then poured back into the grave. That seems to be a method of disposal from which not even the persistent Kathakano has the power to return.

Kelpy (also Kelpie, Each-Uisge)   In Scottish legends there is a very powerful and deceptive shape-shifter called the Kelpy. It is often called the "water horse" because it frequently takes the form of a spirited young horse who, upon being ridden, delights in tossing its rider into the water. Whether it enjoys the fear and death it causes is unknown, though if this is so the Kelpy may be a kind of essential vampire that feeds off of the emotions released during painful death.

The Kelpy legends are many and varied. In some the creature appears as a man—short, hairy, and untidy—who lures the unsuspecting into bogs and swamps; in other tales the Kelpy is a far more romantic figure, appearing as a handsome and sexually appealing man who lures innocent young women to secluded spots before raping and murdering them, sometimes even feasting on their flesh.

When in the form of a horse, it is said that a magic bridle can be used to tame the creature, though acquiring this bridle seems to prove a bit problematical.

In art, the Kelpy has been depicted in the previously mentioned forms, but also as a bull, or as a theriomorphic cross between either man and horse or man and bull. Strangely, and not at all in keeping with the legends, some New Age artists have begun painting the Kelpy as a variation of the mermaid, showing her as beautiful and apparently gentle. Perhaps this is yet another of the many forms this shape-shifter takes in order to deceive its prey.

In Ireland a very similar legend is built around a creature called an Aughisky.

Kephn   Among the supernatural world's sub-species of vampires that are also witches or sorcerers exists a vicious example called the Kephn. This creature is found among Burma's Karen tribe, a people descended from the same ancestors as the Mongolians. The Kephn is one of the most repulsive of all vampires, appearing not as a shambling corpse or even a ball of light, but as the partly disembodied floating head and stomach of a local sorcerer who has made an unsavory deal with wicked spirits in order to acquire vile supernatural powers.

When the Kephn is not hunting it is an ordinary human being, at least in appearance, but when the killing urge comes on it, the sorcerer settles down in a chair and enters a trance. At this point its head and entrails literally tear themselves free from the rest of the body and soar off through the night sky seeking prey. The Kephn is the most deadly kind of essential vampire in that it feeds on human souls.

To kill a Kephn while it is in this monstrous form is impossible unless someone finds the rest of its body and sets fire to it. When the Kephn is in ordinary human form it possesses no magical invulnerability and can be killed by any means, but the Kephn is sly and seldom leaves itself open to attack.

The most advanced sorcerers of this kind can also astrally project their own souls and enter the minds of newly dead corpses. Once there it leaves a kind of energetic residue that is enough to reanimate the corpse, which then rises and attacks the enemies of the sorcerer. These revenants are also called Kephn, and they are virtually indestructible. Only decapitation or fire can stop them, and it takes several men to accomplish this. Only a Ghurkha, one of the highly trained fighting men of Burma, armed with his kukri knife, has even a chance in single combat.

⊣ ASTRAL BODY ⊢

Astral is a term derived from the Latin word for "star" and refers to the spiritual fabric of space and time, or of dimensional places other than physical. An astral body, in supernatural terms, is the part of ourselves that is ethereal and eternal and which can separate from the corporeal form through various kinds of meditations or spells. The astral body maintains its consciousness even while the physical body is in a deep trance. The skill of deliberately doing this is called astral projection.

Khmoch   Khmoch is a Cambodian word that means corpse as well as revenant. Khmoch are nearly classic reanimated corpses with rotting skin, sunken eyes, a foul odor, and a taste for human flesh and blood.

Kigatilik   The Inuits have a legend of a monster that rises from the icy waters to hunt human prey—but not just any humans: the Kigatilik's favorite food is the hot blood and fresh flesh of priests and shamans.

This demon is a servant of evil and revels in corrupting people and turning them away from their beliefs. When it cannot accomplish this through more devious means such as shape-shifting into the form of a member of the village and seducing married men (or women), speaking against religion, or sowing discord through similar tactics the Kigatilik will resort to more drastic measures. It will return to its true form—that of a powerful beast covered in thick white fur like that of a polar bear, but with longer fangs and more fearsome claws, and will hunt down the village shaman and tear him apart, feasting on his heart and other organs.

Kilyakai   In the dense forests of Papua New Guinea there is a race of small and oddly distorted hominids not unlike Neanderthals. These creatures live in the most remote areas and seldom venture near towns, but there are plenty of tales of the Kilyakai sneaking into villages or remote homes and stealing children.

The villagers of the region believe the Kilyakai to be demonic in nature, and they believe that when these beings steal human children they somehow imbue the kidnapped youngsters with their demonic abilities, thus increasing their own population.

The Kilyakai are a malicious tribe and often amuse themselves by lurking in the shrubbery and shooting poisoned darts at passersby, giving the unwary a variety of diseases such as plague and malaria.

Kindermorderinn   A Vengeance Ghost common to Germany believed to be the angry spirit of a child murdered by its mother. See also: *Radiant Boys*.

Kishi   Duality is a common theme in the world of supernatural predators, as evidenced by the human who becomes a wolf (or bat, crow, etc.), the benign household spirit who suddenly turns on its human family, and a variety of other beings caught in the balance between good and evil.

Generally when a supernatural being reveals itself to be a monster it undergoes a process of transformation, but one species stands out as an exception and is both human and evil monster all at once: the two-faced Kishi of the hill countries of Angola.

The face a person first sees is a handsome human face, full of kindness and warmth. This is just a sham, however, for as a person draws near, attracted by the charisma of this person, the Kishi spins around and reveals a second face on the back of its head: the hungry, grinning face of a hyena.

Many tales of the Kishi recount how the monster grows its hair long or wears a headdress to hide the hyena face, and appears quite normal otherwise. Thus disguised it visits a village and becomes part of the community, and actively courts the prettiest young women there. In this guise the Kishi is very social and loves attending parties, dances, and weddings. But once it has made its selection, it lures her away from the crowd to a secluded spot and then reveals its true face.

First the Kishi feeds on the terror of the moment, drinking in the energy released by the unfortunate woman's total horror; and then the Kishi attacks her and devours her. The Kishi is a rare blend of essential vampire, blood-drinker, and flesh-eater.

The bite of a Kishi is more powerful than that of a crocodile, and even if one of the woman's male relatives were to arrive at the first bite he would not be able to open those jaws. The first bite is always fatal.

Fire can drive the Kishi away, and despite its strength and cunning it can be killed with ordinary weapons. But the Kishi is a crafty fighter and possesses far more courage than is typical of a hyena. When defending its prey it is more like a lion. Seldom can one be killed by a single opponent; and by the time help has arrived the Kishi has often fled with the choicest bits of its prey.

Kitsune-Tsuki   In Japan, as with many Asian cultures, one commonly held belief is that a fox who has lived an unnaturally long life will acquire vast intelligence and the ability to shape-shift. During this transformation, the fox becomes a "fox spirit," or Kitsune, and evolves into a kind of pernicious trickster who delights in the seduction and destruction of unsuspecting mortals.

The Kitsune is often female, and can sometimes astrally project its essence out of its own body and enter into the body of a victim, either under the fingernails or through the pores on the breasts. Once inside, the fox spirit drives the woman to commit unnatural acts. This condition is called Kitsune-Tsuki ("Fox-Lunacy") and often leads to murder or suicide.

A number of variations on the fox spirit legend thrive in Japanese myth. Here are the most common examples of how this demonic force manifests itself:

- **Genko:** A black fox—a more benign form generally taken as a good omen

- **Kiko:** A "ghost fox" that, though not essentially evil, is unlucky and its presence often presages minor disasters. (See *Reiko* below.)

- **Kitsune:** The general name for all Japanese fox spirits.

- **Koryo:** Another variation of the "ghost fox."

- **Kuko:** An "air fox," a less physically substantial creature and one that causes tremendous harm.

- **Nogitsune:** A "wild fox" who acts as a messenger to Inari, the goddess of Rice (a deity of major importance to the culture). Though this fox spirit is not evil, it is mischievous and its pranks can cause harm.

•**Reiko:** Most common name for the "ghost fox."

•**Shakko:** A "red fox," but this term is more or less interchangeable with Kitsune.

•**Tenko:** Very old and very evil "celestial foxes." These creatures have reached at least a thousand years in age and have grown nine tails and golden fur.

Kludde   The Kludde is a strange and monstrous black dog that haunts the Flemish countryside looking for isolated travelers to attack. This hound is gigantic—big enough to take down a horse and snap its back.

The Kludde is covered in chains, and some folktales insist that it broke free from Satan's incarceration in Hell and now runs wild on Earth. Though it looks like a dog, the Kludde walks erect on two legs even when giving chase, and on those two legs it can outrun anything short of a fast car.

The best way of defeating a Kludde is to not fight one at all. When the sound of clinking chains is heard in the night, the smartest thing to do is run and then hide in the closest safe place.

The Kludde is a shape-shifter and cunningly changes its form at will into that of a huge black cat, a giant crow, or other shadowy night predator.

Knockers   Like the *Blue-Caps* of England, the Knockers of Cornwall are spirits who live in the darkest and deepest parts of mines and often work along with humans, helping them find things they've lost or even leading them to rich veins of silver, lead, and tin. They find these lodes by rapping their picks and knives against the walls, an action that earned them their nickname.

Some of the legends claim that the Knockers are actually ghosts of conscripted Jews who worked the mines during centuries past. A more extreme version of this legend insists that these Knockers are specifically the ghosts of the Jews who participated in the condemnation and crucifixion of Jesus, and that they are condemned to work in the mines as a punishment, to be released on the Day of Judgment.

Most miners dispute this claim, however, insisting that the Knockers are either some kind of faerie folk or else the spirits of dead miners who have returned to help their living comrades.

For the most part the Knockers are benign and helpful, but they can be vindictive when annoyed. Whistling and swearing angers them and they'll pelt the offender with a shower of stones until he stops and apologizes.

Knockers also appear in the folktales of Wales, where they are called Coblynau.

Kobolds   Household spirits are common throughout the world and many of them share the same characteristic: They are immensely helpful most of the time, but when angered they can turn quite nasty. This is true with the Kobold of Germany and Switzerland as it is with the *Bwca* of Cornwall, the *Brownie* of England, and French goblins.

The Kobold will actually test the atmosphere and disposition of the house and family it has selected by a ritual of its own devising. Before settling in, the Kobold will bring a small pouch of sawdust, dirt, and suchlike into the house, sprinkling some dust, dropping a few grains of dirt into the milk jug, and so on. If the master and mistress of the house are smart enough to recognize these as part of the Kobold's testing procedure and, most important, leave the dirt untouched, then the Kobold will feel that it is both welcome and needed. Then it moves in, settles down somewhere nice and warm (behind the stove is a favored place), and attaches itself to the household for as long as the family members live. Once ensconced, the Kobold will help with cleaning—though never when anyone is looking—and will keep other less helpful spirits out.

If the very last member of the family dies, the Kobold will move on until it finds another compatible family.

If, during the tenure of the Kobold, a new servant joins the household, the other servants must make sure to tell this newcomer how to act and how to respect the presence of the Kobold, otherwise the creature will cause bad luck, accidents, and other problems until the new servant is discharged.

Konaki Jiji Shape-shifters truly do come in all shapes and sizes, and in Japan one of these predatory theriomorphs, the Konaki Jiji, assumes the size and shape of a helpless baby and positions itself by the side of the road, waiting for someone to stop to help. Depending on which story one hears, the Konaki Jiji either instantly returns to its normal rather ponderous size and weight, causing the person who has picked it up to fall to the ground, stunned by the massive creature, at which point the Konaki Jiji runs away; or the Konaki Jiji grows into a large flesh-eating demon and devours the Good Samaritan.

The name "Konaki Jiji" means "old man crying like a baby," and the full-grown creature does indeed resemble an old man, though one of particularly dense mass and great strength. Statues of the Konaki Jiji can often be seen in temples or along roadsides in Japan.

Kornwolf The Kornwolf is a legend from all across Europe (France, Germany, Hungary, Estonia, Latvia, Poland, Russia, etc.) that tells of strangely intelligent wolves that haunted the cornfields and preyed on farmers and their families. The Kornwolf was a true werewolf and ran around in the forms of ordinary wolves, and could be killed by arrows or any other weapon. The tradition of burning a Kornwolf's corpse—either real or in effigy—in ritual fires was used for centuries to chase away evil spirits and bring luck to the coming harvest.

Korreds Some of the world's monsters are harder to understand than others. The Korreds of Brittany are certainly killers, but it is not at all clear what they gain from their murders.

In appearance the Korreds are a race of small people with shaggy hair, extremely wrinkled faces, bright red eyes, goatlike legs, and cat's claws in place of fingers. Despite these deformities they are metalsmiths of great skill and make the most beautiful coins from precious metals. They build strong stone houses called "dolmen," and at night they have wild dance parties and cavort around the dolmen by firelight.

KORNWOLF Reymond Pagé

Should a traveler chance to pass a dolmen, the Korreds will invite that person to join in, treating them to excellent food and wine, and then will encourage the well-fed traveler to get up and join in the dance. However, the dance of the Korred is charged with sorcery and once a human has joined in the dance, he or she must continue to do so until they become so overheated and exhausted that they drop dead.

It may be that the Korreds are a kind of communal-essential vampire, each member of the village sharing in the release of life energy. Or, perhaps they are just mean-spirited little imps who delight in murder. In either case, if you are out walking in rural Brittany and you see a group of wizened little folk making merry around a small stone house—keep walking.

Kozlak (also **Kuzlak)**   Unlike the vampires in novels and film, vampires in folklore as a rule are not killed by stakes through the heart. Generally the stake is merely used to hold the vampire immobile while the ritual of exorcism is performed. This is true with nearly every species of vampire on Earth, however, except the Kozlak of Dalmatia. This one species can, in fact, be killed by a stake of hawthorn being plunged into its heart.

The Kozlak is created in one of two ways. The most common method occurs when a child dies because it has not been properly breast-fed. If such a calamity happens, the spirit of the child becomes enraged and filled with enormous power, and returns to the world of the living as a kind of poltergeist to haunt its neglectful mother and the whole community. The infuriated infant ghost smashes plates and cups, throws objects around the house, and can even summon the strength to overturn a hay cart. Sometimes the creature manifests itself in physical form—usually a bat or small carrion bird—and attacks the family's livestock, drinking blood and spreading disease.

The second method by which a Kozlak is created is the death of a person who was not properly breast-fed as a child but who lived to adult age and then died through violence, murder, or suicide. In this case the Kozlak rises as a true revenant, clawing its way out of the ground and attacking its family in a far more direct manner—by tearing their throats out.

When a Kozlak is suspected the family or their neighbors generally appeal to one of the Franciscan Brothers for aid. The monk creates amulets for the members of the family, blessing them with special prayers against evil. Then the monk hunts for a hawthorn bush growing at a high place in the mountains where there is no view of the sea. From this plant he selects the largest branch and sharpens it into a long stake. Armed with this stake and his own amulet, he journeys back to the place where the suspected Kozlak was buried. There he sits down to pray until sunset. When the Kozlak rises from the grave, the monk springs up and stabs it with the hawthorn stake. The hawthorn possesses a quality that extinguishes the link between demonic possession and the reanimated flesh. The body returns to a normal dead state at once.

The monk then cuts off the Kozlak's head, stuffs its mouth with garlic, and reburies the body, thus ending the threat forever.

≼ HAWTHORN ≽

Hawthorn (*Crataegus species*), one of the principal weapons against vampires, is a member of the rose family. The most common usage for hawthorn sprigs is to hang them above doorways to prevent the entry of evil spirits into a house. When choosing wood for a stake as part of the Ritual of Exorcism, hawthorn is preferred because of its protective powers. These powers weaken the vampire so that ordinary mortals can overpower it. In Dalmatia, the fierce Kozlak is actually killed by the hawthorn stake itself.

Hawthorn extract has been used for centuries to treat circulatory disorders and respiratory illnesses. Considered a "cardiotonic" herb it is used to treat irregular heartbeat, high blood pressure, chest pain, hardening of the arteries, and congestive heart failure.

Travelers in Eastern Europe and also in Great Britain (particularly Scotland) often used hawthorn for walking sticks because a strike from a hawthorn rod hits supernatural creatures with the force of a battering ram.

Krvopijac (also **Krvoijac**) The proper adherence to religious practice is closely linked to vampirism, or rather the *improper* adherence can lead directly to vampirism. In Bulgaria, for instance, a person can become a Krvopijac, a particularly unsavory species of vampire, merely by smoking tobacco or drinking alcohol during Lent. Some become Krvopijac instantly; others are doomed to do so whenever they die. In Bulgaria rural folks do not lightly break their yearly promises of abstinence.

The Krvopijac has a forked tongue and a single nostril, and during the process of transformation its skeleton melts and then reforms as a far tougher and more durable material—the exact structure of which is unknown. This new skeleton, however, gives the Krvopijac fantastic physical strength and a resistance to nearly any weapon short of fire. The process of conversion from newly buried corpse to fully reformed Krvopijac takes forty days, after which the monster rises from the grave to hunt for blood. It is widely believed that the forty-day process is the Devil's deliberate attempt to mock the forty-day-long purification that Jesus underwent prior to beginning his ministry.

Aside from the facial and lingual deformities, the Krvopijac looks otherwise like a standard pallid-faced decaying revenant, with rotting teeth, sunken eyes, and the reek of decaying meat.

Locating a Krvopijac requires certain specific items, namely a naked virgin riding astride a black foal, which she must ride through a graveyard. If there is any spot within the burial ground where the mount refuses to go, then that is likely to be the Krvopijac's resting place. A vampire-hunting monk known as a *Djadadjii* is generally called in to handle the actual disposal of the monster.

The Djadadjii does this by first scattering wild roses all around the grave. Wild roses, along with hawthorn and garlic flowers, have a powerful weakening effect on many species of vampires. The smell of the flowers prevents the Krvopijac from rising to flee or from attacking the cleric. Once the creature is confined the Djadadjii uses a form of church-approved sorcery to draw the creature's invisible spirit out of the ground and then force it into a bottle that he has specifically prepared. The bottle is then hurled into a bonfire. Once this has been accomplished, the body, still in the grave, becomes nothing more than a lifeless corpse and troubles the village no longer.

Kudlak   All around the world a child born with a caul[44] is regarded as a connection with the supernatural world. Sometimes this connection is positive—as with the Celts—but more often it is considered to be a sign of some demonic taint. Sometimes the matter is uncertain, requiring that the wise folk among the people pay close attention to the child to detect signs of demonstrable good or definite evil. On the peninsula of Istria, both the Croats and Slavs believe that a caul is a sure sign that the child will either become a good-natured and heroic Kresnik, or a foul and vampiric Kudlak.[45]

In either case the child will grow to be an adult possessing great supernatural powers. If it is the Kudlak spirit that defines the person, then they will become a kind of living vampire with the power to shape-shift and fly on the night winds, and to whom sorcery is almost second nature. The Kudlak will use his powers to prey on the people of his town, magically learning secrets, causing sickness, and often killing when he knows he can get away with it. After death, however, the Kudlak rises from the grave as an even more powerful blood-drinking vampire.

On the other hand, if the Kresnik spirit emerges, then that person will become a champion of goodness and will be aware that it is in his destiny and in his nature to seek out and confront evil in all of its many forms, and particularly when a Kudlak rises.

A struggle between the Kudlak and Kresnik was recorded in the late nineteenth century by the scholar I. Milčetić in his work, *Vjera u osobita bića*.[46] He wrote:

44. An embryonic membrane sometimes attached to the top of the head at birth and which forms a veil.
45. A common abbreviation for Vorkudlak.
46. Translated by Jan L. Perkowski. Sbornik za narodni život i običaje južnih slavena, Vol. I (Zagreb, 1896), pp. 224–225.

The people believe that each clan has one kudlak and one krsnik. They are two opposite beings. The kudlak plots to do harm to people, and the krsnik strives to protect them. They know how to transform themselves into all sorts of animals, most frequently into pigs, oxen, or horses. The kudlak is usually black, and the krsnik white or multicolored. The kudlak attacks men at night, frightening, striking, and even killing them, but the krsnik jumps in and they engage in a wild battle. In the end the krsnik wins. There are no peasants who do not believe in the vukodlak. For that reason there are few old people who have not seen one. . . . The kudlak most frequently troubles people after its death. If the people suspect that someone who has died is a kudlak, they sever the tendons under his knees before they place him in his grave. They think that in this way he will no longer walk at night nor bother anyone. The most recent kudlaks in Dubašnica were the Čoporići from the village of Turčić (1880). I met one of the Čoporići. . . . He was lame and by reliable testimony a kudlak! I still remember well how in my youth I went past his house with trepidation. However, during his lifetime he had rid himself of the evil spirit, having confessed his sins. From then on there were no more kudlaks in Dubašnica, because the priests had driven them out. The grandfather of this Čoporići was a kudlak even after his death, and at night he plagued the populace and brought harm to them. To be rid of him the people of Dubašnica exhumed him and at night impaled him with a hawthorn stake. This happened at the first half of this century.

Kuei   The Kuei, a ghost of rural China, rises from the grave of someone who has committed suicide or has died by violence. It can also come into being from the grave of a woman who has died during childbirth or, more often, while pregnant. Of these, however, the Kuei of suicides are the most evil and destructive.

The suicide Kuei wears a red handkerchief to hide the fact that its face is inexplicably deformed (it has no chin), and its approach can be detected by watching candle flames—they will suddenly burn green if one of these beings is near.

The best way to drive them off is to set off firecrackers. This works well with all ghosts and spirits in China.

Kumiho The Kumiho is another of the world's many fox spirits, and the basis of a classic tale, "The King and the Kumiho" ("Wanggwa Kumiho"). In this story an unlucky king meets a girl in the woods at night and talks her into having sex with him by offering to assist her financially devastated father. Regrettably for him their resulting dalliance takes place in the dark and he is unable to see the creature's animal body, and the act of mating with her drains him of much of his life force and vitality.[47]

Another fox spirit legend is "The Emperor's Kumiho Daughter-in-Law," in which a Kumiho living in secret among the emperor's household begins draining life energy from court retainers. Only when a heroic monster slayer kills the Kumiho are the remaining courtiers saved.

Kung-Lu (also Dsu-The, Ggin-Sung, and Tok) The timid and docile Yeti is not the only hairy hominid dwelling in the vastness of the high Himalayas; it is also the hunting ground of a far fiercer creature—the Kung-Lu. Both are enormous humanoid creatures covered in thick fur, but the similarities end there. The Kung-Lu, unlike its shy cousin, actively seeks out humans. Any man it finds becomes its next meal; any woman it meets becomes a breeder for its young. Since the newborn of the Kung-Lu are about the size of six-month-old apes, few women survive to bear more than one child. This is, arguably, a mercy.

Apparently the Kung-Lu are all male because no females have ever been

47. This suggests that the Kumiho is some species of essential vampire.

sighted; which makes the fact that all of these creatures are born from human mothers even more curious, if deeply disturbing.

Kwakwakalanooksiwae   Among Canada's Kwakiutl Indians there is a legend of a gigantic man eating raven called Kwakwakalanooksiwae, a creature much larger than a condor, whose wing beats can shake the sky, and who can eat a man in one bite.

Lake Van Monster   A monster found in Turkey's Van Lake, this is the most frequently sighted sea monster in the world—and also one of the most recent. First spotted in 1995, the creature was caught on film in 1997 by twenty-six-year-old local man, Unal Kozak. The video footage shows what is believed to be the creature's head, partly submerged, and a single piercing black eye glaring out of the water. The footage was shown on CNN and other news services and has become something of a classic for cryptozoologists. Since 1995 there have been well over a thousand sightings of this monster.

La Llorona   Tragedy can often result in evil, at least in the world of ghosts and vampires. Often tragic human circumstances create a supernatural aftershock that brings into being one of a variety of spiritual maladies, such as hauntings, possessions, or the creation of a malignant being.

In Guatemala legend survives of a destructive spirit called La Llorona who often lures children to their deaths if they chance to meet her in the countryside. In life La Llorona was a woman who had been jilted by her lover once she had become pregnant. Angry with the child for the loss of her lover she murdered it by drowning it in a pond.

---

48. Heuvelmans, Bernard, Dr., *On the Track of Unknown Animals,* 3rd ed. (London: Kegan Paul International Limited, 1995).

⊰ DR. BERNARD ⊱ HEUVELMANS (1916–2001)— KING OF THE MODERN MONSTER HUNTERS

Bernard Heuvelmans, a native of Belgium and a doctor of zoology, was a scientist dedicated to the discovery and classification of hitherto unknown species of animals. His seminal book, *Sur la piste des betes ignorees*[48] (*On the Track of Unknown Animals*) was published in 1955 and has become the bible of cryptozoology, a term he coined in 1959. Heuvelmans was a true scientist and would debunk an artifact if he could, as he did with the so-called yeti skullcap, an object also debunked by Sir Edmund Hillary, though Heuvelmans disproved it first. Even so, he believed that there are many species of creatures alive in the world that were unknown to science, including sea serpents, hominids, and perhaps even stranger beings.

After her own death some years later, La Llorona returned to the pond where she had committed the murder and is forever shackled there by some spiritual bonds. Far from helpless, however, she constantly seeks fresh prey. When she senses or spots a child coming into her woods, she sings the kinds of songs a mother might sing to a beloved child, luring unsuspecting children to her.

In some stories she springs at them once they're close enough and pushes them under the water; but most frequently the stories say that she sings to the children from beneath the water's surface and tricks them into leaning too far over the bank so that they fall in and drown.

LA LLORONA (Mordideus W. Goodell)

No one is quite sure where La Llorona died, but she has been reported in many places across Guatemala. So perhaps she lives partly in every remote pond, stream, or river, waiting for her next victim.

Children are, of course, warned never to stray too close to the water; and in some villages charms are made with the names of the child's maternal grandmother (a powerful person in those rural families) and the "grandmother stone" keeps the child safe.

Lambton Worm   In Durham, England, they still tell tales of the great local dragon called the Lambton Worm. The creature was actually caught by one
of the younger Lambtons while the lad was fishing. When he netted it he
thought he had found some kind of ugly eel. Not liking the looks of it, young
Master Lambton chucked it down a well and forgot all about it. He grew up
and then left home to fight in the Crusades. Unfortunately the "eel" he'd
caught had been a baby wormlike dragon and it, too, grew up and left its new
home—the well—to launch its own crusade. It slithered out of the well and ter-
rorized the countryside, eating livestock, children, and even grown men.

The Lambton Worm,[49] as it became known, was so vast that it could wrap
itself three times around the hill on which the well was built. That hill is still
known as Worm Hill.

Eventually young Lambton, now a seasoned veteran of foreign wars, returned home. When he heard about the monster, he set out to destroy it. He
made a short visit to a local witch first, however, to get some magical aid in destroying so enormous a creature. She gave him charms and made him promise that after he killed the worm he had to also kill the very next creature he
met. Lambton agreed, figuring that no person would be loitering around the
area occupied by the dragon. So he set out, and using his ensorcelled weapons
slew the worm and cut it into three pieces, at which point he turned around
and set back off for home. Alas, he did encounter someone—the very next living thing he saw—and it was his father, likewise out for a bout of dragon-
slaying.

Lambton could not bring himself to murder his father, so he just reneged
on his promise to the witch. She, however, was not so easily ignored and cast a
curse on the Lambton family that brought misfortune, madness, and other ills
for nine generations.

It might have been better to have let the worm live, at least for the unlucky
Lambtons.

---

49. "Worm" is an Old English name for "dragon."

The story of the Lambton Worm became the basis for the "Dampton Worm" in the novel *The Lair of the White Worm* by Bram Stoker; and in the film version, the modern descendant of the Damptons was played by a very young Hugh Grant. The film also had a folksong that actually follows the original legend fairly closely.

Lamiai The Lamiai of ancient Greece are evil birth demons that prey upon newborns, drinking their blood and consuming their flesh. These creatures are named after a Libyan queen Lamia, who was one of Zeus' many mistresses. Hera, Zeus' long-suffering and understandably bitter wife, was so enraged by the liaison that she murdered any offspring that resulted from the union. Lamia was also understandably outraged and swore that in revenge for this act of cruelty she would kill as many other children as possible. So, to carry out this dreadful mission, she created the Lamiai: female demons with lower limbs like snakes, sharp talons, and wicked teeth.

The Lamiai were shape-shifters and often took the forms of various birds and would fly through the air hunting for prey. Once they spied a victim they would land and reclaim their regular monstrous forms. Their method of attack was to tear out their victim's entrails, devour the flesh, suck out any milk, and drink the blood. The Lamiai even sought out pregnant victims in order to kill both mother and child.

The Lamiai did not confine their murderous attentions strictly to women and children, however; sometimes they would play the role of a seductress vampire and seduce young men, have sex with them, and then at the moment of orgasm they would tear out their victims' throats and drink the spurting blood.

Lampire It is not only political strife and social turmoil that has disturbed the hearts and minds of the people of Bosnia-Herzegovina. It is an ancient land on the Adriatic between Croatia, Serbia, and Yugoslavia, and it has had its shares of unearthly troubles as well. In those hills and forests there are legends

of vampires of great power and unquenchable hunger. It is home to two different monsters: the ferocious *Vlkodlak* and the deadly Lampire.

Belief in the Lampire endured openly well into the 1980s, and is probably
still going on in the twenty-first century. As late as 1878, when the Austrians
took control of the country from the remains of the Ottoman Empire, citizens
were still digging up the recently dead and burning them to prevent their becoming vampires. The occupying Austrians had to pass—and harshly enforce—
laws to prevent this practice.

There had been a wave of suspicious deaths and the Bosnians believed
that this was caused by a spread of vampirism, as the Lampire was one of the
nosferatu—vampires who spread disease and pestilence. The local belief was
that the first victim to perish of the disease was very probably the Lampire itself, and the subsequent deaths were the result of his evil power stretching out
over the whole of the village. The deaths would continue and the disease
would spread until the Lampire was identified and his body disinterred and
burned. For good measure each victim had to be burned to prevent each one
of those persons from becoming the next Lampire. The Bosnians knew this,
but the Austrians put a stop to it.

An interesting coda to this is that one of the other powers of the Lampire
is to sow discord, and since the practice of destroying vampires was forcibly
stopped, that land has seen nothing but internal hatred, strife, and mass
murder.

Langsuir (also Lansuyar)   The Langsuir of Malaysia is included on that
sad and terrible list of vampires created as a result of stillbirths and deaths of
women during childbirth. This paradigm is found throughout the world, but
perhaps with a bit more frequency in Indonesia and India.

In the case of Malaysia, these traumatic deaths lead to the creation of one
and sometimes two separate vampires: the Langsuir and the *Pontianak*. If it is
the woman who has died, she becomes the Langsuir; if it is the child, it is the
Pontianak.

Forty days after a woman dies while pregnant or giving birth, the Langsuir rises from the grave as a ghostly vampire. No matter what her appearance was before death, once she has risen the Langsuir takes the form of a woman of surpassing beauty with long nails and silky black hair that trails all the way to her ankles. However her beauty diminishes somewhat on closer examination, because behind her hair she has a second mouth at the back of her neck. This mouth, filled with needlelike teeth, is what she uses to bite her victims, and her most desired sustenance is the blood of children.

When denied this, she will satisfy her hunger by attacking adults or even livestock, drinking blood and eating raw meat. Though the Langsuir generally hunts alone, there are some frightening tales of several of these monsters hunting in a pack.

Killing a Langsuir is difficult, but preventative measures taken at the time of burial can keep it from rising, such as filling the mouth of the recently dead with glass beads (which, even if it did rise, would prevent its seductive voice to lure prey). Also, placing hen's eggs in its armpits and driving strong needles through its hands and feet are said to keep it immobile.

The Langsuir is one of the very few vampires around the world that can be cured of its demonic nature and restored to a normal healthy life. To accomplish this amazing goal, someone first has to care enough about the Langsuir (or the woman she was before death) to want to undertake the risks. Next, this person has to enlist strong and clever friends because the Langsuir has to be tracked, captured, and restrained. Her long hair must be cut off and stuffed into the second mouth at the back of her neck, and her fingernails need to be cut down to the quick. These steps break the spell that imbues the creature with both its powers and its appetite. If all of this is accomplished, the Langsuir will be restored to normalcy. She can even marry, have children, and live a normal life except in one regard: If she were to make merry and feel intense emotions, she would revert back to her vampiric self. Therefore the Langsuir must be sure to live a dour, somber life.

There is one particularly creepy folktale of a man, insane with grief over his wife who had died during the last trimester of her pregnancy, who had buried her improperly in the hopes that she would rise as a Langsuir. When she did, in fact, rise, he set about trying to capture her with the help of a half-dozen strong men he had hired, then took the steps necessary to restore her to normal life. He managed to do that and felt delighted that he had tricked death and gotten his wife back from the grave. But he never told her what he had done and she had no memory of her previous pregnancy, death, and unnatural rebirth. Months later, the wife realized that she was pregnant. She was filled with such great joy that she ran to tell her husband the wonderful news. By the time she had run from one room of the house to the other, it was the Langsuir who delivered the news. This time her husband had no hired muscle to help him capture his monstrous wife. Death, it seems, seldom enjoys being cheated.

Leanhaun-Sidhe (also Lianhaun Shee, Leanhaun Shee) The Sidhe[50] are many and varied, and their races are spread throughout the Celtic lands. The word means "faerie" or "fay," though it is said that they prefer to be known as the Sidhe, at least those that have relations with humans.

Most of the Sidhe are neither good nor evil but exist according to their own peculiar and exotic natures; they seldom interact with man. However some, like the infamous Leanhaun-Sidhe, are decidedly evil and certainly predatory. These creatures appear as women of such incredible beauty that any man seeing them is instantly enthralled. Using songs and laughter as well as her obvious physical charms, the Leanhaun-Sidhe lures her prey—generally healthy young men—to secluded spots and then either quickly or over a length of time that suits individual appetites, the creature drains away the man's life essence.

The Leanhaun-Sidhe are certainly seductress vampires, and like many of that kind they are also essential vampires.

---

50. Pronounced "shee."

LEANHAUN-SIDHE
Xris Hannah

In quite a few of the tales of the Leanhaun-Sidhe the creature is somewhere between a vampire and a muse, offering to provide unnaturally potent inspiration in exchange for little tastes of the young man's life force. Many struggling poets have yielded to this offer, but these things tend to end badly, and almost always in favor of the monster. In a few tales the man was able to master himself enough to break the enchantment and flee.

The image of the Leanhaun-Sidhe as the "Dark Muse" has been a staple of literature, and even William Butler Yeats, in his book *Faerie and Folk Tales of Ireland* wrote, "This spirit seeks the love of men. If they refuse she is their slave; if they consent, they are hers, and can only escape by finding one to take their place. Her lovers waste away, for she lives on their life. Most of the Gaelic poets, down to quite recent times, have had a Leanhaun Shee, for she gives inspiration to her slaves and is indeed the Gaelic muse—this malignant faerie. Her lovers, the Gaelic poets, died young. She grew restless and carried them away to other worlds, for death does not destroy her power."

Lemure (also Larvae)   In Ancient Rome it was believed that the souls who descended to the Underworld were divided into two groups: Manes and Lemure. A Mane was the spirit of a person deserving of honor, and if his spirit received the proper respect from his living relatives, and if the proper holy rites were performed in his memory, then his spirit would be released from the Underworld and would often serve as a spiritual guide and guardian to his surviving family and his descendants.

A person whose soul was corrupt, and who was therefore unlikely to be revered by his surviving family, was known as a Lemure. This creature often returned to Earth as an evil ghost who delighted in sowing discord and bringing torment to everyone he encountered.

The Lemures were essential vampires who fed on the pain and misery they caused, and they worked at their evil all year long. They are particularly powerful, however, during the Festival of Lemuria, held each May. Since they are ghosts, the Lemure cannot be killed, but they cannot abide loud noise, and the banging of drums will drive them away.

Lidérc Nadaly   The Lidérc Nadaly of Hungary is another of the world's many vampires who is both sexual predator and blood-drinker. In many ways similar to the Incubus and Succubus in that it essentially loves its victims to death, the Lidérc Nadaly goes a step further and drinks the dying person's blood as well. All that is left is a lifeless and desiccated shell.

The Lidérc Nadaly is a theriomorph and can take whatever form it feels will work best to deceive or attract its prey. Often its victims will not see a monster, but rather some desired or beloved person such as wife, husband, or secret lover. Occasionally it even adopts the will-o'-the-wisp form of a ball of light in order to lure the curious into suitably remote spots.

In the rare case that a person discovers that they are confronted by—or know the whereabouts of—a Lidérc Nadaly, the only defense is to drive an iron nail through its temple, which kills it instantly.

⚔ IGNIS FATUUS ⚔

Latin name for "Corpse Lights," the older name for the will-o'-the-wisp. Many of the world's supernatural predators take the form of a fiery ball of light that lures travelers into dangerous places, where they either suffer deadly falls, sink into bogs, or are directly attacked for life-energy.

Also known as Luminous Phenomena, this includes any of a number of paranormal events in which observers see lights, glowing objects, or other kinds of unexplained luminescences.

Lilith   Lilith is one of the oldest creatures in the long history of vampiric beings, with roots buried deep in the traditions of the ancient Sumerians, Babylonians, and Hebrews. The origin of Lilith, from an archaeological point of view, is very like the Sumerian Lilû.[51] But the "Lilith" most commonly discussed is drawn from the Talmud,[52] which suggests that Lilith was created to be Adam's first wife. She was, however, a fiercely independent woman who did not respond well to Adam's attempts at being the dominant partner, especially in a sexual sense. Adam tried to establish sexual dominance over Lilith by making her lie beneath him during sex; Lilith wanted to be the one on top, and this

---

51. See the forthcoming third book in this series, *Beyond Vampire Universe*, for info on this ancient demon.
52. The Hebrew sacred writings on holy matters.

LILITH STEALING THREE BABIES
Lilian Broca

resulted in history's first divorce due to irreconcilable differences. In some stories she was driven out by angels—male angels, of course.

In a different telling of this legend, God had originally created Adam and Lilith as twins joined together at the back. Lilith wanted complete equality with Adam but was denied, so she fled from him in anger.

And in yet a third story, after Lilith left Adam she met Satan and had sex with him.

In all of the stories, however, Lilith goes to the "abode of demons," where she became pregnant (either by Satan or one or more demons), and began producing children at the rate of about a hundred per day, thereby populating the whole Earth with monsters. In many of these legends of Lilith, her children were the first vampires, which makes her the mother of all vampires.

Adam appealed to God, who sent three angels, Sansanvi, Sanvi, and Semangelaf, to drag Lilith back to Eden. Lilith cursed the angels and refused to go. The angels warned her that God would take these demon children away from her unless she returned to Adam and submitted to his will. Lilith refused and was severely punished by God. Her offspring were scattered across the world and cast into demon dimensions. Adam was then placated by the creation of Eve, who was far more docile.

The canonical Bible contains none of these Lilith stories, but the folklore has been passed down through the centuries. Though openly refuted by Hebraic scholars, even as late as the Middle Ages, there were Jews wearing amulets to ward off the Lilim—the vampiric children of Lilith.

In more modern times Lilith is seen as being the victim of a male-centric hate campaign, and she is often regarded as an icon and role model for feminism and equality.

Llamhigyn Y Dwr   In Wales, when a fisherman sets out to fish in a remote stream, and if he's wise, he'll keep an eye out for a nasty amphibious water monster called the Llamhigyn Y Dwr, or Water Leaper. The Llamhigyn Y Dwr looks like a huge frog as big as a hog that has a thrashing tail, leathery wings, and teeth that can bite through a boat oar in a single snap.

The Llamhigyn Y Dwr stakes out its territory and then defends it with great ferocity. If a fisherman ventures into its domain, the monster will bite through fishing lines, tear apart nets, and frighten away all the fish. Moreover, if it manages to upset the boat, it will attack like a shark and devour the unlucky fisherman.

The Llamhigyn Y Dwr generally keeps below the water, raising only its protuberant eyes above the surface in the same fashion as an alligator. When it spots an intruder the creature will leap out of the water, its wings allowing it to jump much farther than even its powerful legs could manage.

Luckily, the creature appears to be mortal and can be killed with a gun, gaffe, or knife. Guns are safest, though, because at close range the Llamhigyn Y Dwr is quick and deadly.

⊰ ACONITE ⊱

In werewolf folklore the plants of the aconite family have potent protective and curative powers. A decoction of the root is a good lotion to wash the parts bitten by venomous creatures, both natural and supernatural. Various species (*Aconitum Orientale, Aconitum Septentrionale, Aconitum Lycoctonum,*) of the plant are used in different herbal remedies and known under a variety of regional names like Auld Wife's Huid, Blue Rocket, Friar's Cap, Helmet-flower, Helmet Flower, Monk's Hood, Monkshood, Mousebane, Soldier's Cap, Wolfbane, and Wolf's Bane.

The most potent variety of aconite in the war against werewolves is *Aconitum Anthora* or Yellow Monkshood. In fiction Wolf's Bane (*Aconitum Septentrionale*) is named as the top protective herb, but this is not accurate according to folk medicine.

The plant is widely used as a homeopathic remedy for treating the initial stages of fever and inflammation resulting from exposure to dry cold and also for healing skin inflammation, coughs, dry skin, exposure to extreme weather, palpitations, panic attacks, and the fear of dying.

Lobishomen   The Lobishomen, another of Brazil's many vampires, preys mainly on women, though it only takes just enough blood for nourishment but not enough to kill. Its bite, however, causes a taint in the woman's blood that leads her to become an insatiable nymphomaniac. These women become even more fearsome predators who attack children for their blood.

Despite being revenant vampires, the Lobishomen is driven off by Wolf's Bane rather than garlic. The herb is planted on the graves of those suspected of being Lobishomen, and that is enough to keep them in their graves. To protect the home the herb is crushed into a paste with sweet onion, then smeared around doors and windows.

The Lobishomen is a horrifying hunchbacked creature who scampers around on stumpy legs. It has a pale face with bloodless lips, jagged black teeth, jaundiced skin, and stiff bristling hair like that of a jungle ape.

Lobizón (also spelled **Lobisón)**   Not all of the world's fox-people are confined to Asia, as seen with the Lobizón of Argentina, cousin to the *Lobishomen* of Brazil. This repulsive beast feeds on dead flesh, excrement, and unbaptized infants.

The Lobizón can be warded off by the herb aconite and killed by fire and steel, but it is extremely fast and powerful. Furthermore, when cornered this creature becomes a savage fighter and has been known to tear apart half a dozen at once.

Lofa   The Chickasaw Indians, originally of Mississippi and now of Oklahoma, have had legends for centuries of a race of flesh-eating monsters called the Lofa. This creature was their version of Bigfoot, only vile and malicious in nature. The Lofa were intelligent but extremely hostile, and often raided Chickasaw camps, killing the men and taking the women in order to mate. Like the *Sasquatch* and the *Shampe,* the Lofa had a horrible body odor that was so pungent it could actually kill.

The Lofa possessed no supernatural immunity to weapons and could be killed. But they would go to great lengths to reclaim the body of one of their dead—even to the point of slaughtering an entire Chickasaw village to retrieve one dead Lofa.

Loogaroo   The Loogaroo of Haiti is one of a number of skin-shedding monsters who transform from old hags into fiery balls of light. To do this, the Loogaroo goes to a "Devil Tree" and tears off her skin, which she then hangs like a suit of clothes on a branch of the tree. Beneath her skin she is a sulfurous ball of fire, and in this form she takes to the air in search of prey.

The Loogaroo is not born with these powers; they are acquired when a witch of Haiti (or one of the nearby islands of the West Indies) makes a pact with the Devil. In return for promising to bring fresh human flesh to the Devil each night they are given a variety of dark magical powers.

Flying through the air, the Loogaroo hunts for a house with an open window and then enters boldly, attacking whomever she pleases. Though it is nearly impossible to survive a Loogaroo's attack, the creature can be deterred by one of the most common methods: spreading uncooked rice, sand, or seeds in front of all of the doors and windows. The Loogaroo will feel compelled to count every single grain before entering. With enough rice left out, the Loogaroo might waste the entire evening and then have to return to its skin before sunrise, unfed and unhappy.

The word "Loogaroo" is a slurring of the French word *Loup-Garou* (see next entry), which means werewolf, and though the creature in question here does change form, she is not in any way lupine.

Loup-Garou   Since the Middle Ages there have been werewolf legends in France, ranging from almost comical folktales to stories of unbelievable cruelty and shocking violence. Known as the Loup-Garou, the lycanthropes of

⊰ ANCIENT WEREWOLF ⊱ CULTURES

In 500 BCE, Herodotus wrote that the Scythians, who lived in the southern part of the Ukraine immediately north of the Greek towns (and who are thought to be the Iron Age ancestors of the Slavs), believed that the Neuri (the probable ancestors of the Balts) turned themselves into werewolves during a yearly religious festival.

France have been very well documented in church records, public records, and literature.

Like most of Europe's lycanthropes, there are three distinct types of Loup-Garou. The first is the true werewolf, a person who transforms completely into a wolf. Though this lycanthrope maintains its human intellect, its powers are no different from an ordinary wolf. These tend to be the oldest of the French werewolf stories, and in many of these tales the person in question became a wolf through magic, often by strapping on an enchanted belt.[53] Beginning in the eighteenth century there were stories of wolf-men, creatures who were only partly transformed into wolves, and who walked on two legs. These monsters possessed incredible strength, were unnaturally fast, and were very hard to kill. The third kind of werewolf is the most modern, beginning in the mid-nineteenth century, and in these stories the Loup-Garou did not actually transform but rather a wolflike spirit took over and the person committed murders and atrocities that included cannibalism and grave robbing. The famous novel *The Werewolf of Paris* by Guy S. Endore (1933)[54] was based on one such case, involving a sergeant in the French army, Francois Bertrand, who robbed a number of graves and cannibalized the corpses before being appre-

53. Wolf Belts are a frequent element in European werewolf legends.
54. This was also the basis for the 1935 film *The Werewolf of London*.

hended in 1840. Many reports of this kind continued well into the twentieth century, and it is one of the factors that has led psychologists to hypothesize that werewolfism was simply the name given to serial killers before modern science understood the nature of that kind of psychopathology.

Lugat (also spelled **Liugat;** also known **as Kukuthi**)   Not all vampires are killers. Some are only minor nuisances—though, sadly, these are only a few.

One such, however, is the Lugat of Balkan legend, which prefers to take just a little blood here and there, leaving its victims weakened but alive. It may harass a single victim for a period of days or weeks, but there are no reliable reports of deaths attributed to the Lugat. However, the bite of a Lugat can leave behind a spiritual, or perhaps psychological, taint in that many of its victims develop a bloodlust of their own. Not a murderous hunger for blood, but rather an erotic one, where they become *sanguinarians*—people who are totally fixated on blood and want to inflict minor injuries on their lovers and drink their blood. Like the Lugat itself, this blood thirst seldom results in death, but it has certainly ruined many a marriage. Furthermore, this practice has landed more than a few of the victims of this sanguine urge in jail or in mental hospitals.

The Lugat is apparently a theriomorph and has appeared as an adult human, a child, a crow, and even a stray dog. The Lugat uses ordinary teeth instead of fangs, and it sucks blood from the welling bite in the same way a bat does. Though not a murderer, the Lugat is still a powerful vampire and nearly impossible to kill. Only the bite of a wolf can destroy it, but this is moderately hard to arrange.

Lupo Mannaro   Italian name for werewolf and similar in almost every regard to the *Loup-Garou* of France.

M

Ma Cá Rông   One of the most disgusting vampires of the world is the Ma Cá Rông of Vietnam who, like the *Asuang* of the Philippines, the *Phi Song Nang* of Thailand, and the Malaysian *Penanggalan,* appears as in the form of a head and floating entrails but no other body.

Unique among all of the world's vampires, the Ma Cá Rông feeds only on cow dung, which—even for a supernatural monster—is pretty nasty. If the Ma Cá Rông is disturbed during its feeding, or if it is prevented from getting to its food, it will attack humans and tear their throats out. Not to feed on them—just to kill.

Mambu-Mutu   The Mambu-mutu is a kind of merman from Lake Tanganyika in Burundi in East Africa who swims near the shores and drags fishermen out of boats to drown them and drink their blood.

Manananggal (also **Wak-Wak)**   One of the most feared creatures from the folklore of the Philippines is the she-creature known as the Manananggal. She is a night-hunter, a shape-shifter, and a predator who feasts on children.

The Manananggal is a kind of were-bat who transforms from a humanoid female—an appearance that may be entirely false—into a winged monster. When

⊲ SANGUINARIANS ⊳

Derived from the Latin word "sanguineus," which means bloodthirsty, sanguinarians are people who have a physical craving for blood. People acting out because of this disorder may be one of the many non-supernatural causes of vampire folktales.

> ## ⊰ WEREWOLVES OF ⊱ ANCIENT ROME
>
> The Roman poet Virgil speaks and writes about a were-
> wolf named Moeris as shown in this excerpt from *The
> Eclogues:*
>
> *These herbs of bane to me did Moeris give,*
> *In Pontus culled, where baneful herbs abound.*
> *With these full oft have I seen Moeris change*
> *To a wolf's form, and hide him in the woods,*
> *Oft summon spirits from the tomb's recess,*
> *And to new fields transport the standing corn.*

she transforms she stands stock still with her legs locked, and then without bending her knees she leans forward and drops to all fours. His hands and feet sprout claws, her long hair stiffens, and her eyes grow huge and luminous. Next, the skin of her back rips open and great batlike wings rise out and spread wide. Then the Manananggal leaps into the air to go hunting, calling out her strange hunting cry: "Wak-wak-wak!"

The Manananggal goes through this transformation every night between six and seven o'clock and will hunt until dawn, or until she finds her prey.

Children who mind their manners, obey their parents, and say their prayers are safe from this monster, and she has no power over them. But children who have been naughty and disrespectful are unprotected. When the Manananggal comes calling, it is these disobedient children who are her prey animal. She slaughters them and feasts on their livers. However, the Manananggal cannot enter a house and must wait for children who linger outside after they've been told to come in for the night.

When she cannot get a naughty child for her meal, the Manananggal turns to the totally unprotected unborn. Since these children have not yet been blessed or baptized in any way, they are open to her attack. And the presence of a pregnant woman in a house somehow opens the barriers that would otherwise keep this monster out. She steals in very quietly while everyone is asleep, and when she finds the sleeping pregnant woman, the Manananggal uses her unnaturally long tongue to enter the womb through the mother's navel. This tongue is hollow and through it she is able to drink the blood of the unborn child.

The Manananggal cannot easily be killed, but it can be harmed and driven off. Garlic is fatal to this monster, and the presence of it is enough to keep the monster out. In addition, a pair of scissors on a nightstand or under a pillow is enough to frighten it off, and travelers at night are advised to carry a thorny branch. Such branches are also the best protection for pregnant women and are generally placed beside their beds.

Mandurugo   Though legends of the Mandurugo have existed throughout the Philippines, this vampire species is mostly a problem to the folks in the province of Capiz, in the northern region of Panay Island. The creature's name means "bloodsucker," and this—unlike many Filipino vampires—is a fairly traditional monster. It uses the classic technique of adopting the appearance of a beautiful woman and then when its victim is nestled into a soft embrace, the Mandurugo reveals its true nature and its sham of beauty vanishes, replaced by a decaying corpse with a mouthful of fangs.

In some tales, however, the Mandurugo is not a revenant but a form of living vampire who can lead a fairly ordinary life, marry, have children, and even attend church. At night, though, when her husband and kids are asleep, the Mandurugo will go to the window, transform into a hideous flying beast, and go out hunting for blood. She seldom attacks her own family, using them instead as a kind of smokescreen.

Whether in human form or in her natural monstrous shape, the Mandurugo has little vulnerability except to fire. Weapons can wound her, but cannot kill her; fire, though, will quickly reduce her to ashes.

Maneden   In the forests and jungles of Malaysia thrives an arboreal vampire called the Maneden. When left alone, the creature will happily stay in its home in the leaves of the pandan trees, eating fruit and occasionally attacking proboscis monkeys. If a human wanders by, the Maneden seldom attack; however, if a human tries to settle in the territory staked out by these diminutive creatures, the Maneden will leap out of their trees and attach themselves leech-like to the offender, sucking blood from the elbows of men and the nipples of women.

If a Maneden has been angered, it's best to appease it with an offering of tubers or nuts. If it takes the offer, the offending human should then hotfoot it out of that part of the forest; if the Maneden does not take the offer, the offender is often later found desiccated and lifeless. They may be small, but they are very tough little monsters.

Mapinguary   The Mapinguary, a murderous monster from the jungles of the Matto Grosso, is both cruel and powerful. One of its favorite pastimes is attacking the largest oxen in the herd and ripping its tongue out by the roots. Like most of the oversized wildmen of the world, the Mapinguary has shaggy brown hair, a heavily muscled torso, thick arms, and a vaguely simian face.

Mara   Like the *Langsuir* of Malaysia and the *Cihuateteo* of Mexico, the Mara of Scandinavia is believed to be the spirit of a woman who had died without ever having been baptized. She is a night-hunter and an essential vampire who adopts one of two classic forms: a seductive beauty or an old hag. In either case, the Mara hunts for the life essence of young men.

The name "Mara" is derived from the old Anglo-Saxon verb "merran," meaning "to crush," and is the root of *Nachtmara,* or "nightmare."

MARA Tim Ogline

Masabakes   In Northern Spain a strange creature exists that blends the essential vampire with the seductress vampire in an entirely unique way. The Masabakes works with a familiar, an evil imp called the Tentirujo, whom she sends out on secret missions to sneak in through the windows of sleeping virgins in order to bewitch them. The Tentirujo strokes the maiden's skin with a piece of fresh mandrake root, then leaves. Within a day the young woman

❧ OLD HAG ☙

Throughout the world legends tell of a withered old crone who appears at night and sits on the chest of her victim while sending him terrifying nightmares, at the same time draining him of life's breath. Known as the Old Hag, this creature is similar in many ways to the *Mara* of Scandinavia. The name is drawn from the Old English term for witch: *hægtesse.*

When the Hag attacks her victim the poor wretch suffers through a terrible night and wakes up to total immobility and a crippling shortness of breath. Modern scientists call this phenomenon "sleep paralysis."

will be filled with an uncontrollable sexual need that will compel her to have sex with any man she can seduce. As the young victim gives in to debauchery, the sexual energy released becomes the food for the Masabakes. This vampire feeds on lust and wantonness, and delights in the emotional, social, and spiritual damage her bewitchments cause.

Masan (also known as **Masand)**   The Masan of Hindu folklore is the ghost of a child that has failed to pass on to its next incarnation and, once trapped here, becomes filled with rage and hatred for the living by doing as much harm and causing as much hurt as possible. The Masan delights in torment and slaughter; and because it died as a child this monster takes its revenge on its living peers. The Masan is so angry and peevish that it will even attack a child that chances to walk in its shadow.

The Masan is a trickster as well as a shape-shifter and will adopt the form of any child—not necessarily looking like it did before death. Most often it takes the form of a village child whom another child might recognize. Using famil-

·iarity as a tool, it ingratiates itself with its living victim, pretending to play and acting like a normal little boy or girl. Then, when there are no adults around, the Masan turns back into a ghostly monster and then bleeds its victim dry.

The Masan has a variety of dark magical powers and can also cast hypnotic spells or lay curses.

Most of the Masan are male, but there are plenty of females, and their predatory habits are different from the male. The females sleep by day in the cold ashes of a funeral pyre and rise at night to harass travelers who past by the cemetery. Though the female Masan also prefers to dine on children, at need she will attack anyone—man, woman, child, even livestock.

Mashan (also **Chudel)** The Mashan is a demonic vampire known to haunt areas in Nepal and parts of India, but the Mashan does not actually live here in this world. For most of its unnaturally long life the Mashan lives in a demon dimension that is very close to ours, and it is constantly searching for places where the walls between the worlds have become weaker. These thin spots, or veils, can allow the Mashan to enter our world. Luckily these veils are rare and a Mashan seldom gets the chance to trouble mankind.

Most often it is a human who is responsible for a Mashan crossing over into our world, typically a sorcerer who conjures the creature thinking that it is a lowly demon who can easily be enslaved. These sorcerers use the divination practice of geomancy to locate these veils and then create elaborate containment fields made from colored sand and herbs. After locating the veil, the sorcerer then casts binding spells so that the Mashan is trapped within a kind of bubble that extrudes into our world.

If the sorcerer errs even a little in his rituals or practices, then the Mashan is set loose. The creature then attacks with great appetite, feeding first on blood and then on flesh. From there it escapes into the larger world, causing plagues of madness and killing wantonly. Only prayers to the god Shiva will stop the killing spree. Shiva benevolently "encourages" the Mashan to return to its own place and then seals the dimensional rift.

Mermaid   Mermaids appear in the folklore of every seafaring nation and very often tales of them are strikingly similar. Generally mermaids are described as intensely beautiful women from the waist up, and fish from the waist down. Like *Sirens,* the mermaids use compelling calls and swim in a very suggestive way—though, considering they are half fish one wonders what it is they are suggesting. Around the world there are thousands of tales of men who threw themselves into the sea to be with one of these creatures. Once there, they discover that, unlike the mermaids, they can't breathe under water; and often they find that the mermaids are carnivores.

In a number of tales the mermaid is seen lying on rocks and combing her hair with one hand while holding a silver mirror with the other; and the flash of the mirror is often what catches the eye of the ship's lookout.

The mermaid of myth and folklore bears no resemblance at all to the lovely, gracious, and affable versions so often presented in film.

Mjertovjec   In films a vampire and a werewolf are distinctly different monsters, but in folklore they are sometimes very much alike. The Mjertovjec of Belarus is one of those creatures that has qualities of both monsters, and even includes some aspects of the witch as well.

At the core of the legend is one of the strangest and most frightening twists of supernatural folklore: In Belarus, when a werewolf or witch dies, the spirit does not dissipate or "move on"; instead it returns to Earth as a very powerful vampire[55] called a Mjertovjec.

There are other ways in which a person can be doomed to the fate of being one of the Living Dead, such as becoming an apostate (deliberately abandoning faith or defying the Church), heresy, or other crimes against God.

Once this taint is on a person, and unless they strenuously repent of their sins, upon death they will transform into a monster who rises from the grave to attack humans for both flesh and blood.

---

55. This legend is explored in my Pine Deep trilogy of novels, *Ghost Road Blues, Dead Man's Song,* and *Bad Moon Rising,* also available from Pinnacle Books.

However, not all of the Mjertovjec rises from the grave: Only its head and upper chest tear free of the corpse and float through the air to hunt for blood. This peculiarity is rarely seen outside of Southeast Asia and is certainly unique among vampires of Europe.

The Mjertovjec is a night-hunter and must return to its grave once a rooster has crowed three times. If it does not, it loses its ability to fly and then flops to the ground, where anyone with a torch and some kindling can kill it.

Though unlike European vampires in most ways, the Mjertovjec does share in that obsessive-compulsive need to stop and count seeds left outside. If a monster hunter is brave and clever enough to track a Mjertovjec back to its grave, he can immobilize the monster by driving a sharpened iron spike through its chest and then burning the body. Only fire will kill the creature forever.

Mokele-Mbeme (also N'yamala, Guanérou, Diba)   In the Likouala swamps and Lake Tele in what is today known as the Republic of the Congo,[56] there have been reports and even sightings of a huge and ferocious monster that would attack and kill any other creature that came near it, and which was more powerful and savage than anything it met in the jungles. Known as "Mokele-Mbeme," which translates as "one who stops the flow of rivers," this mighty beast is a killer and yet it is not a predator. The beast kills to defend its territory, but apparently it is an herbivore.

The Mokele-Mbeme has been described as being somewhere in size between a bull hippopotamus and an elephant, with a thick rounded body, four trunklike legs, a long tail like that of a crocodile, and a long tapering neck and a head relatively small compared to its body. The creature described would appear to be some sort of dinosaur, but what a sauropod would be doing 65 million years past the point of extinction suggested by the fossil record is anyone's guess.

---

56. Not to be confused with the Democratic Republic of the Congo, which is a separate nation.

The local pygmies were the first to spot the creature and have reported sightings for centuries. In 1776, the traveler and naturalist Abbe Proyhart wrote a book that recounted his discovery of what appeared to be fresh dinosaur footprints measuring a meter across. The centuries since have recorded many sightings, and many of these were reported by respected village elders and by persons whose integrity and authority were such that serious and expensive expeditions were launched by scientists as far away as Europe and Asia.

One of the first major expeditions to find the Mokele-Mbeme was mounted in 1980 by Roy P. Mackal, a distinguished biochemist, engineer, and biologist from the University of Chicago. Dr. Mackal[57] took his team into the Likouala and Lake Tele regions of the Congo, but unfortunately all he was able to collect were oral reports of the monster. No physical evidence was collected.

Dr. Mackal conducted extensive interviews of the natives of the region, collecting a variety of eye-witness accounts, including one story of how a Mokele-Mbeme had begun to cause enough damage and death in a certain village and how the villagers built a great barrier across a narrow neck of the river to keep the creature away. The Mokele-Mbeme attacked the barrier, but the villager warriors stood on either bank and all along the span of the barrier and pelted it with rocks and spears, finally killing it. The creature was then butchered and cooked for a celebratory feast, but everyone who ate the Mokele-Mbeme died within a day or two. Whether the meat was poisonous or the creature diseased is not known.

Dr. Mackal never saw the creature himself, but did hear something splash in the water nearby. When he inquired of his guides they insisted that the Mokele-Mbeme had made the splash.

The following year, Marcellin Agnagna, a Congolese biologist who engaged part of Dr. Mackal's team, mounted a smaller expedition and claims to have observed the creature for about twenty minutes.

57. Roy P. Mackal, Dr., *A Living Dinosaur? In Search of Mokele-Mbembe* (Leiden: E. J. Brill, 1987).

A dozen years later, in 1992, a film crew from Japan managed to take some aerial video footage of a creature that could very well be Mokele-Mbeme. With a camera mounted in a small plane they flew over Lake Tele and the surrounding woods, taking scenic footage for a nature documentary. They got a bit more than they had bargained for. One of the crew spotted something big moving across the lake leaving a V-shaped wake; instantly the cameraman used the zoom lens to capture about fifteen seconds of footage before the creature submerged beneath the lake's surface. Though the footage is jumpy and not very clear, it does appear to show a creature that bears a striking resemblance to a dinosaur like a brontosaur, though smaller.

So . . . what is Mokele-Mbeme? Is it bad reportage? Wishful thinking on the part of zoologists hoping to make their mark in the history books? Is it a species of something far more mundane that hasn't been classified yet? Or has the concept of a "Lost World" where dinosaurs still roam the Earth a possibility? In a place as remote as Lake Tele in the Congo, which is as close as twenty-first-century Earth gets to the climate and flora of the Mesozoic era, perhaps ancient monsters still live and hunt.

Mormo   The Mormo of Greece was a female demon who attacked sleeping children for their life's breath. These creatures were invisible and rode the night winds, entering houses through windows that had been left ajar in a child's room. Once inside, this night waster would settle like a deadly mist around the sleeping child and then draw the breath out of him.

A servant of the goddess Hecate, the Mormo is one of the few demons of ancient Greece that has survived into the twenty-first century, though nowadays she is a kind of bogeyman used to scare naughty children into being good, but the original Mormo was no scary story for kids.

Scientists believe that the legend of the Mormo—along with other night wasters that preyed on children—grew out of the need for the unlearned to explain SIDS (sudden infant death syndrome). Since the child had died unexpectedly—without previous illness, and since it was hard to imagine why God would just strike the child down, people had to hang the blame on a deliberate and malevolent force.

Moroi (also **Moroii, Muroni)** The Moroi of Romanian folklore are blood-drinking vampires who rise from the graves of those who have died from violence or from unfortunate circumstances such as being unbaptized,[58] murdered on a Sunday, or whose life is filled with frustrations or regrets. These troubled souls cannot rest easy in their graves and are susceptible to a kind of demonic possession that reanimates their dead flesh.

When they rise, the Moroi possess a variety of supernatural powers including the ability to shape-shift, and often take the form of a dog, cat, horse, black hen, sheep, or even a man. When assuming human form, the female Moroi have flushed red faces and the males are generally bald.

As humans, the Moroi can easily integrate back into society and do not need to return to their graves. These sham-humans can have families and jobs, go to church, and otherwise appear entirely normal. But they are always on the hunt for a person who is walking alone or otherwise isolated.

Mori often use enchantments to lure children out of bed and away from their homes in order to attack them; or they may cast a sleeping spell over the entire house and then enter through the chimney as a fog or mist and then attack children as they sleep.

There are dozens of variations on the Moroi telling different origin myths and speaking of different powers, different preferred prey, and different hungers; but in every case, the Moroi is a cunning and hungry predator that is difficult to detect and even harder to stop.

Motetzdam A generic Hebrew word for "bloodsucker," used to describe any species of vampire.

---

58. A very common cause of vampirism around the world.

Mountain Man   In the forests and mountains of Japan a demon known as the Mountain Man appears as a shaggy humanoid with apelike qualities in the way he walks and in the shape of his skull and length of his muscular arms. The Mountain Man is thought to be the last survivor of an ancient race that was overwhelmed by humans millennia ago. Other stories claim that the Mountain Man was a deformed human who was ridiculed for his appearance and fled the populated areas to live alone in the woods.

Aside from folktales, many stories, poems, and plays have been written about him, notably *The Mountain Man's April* by the great children's writer Kenji Miyazawa (1896–1933). Though in stories this creature is often kinder, in folklore the Mountain Man is seldom affable and is often violent. He can, however, be appeased by an offering of fragrant rice.

Mrat   In Australia, when an Aborigine dies, his possessions are destroyed so as not to lure the deceased's ghost from its grave. In their beliefs, each person has two souls: the good and well-balanced soul that governs their lives, and a second darker soul that is composed of sins, anger, hatred, and corruption. At death, the pure soul ascends, but the darker soul, known as the Mrat, rises from the grave to cause trouble among its own people.

For most individuals, the Mrat remains in the body and decays as the body disintegrates over time; but if a person has died under bad circumstances such as violence, suicide, or in the commission of a crime, then the Mrat takes control of the body and can revive it so that it attacks former friends and neighbors. Knowing that this can sometimes happen, and because one can never tell whether another person's soul is dark or light, the villagers will pile heavy stones on a fresh grave to prevent the Mrat from digging its way out. Another precaution is to break the legs of a corpse before burial. A last precaution is to eradicate the campsite of the recently dead, destroy his shelter (tent, hut, etc.), and erase all traces of where that person once lived, thereby eradicating a spot that could anchor the evil Mrat to the world of the living.

Mullo   When a Gypsy dies there are certain rituals that must be performed to prevent very bad things from happening—such as the creation of vampires. One such ritual is destroying the possessions of the deceased, which is both a tradition and a law among the Romani. If this is not done, then the dead person will come back to life as a Mullo, a dreadful revenant whose sole aim is to destroy human life.

Many Gypsies are wise enough to take precautions to keep the Mullo from rising should it come into being, such as placing slivers of steel in the mouth to prevent it from biting or chewing, driving hawthorn stakes through the legs (or placing splinters of hawthorn in the socks and shoes), and placing steel over the eyes to blind it. That way, even if the person returns to life as a Mullo it will be unable to rise and hunt for food. Without nourishment it will die.

The word "Mullo" means "one who is dead," and in folklore the creature is often described as a ghost instead of a vampire. In either case, the monster is fierce and craves human blood.

The Mullo also has a powerful sexual drive and will often seek out women, relying either on seduction or rape to satisfy its urges. If a child results from that unnatural and unsavory union, it will be a Dhampyr (also Dhampire, Dhampir) and will eventually grow up to become a very effective form of supernatural vampire hunter. There is something about the process of an innocent child being born from such an unholy mating that creates a kind of spiritual shield around the newborn. This child cannot become evil, no matter what happens during its lifetime, and will always discover its calling and will hunt evil. Sadly, the Dhampyr is doomed to die young because of genetic flaws resulting from the mix of human and supernatural bloodlines. The Dhampyr's skeleton will eventually become gelid and by the time the vampire hunter is in his thirties or forties, his collapsing frame will kill him. It is the wish of every Dhampyr to destroy his own Mullo parent before he dies.

Dhampyresa is a female Dhampyr.

Murony   Though Count Dracula was only a fictional monster, the nation of Transylvania does indeed have legends of a blood-sucking vampire: the Murony.

The Murony is a revenant and a shape-shifter who often takes the form of a cat, toad, hound, or a biting insect, using these pseudo bodies to be able to move among humans in order to find just the right kind of target: a person alone and out of sight of others.

After feeding, the Murony returns to its grave to rest; it is only during these trancelike periods that the creature can safely be approached and killed. The standard Ritual of Exorcism is used, which involves decapitation, stuffing the mouth with garlic, turning the head backward, and re-burying the coffin. In order to accomplish this with maximum safety, a long stake is driven through the body to insure that it cannot rise.

Before the Ritual of Exorcism is performed, there are some quick tests to determine that the corpse is indeed a Murony. First, the face should show a flush of health, and the stomach will be bloated from all the blood it has consumed. Blood will also seep out of eyes, ears, nose, and mouth. The Murony have long, jagged fingernails, which is a dead giveaway, and there will be dirt caked under these nails from the Murony climbing in and out of its grave.

Once the monster has been diagnosed and the Ritual performed, the threat of the Murony is ended.

— Chapter Four —
IF IT HAD TEETH
IT WOULD BITE YOU

(The Why Behind the Weird)

EVIL, WHY HAVE YOU ENGULFED SO MANY HEARTS...
EVIL, WHY HAVE YOU DESTROYED SO MANY MINDS...
LEAVING ROOM FOR DARKNESS, WHERE LOST
DREAMS CAN HIDE.
— *"Evil,"* Stevie Wonder

SCIENCE WOULD HAVE US BELIEVE that there are no monsters and never have been. That would be a comfort, but in a way it would also be kind of depressing. Monsters and spirits make our world larger, less clearly defined, and more wondrous, even if also a bit more frightening. Most world religions make the claim that monsters, of one kind or another, exist—so, to deny them is a step in denying the veracity of the religion itself. The argument between the realities of science and the belief in the supernatural is an old one and overlaps with other debates, such as the issue of natural evolution or intelligent design.

But, sticking just to monsters for now...the question remains—did they exist? If so, do they still? If not, then what is behind all of the myth and folklore that forms part of every human culture?

SUPERNATURAL PREDATORS Sandro Castilli

Science takes the stand that there is an explanation for everything, even if we might not know yet what that explanation is. The scientific method is built on the acquisition of information based on scientific investigation in which qualified persons collect and analyze physical evidence to draw conclusions that prove a theorem or explain an occurrence. Using this method scientists believe that they have been able to explain a number of the world's great supernatural mysteries, and that other mysteries will be explained in time. If we are to take the scientific side, just for the moment, then what might be at the root of all of these myths and legends about things that go bump in the night?

Here are just a few of the scientific theories to explain the supernatural:

•**SIDS:** So many of the world's vampiric beliefs are built around the unexpected death of a child—a child who dies in the night with no visible marks, preexisting conditions, or reason. For the parents of such a child, especially those in preindustrial cultures hundreds of years ago, the need to have an answer to the tragedy was of first importance. The unexplained can be unbearable to face, especially when it involves so significant a loss. Simple folk could simply not accept that God had killed their child for no reason, and with no sign of bite or no rash or other mark it seemed unlikely that a plague or a venomous creature was the culprit. So, in order to restore some semblance of balance, of *justice* to their world, they had to accept the possibility that there was something out there that wanted to do harm to their child, which had in fact done harm. A monster. One that came invisibly in the night and stole the very breath from the child, leaving it cold and dead. As horrible as the thought is . . . it was also understandable—a cause (deliberate evil) and effect (the death of the child). Perhaps the early Church took a hand in fostering this belief—and we know from historical records that this was certainly the case—and used these deaths, and the fear they engendered as a way to draw people back to the faith and to the protection of the Church. A family that lost one child to the night-visiting monster and who then prayed for protection in the sanctity of the church often saw that their other children did not similarly die. Nowadays we know that SIDS exists, even if we don't understand everything about it; and we know that SIDS seldom keeps striking the same family. We know this now, and we know that these aren't vampires coming in the night to claim the lives of our children. But are we, I wonder, more comforted in that knowledge than were the peasants of the Middle Ages who believed that their prayers were now keeping their families safe from further harm?

• **Sleep paralysis:** The Old Hag concept, which involves a person (usually a man) waking up, terrified, utterly paralyzed, with a crushing weight on his chest. In some cases the victim claimed to have seen a gnarled old crone hunched over him, sucking out his life's breath. The Old Hag legend is common throughout the world and until very recently it was an inexplicable mystery that was so strange and so persistent that it lent great credence to a belief in the supernatural. Now, of course, we know about the medical phenomenon called sleep paralysis, which consists of a period of inability to perform voluntary movements either at sleep onset (called hypnogogic or predormital form) or upon awakening (called hypnopompic or postdormital form).[59]

•**Disease and Plagues:** The many legends of vampires spreading disease have a fairly strong basis in hard science as well, as does the link to improperly observed burial customs. A body that is not properly prepared and buried in too loose a coffin or too shallow a grave is the perfect breeding ground for bacteria. Disease is invisible and it can quickly spread. Charms against evil won't stop it, and it often attacks children. As with SIDS, it was easier for our ancestors to blame some deliberate force of evil than to try and imagine microscopic diseases. It is no wonder that the name "nosferatu" means plague carrier. All of the great plagues that have swept the world since the days of the ancient Etruscans were blamed, at the time, on vampires of one species or other; and in modern times this brand of logic still holds in more remote third-world countries. In Malawi, for example, and other economically fractured African nations the spread of AIDS is linked to the supernatural; and the dreaded Ebola virus is known popularly as the vampire virus. It may be the twenty-first century, but we are not that far from the view of the universe held by our forebears.

•**Catalepsy:** The sleeping disorder of catalepsy is almost certainly a root of vampire beliefs. Consider how it appeared from the point of view of, say, a villager in rural Hungary or Romania in the seventeenth century. A person who is apparently dead and laid out for burial suddenly awakens. That would have been a nasty jolt. Some of the accounts of vampires awakening and clawing at the insides of their coffins may have been incidents of cataleptics waking up in confusion and dreadful terror. Their desperate wails and howls, and their maddened attempts to claw their way through their shrouds and

59. Meir H. Kryger, Thomas Roth, and William C. Dement, *Principles and Practice of Sleep Medicine,* 2nd Edition. Philadelphia: W. B. Saunders Company, 1994.

coffins, would have frozen the stoutest heart. Certainly that's more than enough fuel to feed the fire of superstitious belief.

•**Porphyry:** Just about every Halloween, when specials about vampires pop up on TV, many experts trot out the disease porphyry, also called porphyria, as being the basis for the belief in vampires. This disease is actually a common name given to seven rare metabolic disorders triggered by enzyme deficiencies that prohibit the synthesis of *heme* (a molecule that serves as a coenzyme in a variety of biochemical processes, and which forms an essential part of the structure of hemoglobin). In its most severe forms porphyry can cause symptoms such as hypersensitivity to sunlight, as well as occasional skin discoloration and tissue disintegration on the fingers and hands. The concept of porphyry-as-vampirism was given a big push in 1985 after the researcher David Dolphin presented a controversial paper to the American Association for the Advancement of Science. It was his theory that, in centuries past, persons suffering from this disease might have craved blood in order to make up for the deficiencies in their own. However this theory was eventually discredited and the hype over porphyry has somewhat died down.

•**Phychosis and sociopathic behavior:** Psychosis is another possible scientific cause of vampire beliefs, and also of beliefs in werewolves and demonic possession. Less than a century ago there was no word for "serial killer." Moreover, there was no understanding of bipolar disorder, borderline personalities, schizophrenia, multiple personality disorder, or any of the many mental conditions that can result in abnormal—or a sudden change of—behavior. This also can be seen in brain tumors and chemical imbalances, and their effect on personality and behavior. We now know that many of the world's worst serial murderers suffered from psychological maladies that resulted in their sociopathic or violent antisocial behavior. But a hundred years ago living with such a mystery without explanation was intolerable, hence the birth of the legends. The reality of this is hammered home by the transcripts of the many werewolf trials of medieval Germany. A psychologist—even an amateur one—would instantly recognize the "werewolves" as prime examples of serial murderers.

•**Eyewitness reporting:** Of course, there is the simple issue of bad reportage as well, which could explain many of the cryptids scattered throughout these pages. Eyewitness accounts of ordinary things are notoriously unreliable. Imagine the first person that saw a giraffe and tried to describe it to his friends. Natural philosophers[60] of the late eighteenth and early nineteenth centuries argued hotly that no such thing as an egg-laying aquatic mammal could exist, despite eyewitness accounts, and the first explorers to describe the duck-billed platypus were openly derided. One wonders how many of the cryptids of the world—hairy beast men, lake monsters, and other strange creatures—are genuine animals as yet unknown to science.

So, taking all of this into account we should be able to simply discount all monsters, perhaps even all superstition, as nothing more than misunderstanding and misinformation. We know better now, so we should be able to sleep tight without any fears of the dark.

Shouldn't we?

Or, is there perhaps a small part of even the most rational mind that harbors a secret fragment of belief that maybe, after all of the scientific avenues have been explored and the answers presented in cold and factual terms, that we could be wrong?

So tonight, will you leave your closest door ajar? Will you swear that the creak of the attic floorboard is really nothing but the house settling? Will you peer into the unknown dark of deepest night and swear that there is nothing—absolutely anything—out there?

I, for one, will close that closet door very tightly.

---

60. Biologists and naturalists.

Chapter Five
VAMPIRES AND MONSTERS
N–R

N

Nachtzehrer (also Nachzehrer, Begeirig, Dodelecker) The Nacht-zehrer of Germany is another of the world's vampires created when a child is born with caul, or amniotic membrane, covering his or her face. From birth the child is doomed to become a vampire after death, no matter how long he lives or how that death comes about. When life closes and the person is buried, the Nachtzehrer emerges and takes over the body and reanimates the flesh and muscle. Immediately the Nachtzehrer will begin tearing at its shroud and bur-ial clothes, often feeding on its own flesh just to have something to eat and to give itself the strength needed to break through the lid of its coffin and climb up through six feet of earth. At midnight the Nachtzehrer claws its way out of the grave and sets off to hunt for the blood of its relatives.

Aside from being a revenant, the Nachtzehrer is also a nosferatu and over the centuries has earned a reputation for spreading plague and other diseases, causing famine, and starting blights that destroy the crops of an entire village.

The best defense against this monster is to place scissors beneath one's pillow with the points facing toward the head of the bed. Garlic is good for warding it off, but will not kill the Nachtzehrer. Only the standard Ritual of Exorcism will do that.

◄ MANDUCATION ►

Manducation is the act of a reawakened vampire eating its own flesh while still trapped in its coffin. In many vampire legends, disinterred corpses show signs of having been partially self-devoured. Some scientists hold that this is proof of premature burial and the resulting starvation and mania; vampire hunters disagree and believe that a reawakening vampire feeds on itself to gain strength so it can rise from its grave.

Nahuelito   Most lake monsters are named after the body of water in which they live and hunt, such as Champ from Lake Champlain and Nessie from Loch Ness; and the same holds true for the Nahuelito who has been causing trouble for centuries in the Nahuel Huapi Lake of Argentina.

Stories of Nahuelito began surfacing in the 1920s, though locals claim to have heard stories about it from their grandparents. The creature is described as being anywhere from a relatively diminutive fifteen feet to a titanic thirty yards from teeth to tail. The creature has been spotted only on calm summer days and rarely bothers humans, though was once reported to have overturned a boat, possibly by accident.

Naitaka   Scotland's Loch Ness Monster has a lot of relatives around the world, and Saskatchewan and Manitoba residents have long reported a giant serpentine creature in their lakes. It was massive, humpbacked, and had flippers like a prehistoric *zeuglodon* whale. There have been well over 200 sightings of this beastie, known as Naitaka.

Though there have been no photos taken of the creature, a vertebral bone was found on the shores of Lake Winnipegosis in the 1930s. The bone was subsequently lost, but based on descriptions scientists believe that the bone in

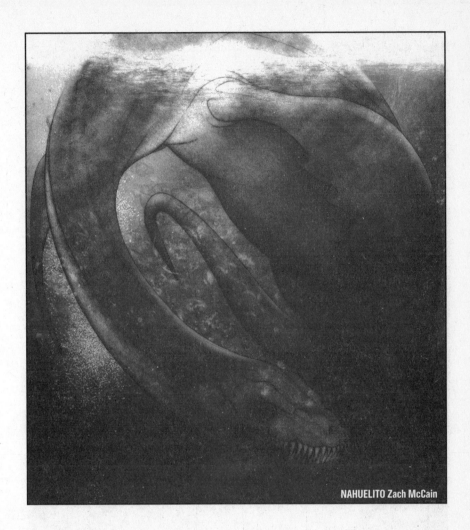

NAHUELITO Zach McCain

question came from some species of prehistoric water creature. Whether it was a Naitaka bone is up for debate, but it does make one think.

N-Dam Kent-Wet In Abenaki Indian folklore from the New England area, there is a legend of a humanoid creature that is part man and part fish, called the N-Dan Kent-Wet. Though not a killer, the creature is nevertheless a vile predator that attacks bathing women to rape them.

Nelapsi Few vampires are as powerful as the Nelapsi of Czechoslovakia, a creature that delights in destroying entire villages, killing every human and

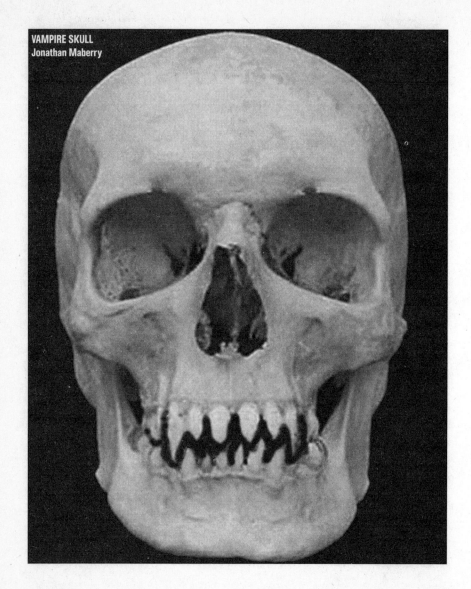

VAMPIRE SKULL
Jonathan Maberry

every animal, and leaving nothing behind but blood-soaked ground and wreckage. The Nelapsi sometimes tears its victim apart with its teeth and other times just crushes them in a bone-snapping embrace. It can also kill with just a glance from its fiery red eyes. The Nelapsi, among other things, is a nosferatu and can cause plagues and blight to sweep through the area.

Because the Nelapsi has two hearts and two separate souls it is extremely difficult to kill. Ordinary weapons seldom do more than annoy it, and an annoyed supernaturally strong psychopathic vampire is not a pleasant thing to be around. When angered it will torture first before it kills, and the Nelapsi is devious and patient, and it can make torture last for weeks.

The best defense against the Nelapsi is to prevent its creation, and fortunately there are ways to accomplish this. The best method is to bang the head of a coffin against the deceased's doorway when carrying his coffin out for burial. This knocks loose any bad luck clinging to the dead person. Also, driving iron nails into the arms and legs of a coffin so that the limbs are made fast to the wood will keep the newly reanimated corpse from rising. Smaller nails likewise pin down the hair so that the creature can't crane its head forward to feed on its own flesh—a necessary step for it to gain the physical strength needed to rise. To double insure this, bandages or a leather strap is wrapped around the head to hold the jaw tightly shut.

If a Nelapsi has come into being, however, the villagers often fall back on the tried-and-true method of spreading seeds, millet, or poppy flowers all around the grave as well as inside the open grave itself. This will keep the monster busy all night and at dawn it will slink back to its coffin. If a Nelapsi has been around for a while and has made a significant number of kills, however, then its brain becomes more active and it is less likely to be distracted by this tactic.

Though it is not harmed by sunlight, the Nelapsi is unable to rise from its grave during the day, which gives vampire hunters a chance to dig it up and perform the Ritual of Exorcism, with the added touch of a blackthorn stake being driven through the skull.

Destroying the Nelapsi does not cleanse the village of evil, and once one has attached itself to a town other vampires may be attracted there. To prevent this a bonfire[61] is built using only new wood and at the same time every other candle or other flame in the village is extinguished. Effigies of evil things such as vampires, witches, and werewolves are thrown into the fire, as well as any an-

---

61. Also known as a need-fire, bone-fire, ban-fire, or bane-fire.

imal that may have come in contact with the vampire and any creature suspected of being a familiar for the Nelapsi. This type of animal sacrifice actually gave the bonfire its name: "bone fire." Once this fire has burned down and cooled a bit, the villagers will quickly walk through the smoky ashes, purifying themselves of any taint of evil. Livestock and even family pets are likewise driven through the ashes to remove any taint of evil from each living thing in the village.

A small part of the fire is kept aside and allowed to burn, and when everyone has passed through the ashes, embers or tapers from this special fire are carried to each person's home and used to re-ignite the hearth fires. Then the ember is extinguished and kept as a talisman against evil. The remaining ashes from the bonfire are scattered along the roads as a final defense against supernatural forces.

Nessie, the Loch Ness Monster (also **Niseag)**   Nessie, the Loch Ness Monster of Scotland, and the world's most famous lake monster, is also the one with the longest track record for sightings. Glimpses of Niseag (Nessie's Celtic name) go back as far as 565 CE when Saint Columba saw the creature shortly after attending a funeral for a man purported to have been killed by it. The most famous encounter, though, took place in 1933 when a couple, Mr. and Mrs. Spicer, saw the creature cross the road right in front of them. The creature had an animal carcass clutched in its jaws and paused to look at them before taking its meal and slipping back into the chilly waters of the loch.

There have been hundreds of sightings as well as very well-organized scientific investigations, but despite some rather questionable photos and some curious sonar readings, no hard evidence has yet been found. Even so, belief in the existence of Nessie is very strong, and not just among cryptozoologists—quite a few scientists, oceanographers and biologists have stepped up to defend the possibility that the monster could really exist.

⊰ SCIENCE VS. ⊱ THE UNKNOWN

In the 1970s a series of expeditions to Loch Ness were sponsored by the Academy of Applied Science of Boston, and team members included scientists from MIT. These expeditions used side-scanner sonar and other tracking devices, along with traps and underwater cameras to try to document the existence of Nessie. In 1975 the cameras recorded images that appear to be the flippers of some large aquatic beast. Harold Edgerton, the inventor of side-scanner sonar; Sir Peter Scott, a greatly respected British naturalist; and Dr. Robert Rines headed the team, and their findings were presented at the House of Commons in London, resulting in the Loch Ness Monster story being taken seriously for the first time.

Neuntoter The name "Neuntoter" means "killer of nine" and refers to the nine-day process it takes certain corpses to transform from dead human to re-animated vampire. This German creature is a known nosferatu and has been linked with the spread of disease for many centuries.

When it rises from the grave, the Neuntoter is hideous to behold, its body covered with open, running sores and necrotic flesh. It is from these open sores that the disease spreads, which kills most of its victims. However the Neuntoter is also a blood-drinker and sometimes kills with its hands just for the sheer evil joy of it.

There are many opinions as to how a person becomes a Neuntoter after death, but the most popular theory is related to that person's birth. A child born with teeth is believed to be filled with unnatural appetites, some of which he will explore in life through gluttony, and others he will explore through death as a vampire.

The Ritual of Exorcism used to kill the Neuntoter differs from the rituals used elsewhere in Europe in that instead of filling the mouth with garlic, after decapitation the Neuntoter's mouth is filled with lemons. Otherwise the usual staking, turning the head backward, and reburial are the same.

Nittaewo   The Agogwe of Tanzania and the Sehité of the Ivory Coast have a close cousin living on the island of Sri Lanka: the Nittaewo. This is another of the world's diminutive wildmen who bear a striking physical resemblance to the Neanderthal, supposedly extinct for more than 30,000 years.

These Nittaewo have been described in the literature of the area as being dwarfish men living in and around the Mahalenama region, which is now within the Yala East Intermediate Zone and the Tamankaduva area. According to the naturalist Hugh Neville, "The Nittaewo were a cruel and savage race of men, rather dark, living in small communities . . ."[62]

He further wrote:

> They built platforms in trees, covered with a thatch of leaves, and in these they lived. They could neither speak Vaedda, Sinhalese or Tamil, but their language sounded like the Telegu of pilgrims to Kattragam. They attacked any intruding Vaeddas, and no Vaedda dare enter their district to hunt or collect honey. Many years ago the ancestors of the informants fought with these Nittaewo and finally drove the remnant of them, men, women and children into a cavern. Before this they piled firewood, and kept up the fire for three days, after which the race became extinct, and their district a hunting ground of these Vaeddas.

According to the descriptions recorded by Nevill and others over the last century or so, the male Nittaewo were described as being about a meter tall,

---

62. Hugh Nevill, "The Nittaewo of Ceylon"; published in his journal *The Taprobanian*, 1887.

and the females slightly shorter, which would make this species about a foot shorter than their cousins in Tanzania and the Ivory Coast. The Nittaewo went naked, stood erect, and had long arms with strong hands that ended in powerful talon-like nails.

The Nittaewo could build structures, but mostly they lived in trees and caves, hunted animals, and were hostile to any human intruders. Though small in size they were fierce fighters and attacked with a viciousness that often surprised and thereby overwhelmed larger humans.

No further stories of the Nittaewo have been recorded since the late nineteenth century, and it is presumed that the Veddas wiped them out entirely.

Were they holdover Neanderthals? Or were they, as anthropologist Osman Hill suggested in his writings,[63] a surviving pocket of pithecanthropus or Java man? If so, that is even more astounding than lingering Neanderthals because the pithecanthropus was supposed to have become extinct half a million years ago!

Moreover, were they wiped out or did this tribe of small but fierce warrior-creatures merely migrate to another place? With all of the reports of savage wildmen around the world—and especially in that area—anything is possible.

Nobusuma   The Nobusuma of Japanese folklore begins life as an ordinary bat, but if the creature somehow manages to live a prolonged life (and how this is accomplished is seldom made clear in these tales) it evolves into a supernatural being that looks like a cross between a bat and a flying squirrel with leathery wings that are attached to all four limbs. Nobusuma means "most ancient" and it is an essential vampire that feeds on human breath.

It glides through the night until it either comes upon a person sleeping out of doors or an open window through which it flies to find someone in bed. In either case it lands on the victim's chest and begins tapping the sternum, triggering a series of coughed exhalations. It sucks in the breath faster than a

63. Osman Hill, *Nittaewo—An Unsolved Problem of Ceylon*, Loris, 1945.

person can breathe in new air, eventually killing its prey. Some victims will linger for three days, but will then pass away, gasping for air.

If, however, someone witnesses this, then the effect of the attack is reversed and the victim will go on to live a very long life marked by unusual good health.

Nodeppo   The Nodeppo of Japan is an even more ancient creature than the Nobusuma, and its origins are not clearly known. The Nodeppo is a night-hunter of great size and physical strength; it swoops down on its prey, enveloping them in its leathery wings, and sucks all of the breath of them. The victims die immediately.

Unlike the Nubusuma, if a person chances to see someone getting killed by the Nodeppo, then they are marked by a death curse and will become sick and waste away within a few weeks or months.

The best protection against the Nodeppo is to carry nanomani leaves in pockets inside one's clothes, close to the skin.

Nora   The Hungarian Nora is one part evil imp and one part vampire. It may or may not ever have been a human (opinions in Hungary differ), but it certainly takes a human form: small, hairless, and fragile looking at first glance. When it moves, however, it runs on all fours like an animal.

The Nora can make itself invisible and then finds a dozing prostitute and bites her on the breast, lapping up the welling blood. Because it most commonly attacks prostitutes and other "impure" women, it is believed that the creature feeds on tainted blood.

However, the Nora is a pest rather than a killer, and its bite is seldom worse than that of a hornet. A poultice made from crushed garlic applied liberally to the breasts will reduce both redness and swelling, and prevent further attacks.

Nosferatu   Because of Bram Stoker's novel *Dracula,* the word "nosferatu" is widely believed to mean "undead" or "not dead," referring to creatures that

have risen from the grave. This is incorrect, however, because Stoker's translation was wrong.

Nosferatu means "plague carrier," and refers to any of the many ghosts or
vampires who spread disease. This term is drawn from the Greek term *nosophoros*,
which also means "plague carrier."

Disease-carrying vampires abound throughout the world; and even now,
in the twenty-first century, the link between the spread of disease and evil is
common. Evil spirits of one kind or another have been blamed for everything
from Ebola[64] to AIDS.

Nymphs   Nymphs are female supernatural spirits who range from completely passive to murderous. In poetry and art, particularly in the works of the
pre-Raphaelite artists of the late nineteenth and early twentieth centuries,
nymphs were generally portrayed as gorgeous and sexually available young
women who—apparently—existed for no other reason than to pleasure a passing young knight. In folklore the picture is a bit different and the nymphs
were, despite their appearance, not at all human and who often enchanted a
young fellow to his death. This version of the nymphs was related in the ancient Greek story of Hylas who met such a fate at the hands of the nymphs,
and though pre-Raphaelite master John William Waterhouse rendered a mag-
nificent painting of this tale, he focused more on the obvious charms of the
nymphs and significantly downplayed the impending fate of young Hylas.

There are two primary categories of Nymph in Greek mythology: water
and land.

Land Nymphs include Alseids (groves), Auloniads (pastures), Dryads
(woods), Hamadryads (trees), Ieimakids (meadows), Meliae (manna ash trees),
Napaeae (mountain valleys), and Oreads (mountains).

Water Nymphs include Crinaeae (fountains), Eleionomae (marshes), Lim-
nades or Limnatides (lakes), Naiads (rivers, brooks, streams), Nereids (the

---

64. Ebola is popularly known as the "vampire virus."

Mediterranean Sea), Oceanids (salt water), Pegaeae (springs), Potameides (rivers), and Sirens (shores and rocky coastlines).

O

Obayifo (also **Asiman)**   Many of the world's vampires blur the lines between species distinction, and none more so than the creature found among the Ashanti people of Ghana (formerly known as the Gold Coast). This culture has a particularly vicious species of witch-vampire that is also one of the world's many will-o'-the-wisp predators. The Obayifo is a living vampire, usually a sorcerer or witch, who actually sheds its skin at night and rises into the air in the form of a blazing fireball.

The Obayifo is born with these abilities rather than being the result of a curse; and the sorcerer-vampire revels in the vast powers its possesses. The Obayifo is malicious and though it is a blood-drinker, it apparently also feeds off of the pain and misery caused by its attacks, making it an essential vampire as well. Furthermore, it is a nosferatu—spreading disease through its bite.

The Obayifo focuses its attacks on children or infants, and comes by night as a ball of fiery light, drifting in through open windows. Then it lands on its victims and makes a small bite that is so subtle that the child never wakes. The Obayifo only takes a small amount of blood, but either its bite is poisonous or its saliva carries disease germs. The loss of blood is marginal, but the onset of disease is often fatal.

If a village suspects that the Obayifo is preying on the children, spells and charms can be used to seal the house against invasion; and denied its food the Obayifo can bide its time by feeding on fruits and vegetables. Apparently it does not need blood for its survival, and the Obayifo is a patient monster. Also, to amuse itself it may wither the plants and bring on a crop blight that will do as much harm as the blood-borne disease would have done.

There have been tales of Obayifo, in their human form as sorcerers, selling their services to a village to actually combat the invading vampire. This scam is

OBAYIFO Ruth Lampi

largely built around a very human greed for money, wherein the sorcerer charges hefty fees to perform spells and incantations, and sells charms and talismans at exorbitant prices. The villages, dreadfully afraid of their children becoming victims of this monster, will pay anything; and the Obayifo gets rich. Then, months later and after the vampire has, apparently, been driven off, the creature returns in its will-o'-the-wisp form and once again attacks the children.

Though the Obayifo is an Ashanti creation, either its legend has spread to other areas, or it has close relatives elsewhere. In the legends of the Dahomean, for example, it is known as the Asiman, and by other names in nearby places.

The only person capable of defeating the Obayifo was the village shaman,[65] but to do so he had to identify the real living person who possessed the powers of this vampire, and then could curse him with sickness so that he, instead of his victims, would die.

Obur (also **Ubour)**   In Bulgaria there is a spirit called the Obur, a strange blend of vampire and poltergeist. It is another of those beings that comes into the world to inhabit the corpse of someone who has died a violent death. After burial, when the soul is supposed to ascend to Heaven or descend to Hell, the Obur stubbornly remains in the body hoping to exact revenge for its death. Even if it accomplishes this, however, the Obur is trapped forever in a decaying corpse. This does nothing to ease its temper, so from then on it takes out its frustrations by any means necessary: creating destruction, hurling things about, destroying furniture, and attacking its own family. The creature is fond of making earsplitting, unexpected noises, like firecrackers, and upsetting any tranquility its former family members might have.

Most of the time the Obur is invisible—more of a presence than a physical being, heard more than seen—but if it gets it into its head to manifest in corporeal form and attack it usually does so for blood. It does not actually require blood to continue to exist, but when it bites and tastes blood it becomes so intoxicated by the flavor that it keeps sucking until the body is drained completely. This ties in to the fact that its name comes from an old Turkish word meaning "glutton."

This rapacious appetite is often its undoing, because a special vampire hunter called a Vampirdzhija uses blood as bait to lure the creature into a trap. Like the Djadadjii who exterminate the *Krovoijac,* the Vampirdzhija lures the Obur into a bottle, which is then burned.

Ogoljen   Bohemia, in the Czech Republic, shares many of its vampire myths with other Eastern European nations, but also has its own unique monster,

---

65. Pedrito U. Maynard-Reid, *Diverse Worship: African-American, Caribbean & Hispanic Perspectives,* InterVarsity Press, 2000.

the Ogoljen, a bloodthirsty revenant who appears as a bald, naked man with rotting skin and breath so foul that it can make a strong man swoon from ten feet away.

The Ogoljen can be destroyed by fire. or beheading, though if this latter method is used the body has to be properly buried to keep it from rising again. Dirt placed in the navel of the resting Ogoljen will prevent it from rising from its grave. Dirt from its grave, when added to a locket or pendant, also works as a charm against it. Another method of destroying this monster is to dig it up during the day and then rebury it at a crossroads, taking time to first open the coffin and stitch its shroud to its navel. This spiritually binds the creature to its grave.

Ogopogo (also N'ha-a-itk, the Lake Demon) Ogopogo is a plesiosaur-like creature believed to live in and around Lake Okanagan in British Columbia, and is similar in many ways to *Caddy* of Cadboro Bay. Stories of this monster date back to the Okanekane Indians, who believed that the monster was originally a man possessed by a demonic spirit that drove him to commit murder. The gods of the tribe exacted a peculiar punishment on him, transforming him into a sea monster so that he would forever be near his original people but unable to rejoin human society. The transformed creature was called N'ha-a-itk, which can be variously translated as "water god," "lake demon," or even "sacred creature of the water," though he is more popularly known as Ogopogo.

Ohyn Like the *Kudlak* of Croatia, the *Wume* of Togo, the *Nachtzehrer* of Germany and the *Strigoi* of Romania, the Ohyn of Poland is a vampire created when a person who had been born with a caul over his face dies. Though this individual will not transform into an Ohyn until after his mortal life has ended, it is generally believed that such a person is to be "watched" with great care and buried with close attention to all proper religious ritual.

If a stillborn baby has teeth at birth, it is another sure sign of impending evil, and there is a fear that the Ohyn will use these milk teeth to chew through its shroud and then feast on its own flesh until it is strong enough to break free from its coffin, then begin feeding on the flesh and blood of its living relatives.

As a result of these fears, a caul is removed at birth and milk teeth pulled (even from living children) as the first step in preventing evil from flourishing. The caul and/or teeth are rinsed with holy water and buried in a church grave-yard. Weekly prayers are said for the child until he takes his first Holy Communion, at which point the individual may be safe from damnation as a vampire.

Orang Pendek   A Sumatran wildman who stands about five feet tall and is covered in dark hair. Though European settlers tried hard to convince the natives of Sumatra that what they were describing were orangutans, the natives held fast to their assertions that they did, indeed, know the difference between an ape and a monster.

According to the natives, the Orang Pendek's fur is short and brown as opposed to the longer orange-brown hair of the apes. Moreover, whereas the orangutans were passive and even genial creatures, the Orang Pendek was a savage killer. And, unlike the apes, the Orang Pendeks were capable of speech and had their own guttural language.

So what is the Orang Pendek? Is it, as some folks have argued, an offshoot of the great apes who learned to mimic human speech; or are they an entirely different species of hominid? Perhaps we will get to find out, because sightings of the Orang Pendek linger to this day.

Otgiruru   The folktales of the Herero people of Namibia speak of a rather unique species of vampire called an Otgiruru, which does not merely rise from the grave but instead constructs a new body of the mean things of the earth: dirt, offal, insects, and other horrible objects. And, stranger yet, the body it most often constructs is not one that approximates its former human form, but resembles that of a dog.

The Otgiruru are the ghosts of sorcerers who come back from death, or who are unwilling or unable to make the journey to the afterlife. Bound to this physical plane, they are angry and confused and take out their supernatural frustrations on living humans from their own village.

Prowling the night in the shape of a hulking dog, the Otgiruru entices its victims with plaintive and compelling howls and then viciously attacks whoever comes to investigate the sounds. A common tactic of this predator is to imitate the size and call of a beloved family pet, luring family members into secluded spots by making them believe they are chasing the family pet who has gotten off his leash. Once the Otgiruru has its victim alone it reveals its true nature and attacks with horrible ferocity, ripping the person to pieces and feeding on both flesh and blood, and cracking the bones to suck out the marrow.

Despite its size and strength, the Otgiruru will never attack more than one person at a time. It will flee even from two children; this cowardice is inexplicable since it can easily slaughter a full-grown man.

Spears are used against it, but not to destroy it. In the same way that stakes are used against European vampires, the spears are used to pin it to the ground and hold it immobile so that other villagers can rush forward with knives and swords and hack it to pieces. Once it has been dismembered the pieces are burned, each in a separate fire to prevent the Otgiruru from reforming its body.

O-Toyo O-Toyo was a legendary were-leopard from Japan who took the form of a beautiful courtesan to seduce Prince Hizen. The real courtesan of the same name had already been murdered by this essential vampire, who was able to take her face, form, and even memories. In the household of the prince she began to systematically drain the life from him until one of his bodyguards, a cunning young samurai, Ito Soda, was able to uncover the deception and eventually kill the beast. The legend of O-Toyo and Prince Hizen has since become the basis for many songs, stories, poems, and operas.

Oupire The Oupire is one of the many Slavonic revenants that rises from its grave to prey on its own family, friends, and neighbors. It is also a nosferatu and is known to be the cause of many of the diseases that swept the region in the Middle Ages. There are tales of the Oupire in Moravia (now part of the Czech Republic), Poland, Silesia, and Hungary.

In direct confrontation a human cannot overcome the Oupire because the monster is incredibly strong and agile despite it being a decaying corpse. If taken by day, however, the creature can be disinterred and the standard Ritual of Exorcism will effectively destroy it. Generally though, after the normal steps of using stake, garlic, and beheading, the Oupire's body is burned and the ashes placed back in the coffin before it is reburied.

Owenga Not surprisingly, blood rituals—the procedures for handling and disposing of blood—are linked to vampirism around the world. In the North African nation of Guinea the issue of vampirism and blood rituals takes a number of difficult twists and turns.

The vampire species in question is the fierce Owenga, a blood-drinking monster that rises from the grave of dead sorcerers and witches, or from the graves of people who have led lives heavy with corruption, sin, and avarice. The Owenga may take physical form, or it may exist as a ghostly presence manifesting just enough of a corporeal form so that it can feed; but whether revenant or ghost, it craves blood.

The villagers in Guinea have long since learned that the best protection against the monster is appeasement, and offerings of blood (animal is okay) left in wooden bowls outside of the house or just beyond the gates of the village will usually be enough to satisfy the monster. It is a predator, but not a glutton, and can exist on a bowl of blood per week.

The fact that it can be appeased is a lucky break for the villagers, since no method of destroying the Owenga has been discovered.

If the rituals of slaughtering an animal for its blood are followed with great care so that no blood falls to the ground, and if the bowls of blood are

OUPIRE Reymond Pagé

placed in their proper spots with no spillage, then the Owenga is appeased. But the creature is stern in its demands and if any part of the rituals are not carried out with reverence and precision—especially if blood is spilled and not immediately cleaned up—the Owenga will become both angry and malicious, and begin a systematic attack on the village. Sometimes the Owenga will slaughter the farm animals or house pets; sometimes it will kill humans; and sometimes it prefers the slower entertainment of spreading disease throughout the town—or even the region.

To this day in rural Guinea, if blood is spilled it is immediately cleaned up and the rags and other objects used to clean the spill are thoroughly burned so that the Owenga is not angered.

Pelesit and Polong　Vampire symbiots are rare, but in Malaysia the Pelesit and the Polong form an unholy predatory union and work in harmony to destroy a victim. Both creatures are tiny, about an inch in length. Initially the Pelesit, taking the form of a cricket, enters the household and finds a sleeping person. It cuts a hole in the victim's skin and then chirps to signal for the Polong to come. The Polong is a witch-imp that enters the body and possesses it.

The possessed person goes insane and thrashes around causing harm to everyone around and himself. Moreover, for some reason that has never been clearly understood, he raves about cats.

Penanggalan　In Malaysia a few different species of vampires appear as a floating head and entrails, but in the legend of the Penanggalan a reason of sorts is offered for how this vampire came about. These peculiar creatures are produced when a woman who is deep in prayer is startled by some great noise or alarm. The shock causes their heads to literally leap from their bodies, dragging along their entrails and a twisted spine. The disruption from prayer somehow causes the woman to be damned as a sinner and remain trapped on Earth as a monster forever, which seems to be a bit harsh considering she was actually deep in prayer prior to being surprised.

The Penanggalan can fly and often lurk in trees, their entrails draped over the branches, waiting for some unfortunate animal or person to walk by. She prefers to feed on children, but isn't a finicky eater. If she has to settle on an adult, so be it.

One additional oddity is that if the Penanggalan lingers too long in one spot the fluids that drip from her entrails will soak into the earth and from that place a thorny, bioluminescent plant will grow.

Malaysian women who fear the coming of a Penanggalan scatter dried thistle along their windowsills. The vampire will not come near these sharp thorns, fearing to get them caught in her entrails.

Pey/Peymakilir   In Hindu folklore the Pey is a vampiric demon who haunts battlefields and drinks up the blood of wounded or dead soldiers. The Peymakilir is the female of the species and is more of a flesh-eater than a blood-drinker, and often engages in a frenzied dance while eating human flesh.

Phi Krasue   The Phi Krasue is yet another head-and-entrails vampire, this one from Thailand. When not out hunting it is fully human but when the bloodlust is on it the monster rips free from its human body. Unlike similar monsters, the Phi Krasue does not fly, but rather crawls along the ground using its unnaturally long tongue like a snail's pseudopodia to pull itself along, dragging its entrails behind. Like the Ma Cà Rông of Vietnam, the Phi Krasue's preferred meal is excrement, through which is absorbs traces of human life essence. It feeds by attacking sleeping humans and burrowing into their bowels.

Few creatures in folklore conjure up a less wholesome or more thoroughly disgusting image.

Though the Phi Krasue cannot be killed by any means, it can be warded off by charms made by a special kind of seer called a Maw Du.

Phi Song Nang   The Maw Du who create charms to ward off the Phi Krasue are also called in when another of Thailand's monsters makes an appearance: the Phi Song Nang. "Phi" is a general category of supernatural creature that includes witches, ghosts, goblins, elves, and, of course, vampires. In this particular case, the Phi Song Nang is a Succubus who takes the form of a ravishing woman and comes to men at night, having sex with them, but taking either life essence or blood, and sometimes both.

Occasionally a man killed by a Phi Song Nang will rise from the grave to become a vampire as well, though this type of revenant is neither as smart nor as powerful as the Phi Song Nang.

The Phi Song Nang is the ghost either of a woman who has died in childbirth, one who was buried without proper funeral rites, or even one who has been killed by animals.

If someone is attacked by a Phi Song Nang and survives, the Maw Du is called in to cure him of the evil taint so that he does not become a monster. Charms, spells, and prayers are used to cleanse his spiritual energy, but even after the cure is complete the man needs to pray daily in order to maintain the strength of the Maw Du's protections.

Pijavica   Pijavica means "one who is red-faced with drink." One would like this definition to refer to a florid-faced drunk slouched on a barstool, but in Croatia, Slovenia, and Czechoslovakia the Pijavica is a deadly blood-drinking vampire.

The creature is created a number of ways, none of which are particularly wholesome. Incest, especially between mother and son, is a very common method of bringing forth this monster as it is regarded in Eastern Europe to be a deliberate perversion of the sanctity of birth demonstrated by Mary and Jesus. Also, a person who has led a deliberately evil or sinful life may, upon dying, rise up again as a Pijavica. However this beast is brought into the world, though, the Pijavica is a flint-hearted killer. More often than not it will return from the dead to prey on its family—the sinful and the innocent alike.

The creature is hugely strong and not easy to kill. When it's awake and in the full flush of its power only fire can destroy it; if caught sleeping in its grave by day, then the standard Ritual of Exorcism will work.

Charms and protective icons do not keep a Pijavica from entering; only by pasting a mash of garlic and wine around all doors and windows can someone drive it away.

Pisacha   The Pisacha are hideous flesh-eating ghouls from India who rise from the grave as revenants to hunt humans. Though horrible in nature and action, the Pisacha are somewhat pitiable creatures in that they are caught between Heaven and Hell and are unable to redeem themselves or move on, and therefore suffer terrible spiritual torment. Since they are denied any chance at redemption, the Pisacha take their frustration out on the living, who still have a shot at making it to Heaven.

Though the Pisacha can be killed by a sword, only their physical forms can be destroyed. Their malevolent spirits remain and will haunt the site of their second death forever.

However, there is one single way in which the Pisacha can be sent on its spiritual path, but it requires the presence of a holy sage and the secret knowledge of the creature's true name. Since the monster seldom resembles the person it had once been, obtaining or discovering this information is almost always impossible. But in those rare cases when the sage does learn the name he must say it during a second burial ritual following the Pisacha's death by sword. If the true name is spoken during this burial then the bonds holding the tortured spirit to Earth are broken and the soul is free to move forward along its intended spiritual path. Generally, though, the Pisacha remain on Earth, either in their flesh-eating physical bodies or their ghostly forms. Since the Pisacha essentially live in the realm of ghosts they are not subject to the normal laws of time and space, which gives them a great deal of knowledge about the past, present, and future. Because of this knowledge these monsters are often captured by sorcerers and enslaved, and then forced to reveal any secrets they possess.

⊰ GHOUL ⊱

The Ghoul is a common name given to any of the world's necrophageous (flesh-eating) monsters. The name comes from the *Ghul* of Muslim folklore, though it is used openly now in most European countries to refer to any creature who robs graves and feeds on the recently dead.

Poltergeist Any of a number of uneasy spirits who inhabit houses and manifest their presence by making noises, moving objects, breaking things, and in some cases even assaulting people and animals. The term "poltergeist" comes from the German words poltern, "to knock," and geist, "spirit"—hence a "noisy spirit."

Pontianak The Pontianak is a monster that rises from the grave of a still-born child. This creature, found in Java and Malaysia, is a truly dreadful being with a particularly violent appetite.

Though it died at birth, the demonic force that takes possession of the tiny corpse is far older and more worldly, so when the Pontianak rises from the grave it takes the form of a beautiful woman, though it uses the haunting cry of a lost child as a lure to attract its prey. Whether drawn by the cry of a child, or compelled by the image of beauty, the victims of the Pontianak go willingly to their rendezvous with death. Once the victim is within striking distance the Pontianak eviscerates him and feeds on the spilling entrails.

Pooka (also Puca, Phouka) The Pooka is a creature from Irish folklore that hunts the countryside by night, often taking the form of a great, sleek dark horse with burning yellow eyes and a wild mane of silky hair. The Pooka is a foul-tempered and spiteful spirit that delights in creating mayhem and damage. It tears down fences, upsets carts, breaks windows, scatters livestock, smashes down crops, and kicks holes in walls. The very sight of the Pooka is enough to turn cow's milk sour in the udder, keep chickens from laying eggs, and make dogs howl piteously through the night.

But the horse image is just one shape this theriomorph can assume. It also sometimes appears like a humanoid goblin, particularly in County Down, where it demands that it be given a share of every harvest. Even today farmers will portion out a small amount of each crop as the "Pooka's Share."

Another shape it frequently takes, especially in County Laois, is that of a winged creature like a flying ape; in County Roscommon it often appears as a huge black goat with great curling horns; and in Wexford and Waterford, it takes the shape of an enormous eagle. In these latter cases the Pooka often swoops down on travelers and either knocks them into canals or picks them up and drops them into muddy pools.

Pret The Pret of India is another of the ghostly predators created from the death of a newborn. Generally a person's spirit passes on peacefully after the proper burial rituals are attended to, but every once in a while those rituals are mismanaged and the spirit lingers. If trapped on Earth because of such a blunder, the spirit becomes violent and angry and is caught there for a full year, during which it vents its rage at the living.

The Pret is only the size of a man's thumb, and for the most part it lacks the power to do much substantial harm, especially if food offerings are left out for it. When it becomes fixated on a person and wishes to do harm, the Pret will return each night and take a little bit of blood—not enough to kill, but more than a person can replenish in a full day. After enough feedings the victim begins growing weak and will eventually die from pernicious anemia.

After a year has passed, the Pret will dissolve and its spirit will finally move forward.

Pryccolitch Another of the world's strange werewolf-vampire crossbreeds shows up in Romanian folklore in the form of a cunning and very destructive Pryccolitch. The Pryccolitch is a living vampire, rather than a revenant, and is created when a person who feels great animosity toward someone lays a curse on them. Witches can also lay these curses, but the most powerful ones are cast by someone who feels hatred on a profoundly deep level, such as a scorned lover or a business rival. However, even cursing someone in jest can, on rare occasions, transform them into the Pryccolitch. Perhaps it's something in the water there, but being turned into a savage monster really shouldn't be that easy.

Once cursed, the doomed person's soul either turns cold or actualy leaves the body entirely. This absence allows evil demonic spirits to enter and these spirits do not actually possess the body—instead they teach the cursed person the secrets of darkness and the power of supernatural hate. Once the Pryccolitch has begun its campaign of terror, the inhabiting spirit remains like a co-pilot, offering advice, advising caution, and helping to choose the right victims.

The Pryccolitch feeds on blood but unlike most vampires it has to transform into a monster shape in order to do this. This change can only be accomplished while no one is watching, and then there is a quick though painful metamorphosis into a wolflike monster. The process is not unlike the were lycanthrope transformations in movies like *The Howling* and *An American Werewolf in London.*

In the earliest accounts, prior to the eighteenth century, the Pryccolitch would attack and slaughter whole families and then over a period of months destroy an entire village; but from the early eighteenth century onward the Pryccolitches of those tales have only been reported killing livestock.

P-Skig-Demo-Os (also **M-ska-gwe-demo-os**)   The P-Skig-Demo-Os is a man-eating predator from the Abenaki Indians of New England. She appears to be a human being—and may once have been—but now she haunts the shadows and uses a peculiar plaintive cry to lure children and men to her, and then she slaughters them and eats their flesh.

This creature is pure evil and deeply spiteful. Anyone who pities her, even in his private thoughts, is likely to suffer ill fortune and will probably never find love.

For the modern Abenaki, the P-Skig-Demo-Os is the equivalent of the bogeyman and is used to coerce children into good behavior.

Pugut   The Pugut of the Philippines is a night-hunting shape-shifter who often takes the form of a wild dog or a black cat, but in its actual form it is vaguely manlike, walking upright, though taller and more muscular than a man. In some cases it appears as a headless thing that has smoky fire erupting from the stump of its neck.

The Pugut hunts humans for food and is very difficult to drive away, and nearly impossible to kill.

Qiqirn   Among the Inuit a recurring story is told of a brutish dog-creature called the Qiqirn whose very presence caused both men and their dogs to have epileptic fits. The Qiqirn is hairless except for tufts on its mouth, feet, ears, and tail-tip, though the cold of the arctic does not seem to adversely affect it. Despite its size, the Qiqirn is a complete coward and will run away when chased.

Radiant Boys   Throughout Europe and particularly Great Britain there are tales of the Radiant Boys, who are believed to be the ghosts of children who had been murdered by their mothers. This would suggest that they are some kind of Vengeance Ghost. The sad, angry ghosts glow like phosphorus and have been known to chase people for miles, or even lure them into bogs.

It is very likely that the Radiant Boy legend is an outgrowth of the somewhat older tales of the *Kindermorderinn* of Germany.

Ramanga   The Ramanga of Madagascar[66] is one of the world's more bizarre species of human vampire, and one that bears many of the qualities of the European "sin eater."

The name, Ramanga, means "blue blood," and these are otherwise ordinary human beings who are actually hired by village elders to eat those mean

---

66 The first English-language description of the Ramanga was presented in *The Golden Bough* by James G. Frazer, originally published in 1890; currently published by Touchstone Books, 1995.

parts of the body that are ordinarily disposed of: nail clippings and spilled blood, for example.

Though this rather disgusting arrangement is hard to accept by the standards of most civilized cultures, the behavior is quite in keeping with the beliefs of the people of rural Madagascar. They believe that these grisly disjecta membra are linked to the person from whom they come, and therefore possess strong magical properties. If they were to fall into the hands of a sorcerer or witch then great evil magic can be worked. Only an official Ramanga, through the process of ingestion, can effectively neutralize the supernatural properties of these items.

The richer families often retain more than one Ramanga, and often have a special Ramanga for traveling so that this grisly task will always be handled quickly and efficiently, keeping them safe from sorcery.

Redcap   The Unseelie of Scotland are the tainted versions of the Seelie, whose name means "blessed"; Unseelie, then, are unblessed and evil beings and include a variety of faerie-like creatures, including the nasty Redcaps.

Recaps loiter around graveyards, castles, and other ruins, and seldom venture far from their staked-out territories. The Redcap draws much of its strength from the atmosphere of its dwelling place, and if a locale has seen a lot of violence, pain, bloodshed, grief, or death, then the Redcap becomes stronger. It is one of the few essential vampires who feeds (partly) from the energy of a place rather than from the energy of a living person.

They are well known for playing the trickster and luring travelers into deadfalls, over cliffs, and into thorn thickets; or leaping out to startle a horse so that its rider is thrown and injured. Once they've caused a victim to become mortally injured, this Unseelie[67] dips its hat in the flowing blood, and it is from this unsavory practice that it has earned its name.

In appearance, the Redcap is a short and stocky old man with long tangles

---

67. Other Unseelie in Scottish and Irish lore include the Kelpies and the *Will-o'-the-Wisp*.

of greasy gray hair over which he wears his bloody red cap. In place of hands he has claws like a cat's, and he wears iron boots, though despite these he can run remarkably fast. The Redcap's strength is legendary and he can overwhelm any ordinary man. The only way to stop him is to quote Bible passages at him, which instantly shames him and makes him flee.

Revenant Though often used as a general term for any creature that has returned from death as a vampire, ghost, and so forth, the word "revenant" is also used to specifically refer to the living dead of the British Isles. The English revenant is a corpse with rotting skin, sunken eyes, breath that is indescribably foul, and a thirst for human blood.

English revenants are seldom shape-shifters, though in some folktales they can turn in to giant hounds (not wolves). Revenants often retain some or all of their memories, but there is no emotional connection to these memories. Instead they use knowledge of former friends, relatives, and locations as part of their hunting strategies.

Becoming a revenant is not dependent on being bitten by a vampire, but simply by dying with an evil nature. That alone can bring someone back from the dead to be a predator with unnatural appetites.

Runaturunco The Runaturunco of Argentina is a shape-shifter who can take the form of any animal, though it often takes the form of birds or dogs. The Runaturunco is a human sorcerer who makes a pact with the Devil to acquire supernatural powers, including theriomorphy. By day he looks and acts quite normal, blending in with society and going about normal life, though secretly he is constantly scouting for his next victim; when the sun goes down the Runaturunco transforms into an animal and hunts down that person to make a kill.

The Runaturunco is a selective hunter and will only prey on those persons who are of Indian ancestry, refusing to touch anyone of Spanish or Caucasian blood.

Killing a Runaturunco is easy—just a bullet in the brain will do it—but keeping it dead is a bit harder. Even if its corpse is incinerated, the creature will rise again from its own ashes. The key is to shoot it, burn it, and then scatter the ashes along miles of roadways, causing the monster to spread its spirit so thin that it lacks the power to return to corporeal life.

If the Runaturunco does rise from its own ashes, it can only be killed the second time by the father of a virgin. This slayer must be blessed by three priests and wear a charm containing hairs from the Runaturunco's first body. For this reason, if a Runaturunco is ever caught, some hairs from the creature are always kept.

Rusalka (also **Rusalki)** Legends are told of mer-people in all the world's lakes and oceans, and sightings have been recorded as recently as the mid-twentieth century. Many of these creatures share qualities with *Sirens* in that they often lure sailors to their deaths, but in Russia a frightening twist on this monstrous paradigm is known as the Rusalka.

The Rusalki are an amphibious race of creatures thought to be the tortured souls of children who had died unbaptized, babies drowned by unwed mothers, or the ghosts of drowned virgins, particularly those who committed suicide because of broken hearts. When a soul in this kind of torment leaves the body it is caught and can return as a Rusalka.

The creatures live at the bottom of lakes and can come onto land and disguise themselves as humans by stealing clothing. When on land they walk upright on two legs, but when they return to the water their lower quarters once again become scaled fish tails.

In some of the more romantic tales of the Rusalki the creature is a lovesick immortal looking for a human man that she can seduce and enchant into joining her in her vast underwater palace. Sadly, her suitors tend to drown, which sounds like a bit of Disney storytelling with just a dash of the Brothers Grimm.

In the villages of the seventeenth and eighteenth centuries, however, the

RUSALKA Sharon George

Rusalka was anything but a lovelorn fish princess; instead she was a sly predator that stole into villages in hopes of finding stray children to suck the life
from.

Yet other Rusalka tales recount how the creature seduces men and whisks
them off to some enchanted place—perhaps an alternate dimension—where
she has her way with them for many years while using her magic to keep them
from aging. This all sounds good until the mortal reemerges into the physical

world and time instantly catches up with them and he crumbles to dust and bones.

In the folktales of the last 300 years the sign of the cross made in the air can drive off the Rusalka; and a wooden cross made from a tree that grew in a churchyard will likewise frighten it.

There is a wonderful opera by Antonín Dvořák called *Rusalka*, in which Rusalka is a water nymph and the daughter of the Water-Gnome (a benign character from Russian folklore). She falls in love with a mortal prince and everything ends badly, with curses and fatal kisses and the usual grand stuff of opera.

A. S. Pushkin, the great Russian poet, wrote a marvelous poem about Rusalka that can be found at www.vampireuniverse.com, the Vampire Universe website.

— *Chapter Six* —

AND IN THIS CORNER . . .
THE GOOD GUYS

(*Vampire Slayers and Other Enemies of Evil*)

BUT THAT'S THE WAY HEROES ARE MADE
THEY DO THEIR BEST WORK IN THE DARK
— *"Hero in the Dark,"* Eric Hansen

IN THE MOVIES, whenever a vampire starts putting the bite on the locals there is always a Van Helsing ready to provide sage advice for the heroes and often to take a hand himself in slaying the toothsome predator. The concept of Van Helsing, a wise, strong, and confident force for good who has the correct (and often arcane) information and a good head for battle strategy is a comforting one, since the creatures of darkness tend to be extremely hard to kill.

But fiction is often inspired by fact and throughout the world's folklore of the supernatural there are many examples of the enemies of evil. Some of these are human, a few are on the fence between human and superhuman. Some are monsters themselves, and a few are even gods. Like the monsters they fight, heroes come in all shapes and sizes.

Here are just a few of these adversaries of the unnatural:

STREGONI BENFICI Andy Jones

•**Amagqirha:** "Witch-sniffers" from among the Bantu of South Africa who can sense evil in all of its many forms, and in particular the evil Hag-monster, the *Uthikoloshe*.

•**Batak:** The Batak of Java are witch-doctors who hunt the *Pontianak,* a particularly vicious vampire. The Batak can actually reclaim the souls of those lost to vampirism.

•**Benandanti:** Good-natured werewolves from Italian legend who enter a dream-state and descend into Hell to do battle with the forces of darkness. Known as "good-walkers," the Benandanti legend lingers even today.

•**Boloi:** A caste of witch-doctors, tribal healers, and clerics who practice religious sorcery to protect the people of Botswana, Africa.

•**Chung K'uei, the Demon Queller:** A supernatural warrior ghost from China who returns from death to battle ghosts and demons.

•**Dervish:** Iranian Sufi mystics who use dance-induced trances to drive evil spirits out of rural villages.

•**Dhampyr:** The semi-human offspring of a vampire and human parents, found throughout Gypsy culture. The Dhampyr (female is Dhampyressa) has a tragically short life span but while at the peak of its strength has vast psychic powers, and can detect and destroy vampires.

•**Djadadjii:** A Bulgarian monk who specializes in fighting vampires that take the form of pernicious poltergeists.

•**Hino:** The "thunderer" of Iroquois legend who rides the sky with his bow and arrows eternally seeking evil to combat.

•**Houngan/Mambo:** The priest and priestess of Vodoun (Voodoo) who use positive magic to protect their people, heal the sick, appease spirits, and defy the Bokor—the evil sorcerers of that religion.

•**Kishimo-Jin:** Japanese Buddhist patron goddess of little children who protects them from evil.

•**Kresnik:** The good-natured twin of the *Kudlak*, a fierce Croatian vampire. The Kresnik has powers like a superhero and is the only one who can stand up to the equally powerful Kudlak.

•**Machi:** Wise women from the Mapuche Indian culture of South America, who use animal familiars as allies in their ongoing battle against a species of vulture-headed witch-vampires called the Chonchon.

•**Monster Slayer and Born for Water:** Navajo "Hero Twins" whose parents are the Sun and the Earth Mother. The Hero Twins feature in many exciting tales of that culture and have labored for centuries to rid the world of destructive monsters.

•**Moshanyana:** A mythic hero from the Sotho people of South Africa who saved all of mankind from a world-devouring monster called Kholumolumo.

•**Sabbatarian and the Fetch Dog:** A Sabbatarian is a person born on a Saturday who has the power to cure illness as well as detect—and defeat—supernatural creatures such as vampires. The Sabbatarian is often accompanied by a Fetch Dog, a spirit that acts like a supernatural hunting hound.

•**Stregoni Benefici:** In Italy, a vampire who repents of his evil ways and performs great acts of contrition and is officially forgiven by the church and thereafter becomes a monster-hunting weapon of righteousness.

Chapter Seven

VAMPIRES AND MONSTERS
S–Z

S

Sampiro   There has long been tension between Albanians and Turks, and a long-standing belief in Albania suggests that anyone of Turkish ancestry will, upon his death, rise again as a vampire called a Sampiro. Once it rises from the grave, it makes itself a pair of high steel shoes, wraps its shroud around its wasted body, and then travels through the countryside spreading pestilence and disease. Sometimes it takes the form of a will-o'-the-wisp, which is actually one of the ways in which this creature can be destroyed as it can lead vampire hunters back to its own grave.

The Sampiro is a fairly typical revenant who sleeps in his grave by day and hunts mostly at night. Though its body is that of a decaying corpse, the Sampiro does not appear to rot away into dust as long as it continues to feed. The disposal method is the standard Ritual of Exorcism.

Sansuisuga   A general Latin term for vampire that means, literally "blood sucker." This term was used for centuries to describe these monsters until the more modern term "vampire" came into common usage.

Santu Sankai   The Santu Sankai (translated as "Mouth Men") are lycanthropic creatures from the forests of Kuala Lumpur that hunt in packs and can tear their prey to pieces in seconds. Like the werewolves in movies, the

Santu Sankai stand upright on their hind legs and are as tall as men. Their arms are packed with wiry muscles and they sport wolf snouts and savage fangs.

The most recent reliable account of the Santu Sankai was in 1967, when a hunter, Henri Van Heerdan, reported that two of the creatures attacked his truck. Police investigated and saw that the truck had, indeed, been badly battered. In addition, they found deep scratches and splashes of blood. Since then the sightings have become less frequent, but the Santu Sankai is still believed to haunt those remote forests.

Sarut   In the Philippines there is a bizarre predator called the Sarut that takes the shape of a small dog (similar in some regards to the *Bagat*) but can also appear as an insect. Though supernatural, the Sarut's nature is much like that of an ordinary animal in that it is generally harmless, even indifferent to humans, unless injured, chased, or otherwise provoked, at which point it attacks. The method of attack used by the Surat is to radiate an energy that causes illness in the offending human.

Sasquatch (also Bigfoot)   The most famous of the North American hominids, Sasquatch gets his name from the word "Sésquac," which means "wild man" in the Stó:lõ dialect of the Halkomelem language used by the Salish Indians of the Fraser Valley and parts of Vancouver Island, British Columbia. The name is apt, because Sasquatch stands upright like a man and even walks like a human, though his body is covered by thick hair and his face is simian in appearance.

The nickname "Bigfoot" was coined by journalists in the mid-twentieth century following a number of sightings in northern California and is also appropriate, since the creature left behind footprints so large that they make Shaquille O'Neal's feet look like a child's.

The Sasquatch legend got its biggest media boost in 1967 when former rodeo rider and Sasquatch aficionado Roger Patterson took 16mm film of the big hairy fellow walking through the forest. Though this footage has seldom been accepted by anyone associated with the hard sciences, many cryptozoologists aver that it is real.

Since then many researchers have intensified the hunt for this creature, with John Green leading the pack. Since the 1950s Green has been compiling eyewitness accounts of Sasquatch and has documented more than 3,000 of them. He has also written a fairly definitive book on the subject.

Another researcher, the anthropologist Dr. Grover S. Krantz (1931–2002) late of Washington State University, who also collected Sasquatch artifacts including castings from footprints, argued that the creature was likely a surviving member of a species of prehistoric ape called *Gigantopithecus Blacki,* which crossed over the ice bridge during the ice age 10,000 years ago. It was Dr. Krantz's guess that there are likely as many as 2,000 Sasquatch hidden in the massive forests between northern California and British Columbia.

◁ CRYPTID ▷ CLASSIFICATION

There are five primary categories into which all cryptids, or unknown species, are placed by cryptozoologists:

- Creatures known from native tradition (i.e. folklore, myths, oral tales, etc.)
- Creatures known by witness accounts (sightings)
- Creatures known by their interaction with matters (sonar, photography, footprints, injury marks, etc.)
- Creatures known by anatomical evidence (blood drops, bone fragments, excrement, feathers, fur, scales, teeth, etc.)
- Creatures know by complete specimen

Sehité   One of several similar wildmen of Africa. These brutish hominids are about four to four and a half feet tall, covered in rust-colored shaggy fur, and resemble a cross between humans and apes. In many ways they are similar, at least in terms of height, general build, and facial features, to Neanderthals; though according to recent thinking in the paleontological world the true Neanderthals were not very hairy.

Like the *Agogwe* of Tanzania and the Nittaewo of Sri Lanka,[68] the Sehité is rarely seen and there have been only a handful of reported sightings in the last seventy-five or eighty years. Also like the Agogwe the Sehité only rarely attacks humans, and even then it is usually children that it carries off. It is not known if the Sehité feeds on human flesh or whether it takes human children as either slaves or for company; but folktales usually tell of a splash of blood on the ground whenever a child has gone missing and a Sehité is suspected.

A similar and less violent version of the Sehité, called the *Kakundakári,* appears in the folklore of Zimbabwe.

Selma   Selma is a lake monster from Lake Seljordsvatnet in Norway that was first sighted in 1750 when it attacked a small fishing boat. The creature, variously described as being ten, thirty, or forty feet in length, was sighted frequently during the 1800s, and one story claims that a woman was confronted by the creature and cut it in half with an axe. According to the woman's report, one half fell dead to the ground while the remaining half lumbered back into the water.

Senotlke   A sea monster, generally described as looking like a gigantic serpent, that has been reported by the Squawmish Indians of the Pacific Northwest Coast. Sightings are rare these days.

Shachihoko   A sea monster occasionally spotted in the waters of China during the Middle Ages, it has the striped head of a tiger and the wriggling

---

68. Scott Weidensaul, *The Ghost with Trembling Wings; Science, Wishful Thinking and the Search for Lost Species,* North Point Press, 2002.

body of a great fish covered with poisonous spikes. Unlike most sea monsters, Shachihoko can climb out of the water, and once on land it transforms fully into a tiger. In architecture, particularly in Japan, carvings of the Shachihoko are used as gargoyles.

Shampe Deep in the forests of western North America there is a race of demonic hominids called the Shampe who have preyed on the Choctaw for many centuries. These hulking killers keep their hiding places secret and emerge only when the urge to feast on human flesh is on them. The Shampe are night-hunters and, unlike many vampires of folklore which do *not* fear sunlight, this race of wildmen actually does shun sunlight. It weakens them and makes them sick.

Beyond that one vulnerability, the Shampe are virtually indestructible. They have unnaturally acute senses, with sight as keen as an eagle's and a sense of smell to rival a shark's in that they can smell blood miles away and will relentlessly stalk anyone who is injured or carrying freshly killed game. Once they've scented their prey, they are relentless.

The best way to thwart the pursuing monster is to drop the bloody game and hot-foot it out of there. Better to lose a day's catch than to become one. When not carrying game, a Choctaw who suspected a Shampe was on his trail would shoot the first animal he could and leave it dead or dying as a lure while making his escape.

The Shampe is generally described as being covered with coarse brown hair, but some accounts describe a hairless monster, suggesting either a different species of the creature, or perhaps the existence of males and females.

Reports of the Shampe had all but disappeared in the last half of the twentieth century, but in recent years the Choctaw people have reported hearing its eerie whistling cry in their woods.

Shíta Vampires in the classical sense seldom appear in Native American folklore. Other kinds of monsters abound, but they are generally pretty far removed from the concept of the blood-drinking revenant. However, among the

Hopi people of the Southwest there is a legend of a cannibalistic creature called a Shíta who could only be killed by a wooden shaft through the heart.

This monster preyed on the village of Oraíbi, attacking any children it could catch and devouring them; or attacking any person within biting distance if it could not catch young prey. The villagers appealed to two magical brothers, Pöokónghoya and Balö'ngahoya, who lived in a nearby village and who had a reputation as supernatural problem solvers. The brothers asked the villagers to make each of them a special arrow, and then they went and ambushed the Shíta; but instead of fighting it outright, they allowed themselves to be swallowed whole by this enormous beast. Once inside the creature the brothers shot their magical arrows into its heart, slaying it.

Although the Shíta never returned to Earth to again trouble the living, the story is still told how Pöokónghoya and Balö'ngahoya defeated it . . . just in case the knowledge will ever come in handy again.

Shtriga (also Striga, Strige, Strigele)   The Shtriga is a witch-vampire whose predatory nature is linked with sudden infant death syndrome (SIDS). This vile monster preys on sleeping children, sneaking into a house through magical means and drawing the breath and life out of slumbering babies. Throughout Moldavia, Albania, and Transylvania people believed that children who died in the night for no discernible reason had to be victims of this pernicious monster.

To enter a house, the Shtriga transforms into a moth or other flying insect and flies in through an open window. It is one of the reasons that, for many centuries, people believed that it was bad for the health to leave the windows open at night, especially in a nursery.

Children are not the Shtriga's only victims. These evil creatures also prey on adults by spreading diseases and bringing discord to the community.

During daylight hours the Shtriga is able to live among ordinary people, passing herself off as a kindly old lady and a member of the community, even to the point of attending church services. However, she has to be careful because if she were to accept a piece of the Host she would be visibly repelled by it, thus alerting those around her that there is an unclean monster in their midst.

Another way of detecting the presence of a Shtriga in a church is to wait for everyone to enter and then place a small cross made from the bones of a pig on the threshold after the service has begun and everyone is inside. When the service is concluded, the Shtriga will not be able to cross the threshold to exit the church. Trapped in the church, the Shtriga may be dispatched by ritual exorcism, or if the need is great, through violence.

For variations of this legend, see the *Striga*.

Singa   The word "Singa" means "lion," but the creature that goes by that name and who hunts in the mountains of Sumatra bears no resemblance at all to any lion from the natural world. This monster is closer in size and bulk to a bison and has a weirdly human face. The Singa appears in decorations and carvings, particularly of the Batak people of that region and is used in much the same way as a gargoyle is used in Europe—a creature so fierce that it can even frighten off other monsters.

Sirens   Sirens are women from various world mythologies who live in or near the water and who lure sailors to their doom. In Greek mythology, the Sirens had a woman's head and the body of a great bird, and they made their nests in craggy rock outcroppings and atolls. Sirens have the most beautiful and compelling singing voices and their songs would draw the sailors inexorably to them, resulting in wrecked ships and drowned men.

The Sirens were confronted by both Odysseus and by Jason and the Argonauts, and escaping them in both cases was a near-run thing. For Jason, only the sweet music from the harp of Orpheus—a sound more beautiful even than Siren song—saved the crew of the *Argo*. For Odysseus, the song of these seductive killers was a challenge to him and he ordered that his men stop up their ears with wax and that they lash him to a mast so he could hear them. The experience nearly drove him insane.

According to Ovid, the Sirens are a species of Nymph, which is a class of female supernatural spirits found in various parts of nature. Originally the Sirens were simply Nymphs who were playmates of Persephone, but when she was kidnapped by Hades, Persephone's mother, Demeter, punished them for not stopping the abduction and cursed them so they turned into birdlike monsters.

Sluagh (also Sluagh Sidhe)   According to legends of the Sidhe, the faerie folk of Ireland and Scotland, the Sluagh are the hostile spirits of dead sinners who plague the living, hoping to capture and enslave less tainted human souls. When taking corporeal form, the Sluagh are ugly, pallid creatures with piercing dark eyes and toothless mouths that, through magic, manage to appear compelling and even seductive.

The Sluagh always appear from the west, and for this reason when a person is dying or very ill all of the westward-facing windows are sensibly kept shut to prevent these beings from stealing the dying person's soul. Once captured by a Sluagh, a person is condemned to eternal damnation rather than being allowed to pass on to a more positive spiritual reward.

The Sluagh are most easily detected by their strong smell, which is like rotting meat, and the older a Sluagh is the more powerful this reek becomes.

Some Sluagh are so attached to the Earthly plane that they constantly maintain a physical form and dwell in ruined houses and crumbling castles; a few even live in sewers and in the hearts of garbage mounds. Other Sluagh remain invisible and possess houses with living occupants, sowing discord and creating the kinds of illnesses that will yield up a departing soul for them to harvest.

Soucouyan (also Soucouyant)   The Soucouyan is a skin-shedding monster from the tiny island nation of Dominica[69] in the Lesser Antilles, between Martinique and Guadalupe, who removes her outer form like a suit of clothes

---

69. Not to be confused with the Dominican Republic.

SOUCOUYAN Pete Brown

and flies into the air as a ball of fire each night. This fiery monster flits through the forest looking for human prey and then slams into them, knocking them down and draining them of either life energy or blood.

Though the Soucouyan seldom kills its victims—preferring to leave them wasted and weakened—if a victim should die it, too, will rise as a flaming will-o'-the-wisp monster.

It is vital for the Soucouyan to return to where she left her skin and wriggle back into it before she is touched by the first rays of the morning light. Sunlight will not kill the Soucouyan, but it will dissipate her, the effect of which would be like tossing a bucket of water into the ocean. She will still exist, but will lack the power to become a single entity again.

The skin of a Soucouyan is highly prized in the making of charms and potions of Obeah magic.

Spunkie The Spunkie is a night-hunting Scottish goblin who preys on travelers. It is so evil that rural Scots believe that the Spunkie is a highly prized servant of Satan whose sole purpose on Earth is to murder. The Spunkie is distantly related to the *Will-o'-the-Wisp* in that it projects a fiery ball of light that it sends out to attract the attention of travelers and then lures them into the woods. While the travelers are chasing after the light, the Spunkie sneaks up on them from the shadows and begins ripping and tearing. When in a more playful mood, the Spunkie uses its ball of light trick to lure travelers over cliffs.

Sriz The Sriz of Poland is a ghostly and murderous spirit whose very voice possesses a deadly magic. The creature, which is most often invisible, climbs to the top of a church steeple and calls out the names of its victims. The victims invariably die, some from heart failure, others in violent accidents, still others of various wasting diseases.

The Sriz is an essential vampire who feeds on the release of pure terror projected by those who succumb to its call. Luckily tolling church bells, especially during times of prayer, will drive it away. Failing that, any kind of religious or sacred music should do the trick.

Stihi In Albania there lives another of the world's many breeds of treasure-hoarding, fire-breathing dragons, this one known as the Stihi. Like all dragons the Stihi knows her treasure to the last penny and can tell when any of it has been taken or even touched. And, also like most dragons, she is not particularly forgiving to those who try to rob her.

Striga   The Striga of ancient Hebrew legend, the Albanian *Shtriga*, the *Striges* of Greece, and the *Strix* of Roman folklore share many of the same evil qualities and may in fact be slightly different species of the same monster.

The name is a variant of the Italian word for witch, strega; and in all cases this creature is a witch of great and varied power who can shape-shift (often into magpies, crows, or other dark birds), possesses great intellect, is physically very powerful, and who feeds on the blood of innocent children.

For many centuries it was widely believed that evil witches[70] could adopt animal forms, and particularly the form of a night owl. Many representations in art show the Striga as wholly or partly transformed into an owl in order to hunt. In his book, *Fasti,* Ovid wrote that the Striges used their beaks to tear wounds in the chests of infants and then feasted on the blood that welled from the gashes.

The surest proof against a Striga is to place whitethorn in the window of the infant's room. Thereafter the Striga cannot enter.

Strigoi   The Strigoi is a general term for ghostly entity of evil intent from Romanian folklore. Like the Striga, the name is a variant of "strega," meaning witch; and the Strigoi are often reputed to transform into screech owls or other night birds.

In some legends, particularly those of the later nineteenth and early twentieth centuries, the Strigoi shifted from being a witch-vampire to being a revenant vampire, but this may have more to do with the publication of Bram Stoker's *Dracula* than with any folkloric origins.

See also *Shtriga* and *Striga* for variations on this legend.

Succubus (also **Buhlgeist)**   The Succubus is a female essential vampire who preys on men while they sleep, seducing them by means of magical power. The man will not be able to wake up during this seduction, but in the morn-

---

70. Not to be confused with Wiccan believers, who are generally a very positive group dedicated to preserving and cultivating life in all of its many forms.

ing will waken very listlessly, drained of vital energy. The Succubus (plural is Succubi) often returns night after night, draining a man of all of his life energy until he is so weakened that his body shuts down and he dies.

The Succubus can mate with a human and produce a child, called a *Cambion,* who will be corruption and evil incarnate.

Sukuyan   The Sukuyan of Trinidad is another witch-vampire that sheds its skin at night and takes to the air as a fiery ball of light to prey on sleeping humans. The Sukuyan can also adopt various corporeal forms such as fierce jungle cats, large dogs, and predatory night birds. Like its close cousin, the *Soucouyan,* the Sukuyan must return to its skin before dawn.

Sundal Bolong   If the supernatural world ever needed a spokeswoman for the dangers of casual sex, then the Sundal Bolong of Java would get the job. She is a revenant who takes the form of a seductive woman dressed in white and flirts with men in order to lure them to secluded spots in the forest, where she then transforms back into her normal self—a decaying, fetid corpse—before tearing their throats out and drinking their blood.

Sometimes the Sundal Bolong eschews outright murder and instead infects the man with a horrible wasting disease that often manifests as dripping lesions on the skin, particularly around the genitals. These sores erupt almost at once and the Sundal Bolong will allow her victim to escape and then harass them all the way back to their village, allowing the injured man to believe he was on the verge of safety, and then she'll pounce and kill him within inches of his front door.

In some versions of the Sundal Bolong legend, it possesses similar qualities to the Polong (see *Pelesit and Polong*) of Malaysia in that it is a diminutive creature that sneaks into bedrooms at night and drinks blood from the thumbs of sleepers. In this variation of the Sundal Bolong tale, the vampires can be captured and placed in bottles specially prepared by priests.

T

Talamaur   The Talamaur are sorcerer-mediums from the Bank Islands off the coast of Australia who possess the ability to speak with the dead, sometimes for nefarious purposes, and sometimes serves as a link between the departed and their living relatives. Those Talamaur who work for the good of their fellow men are in the minority, however, and the darker-natured ones use this otherworldly ability to contact the dead in order to control them and enslave them, using these servant ghosts to do all manner of mischief.

To be a Talamaur is not a crime, and some even advertise this service in order to make a living. However, being a Talamaur is risky because whenever something unlucky or disastrous occurs in a village the Talamaur is generally blamed, fairly or not, which results in the somewhat traditional throng of angry villagers with torches and pitchforks.

Tamawo   Tamawo are Filipino faerie folk who live in anthills, wasp nests, and other hives, but who can shape-shift into both male and female human forms. Though they use seduction and physical beauty—or at least its illusion—they are not essential vampires. Their goal seems to be to mate with humans, which they transform into their own diminutive species. If one of these abducted humans eats, by chance or coercion, the food of the Tamawo, then he or she will automatically transform forever into one of those creatures. However, if the captive resists eating the food for four days, then he or she is released and returned to normal size.

Tarunga   Among the Talamaurs of Australia's Bank Islands there is a subgroup that are sorcerers who have gained so much power that they can separate from their bodies and become invisible essential vampires, feeding on the lingering life energies of the recently deceased. The presence of a Tarunga is most often detected by villagers having unusually vivid dreams or visions, and at this point watchers will be set at the graves of anyone who has died in the last few weeks. The Tarunga will generally not feed while someone is around, and after a few weeks the spiritual essence will have completely departed the corpse.

Tenatz   It is in the legend of the Tenatz of Bosnia that we learn the secret of how many of the world's vampires can rise from the grave without disturbing the soil. These monsters are theriomorphs who can transform into mice or other small burrowing animals. In those forms they easily can tunnel their way to the surface. Once out of the grave they regain their revenant appearance and go lumbering off in search of fresh blood.

To prevent a suspected Tenatz from rising and walking, Bosnians sometimes sever the hamstrings of the dead before burial. If the creature does rise, fire and the standard Ritual of Exorcism will work.

Thags Yang   In Tibet there is a murderous race of shape-shifters called the Thags Yang that attack travelers, wrestle them to the ground, and suck out their life's breath. These theriomorphs can change from human form either into tigers or half-tigers. Only persons who are deeply spiritual exude a protective aura that can drive a Thag Yang away; a person whose religious practices are less stringently observed will actually attract the hunger of these monsters.

⊰ AURA ⊱

The energy field surrounding and permeating all living things, including humans, animals, and plants is called the Aura; and Auras change color according to the nature and/or health of the being. Reading the color of a person's aura often reveals vital information about that person.

Tlacique   The Tlacique is another of the vampire-witches who can become a fiery will-o'-the-wisp in order to hunt. They have appeared in legends of Mexico's Nahautl Indians, and these bizarre creatures attack their prey in these fiery shapes. For some unknown reason, however, their touch does not burn their victims, but merely mesmerizes them. The victims then slip into a stupor while the Tlacique drinks their blood.

When pursued, the Tlacique can shape-shift into various fowl like turkeys or chickens, blending innocuously into the local scenery, and then later changing back into human form before beginning their hunt anew.

Tlahuelpuchi   The Aztec vampire known as the Tlahuelpuchi preys exclusively on children, and is a remorseless blood-drinker. In order to get close to families with young kids, the Tlahuelpuchi takes the form of a household pet, or common bird. However, their preferred shape is that of a turkey, a bird found in every farmer's yard. In this perfectly ordinary disguise they seek out their prey and then wait for nightfall to sneak into the house and drink the blood of the sleeping children. Unlike most vampires, the Tlahuelpuchi needs to feed only once a month. It may feed more often if possible, but should it miss its monthly feeding it will die.

If detected, the Tlahuelpuchi will shape-shift into a flying insect and flit out through the window, or even change into a flea and hide in the hairs of the family dog or cat until the searchers stop hunting for it. In this disguise, the creature can remain close to its intended victim.

The Tlahuelpuchi is not a revenant but is actually a person born under a curse, doomed to be a living vampire. Though the Tlahuelpuchi can be male or female, the females are far more common and much more powerful. By day they live and act as ordinary humans, their evil nature unrevealed.

Though the Tlahuelpuchi may enter any house without invitation they are bound by strange rituals. Before entering they must assume bird shape and fly over the house from north to south then east to west, forming a cross pattern. This casts an enchantment that allows them entry. To save the victim's

TLACIQUE
Jason Beam

soul, a local shaman must disenchant the victim by "uncrossing" them. Other precautions include placing garlic and onions around doors, windows, and an infant's bed. The Tlahuelpuchi also fears sharp metal, so an open pair of scissors left on a night stand near a crib is often enough of a deterrent to keep the child safe.

Tokebi   The Tokebi is a species of goblin from Korean folklore who is decidedly mischievous though not actually evil. They love to frighten and cause small-scale mayhem, but they do little actual harm. Much of their time is spent eating, drinking, and singing, which they approach with great gusto.

Some Tokebi are active in human affairs, seeking out good-natured humans to reward and wicked humans to punish.

Tokoloshe (also **Tikoloshe, Hili)**   In Bantu folklore there is a recurring story of a short, hairy, and very nasty dwarfish monster called the Tokoloshe who can be conjured by malevolent people in order to do harm or carry out acts of revenge. The Tokoloshe causes sickness and can even kill with its very presence. Only a N'anga (witch-doctor) has the power and skills needed to drive away this monster.

Trazgos (also **Trasgos)**   If you can imagine a prehistoric velociraptor that partly evolved into a chicken you'll have some idea of the Trazgos, one of Spain's strangest supernatural predators. The Trazgos stands only about four feet tall and struts around on legs that are more humanoid than avian, but which end in clawed toes like a bird's. The creature has abnormally short arms much like those of some species of dinosaur like the velociraptor; unlike a dinosaur the Trazgos has no tail. Its skin is reddish and, though similar to human skin, is very rough.

The Trazgos is cunning and enjoys setting elaborate traps for travelers much like a woodland hunter, using tactics like deadfalls and foot snares. Once a traveler has been trapped and, frequently, injured or incapacitated, the Trazgos darts in to spit venom in the helpless person's eyes. Afterward the Trazgos slashes and bites the person to death, feasting on blood and flesh.

A sword or axe that has been soaked for three days in a mixture of sweet oil and mashed garlic can destroy this monster; and this weapon must be handled deftly so that the Trazgos is dispatched by a single blow. A wounded Trazgos will turn into a will-o'-the-wisp and escape, regenerating completely by the time they return to physical form.

If a Trazgos has been slaughtered, its body must be rubbed down with garlic paste, wrapped tightly in shroud cloth, and tied at three points (neck, waist, and ankles) with seven turns of grapevine. Then it should be staked through

⚞ TRICKSTER ⚟

The Trickster is not a specific creature but rather a paradigm for a type of supernatural being. This being delights in creating confusing and unpredictable situations that force a person to make a choice that (quite often) works out badly for the person in question. In some cultures the Trickster is neither evil nor good, but exists to create circumstances in which a person is forced to make a moral decision without necessarily making it clear which is the correct path.

Tricksters appears in every culture, from the Coyote of Native American legends to Loki of Norse myth.

the heart with a fire-hardened holly shaft and buried beneath an evergreen. Skipping or mishandling any phase of this exorcism will result in the Trazgos' returning to life twice as strong as before.

Tsutsuga   Japanese rural villages of the sixth and seventh centuries were plagued by an evil and monstrous theriomorph called a Tsutsuga who could take a variety of forms, such as insects, birds, vermin, will-o'-the-wisps, fog, and even the likenesses of holy people.

Using tricks and deception, the Tsutsuga sneaks into houses at night to infect sleeping humans with a variety of diseases. The Tsutsuga is part nosferatu, but it has qualities of the essential vampire in that it also feeds on the misery of those persons whom it makes ill. Many of the victims of the Tsutsuga are so overwrought by the pain and discomfort of these illnesses that they commit suicide, and the release of that kind of terminal despair also feeds the monster.

Tulivieja   The *Bogey Man* is often the culprit in stories designed to scare children into good behavior, and this holds true around the world. But in rural areas of many countries the stories of the Bogey Man—under whatever name it is called—hold more weight and are believed more deeply.

This is particularly true in Panama, where the story of the evil Tulivieja is known by everyone. It is a grim story passed down from generation to generation, from parents to children, and even from sibling to sibling. This old tale is as frightening as it is sad.

In the most common version of the story there was once a race of spirits that lived among mortals and with which mortals could see and interact. Most of these spirits were benign and even helpful, but they pursued their own fates and generally left humans to theirs as well.

One spirit envied the grace and beauty of human females and wanted to prove that she was better than any of them, so she created for herself a mortal body and went to live among them. She pretended to be a traveler who had chosen to settle in the town and immediately she was hailed as the most strikingly beautiful woman anyone had ever seen. Men fell over themselves courting her and all of the women in the town were jealous of her. Yet they respected her at the same time for she was queenly in her beauty. Soon it was that the town began to brag of her, saying that they had among them the most beautiful woman in the world.

One young man—the handsomest and most talented of the town's hunters and warriors—fell in love with her, and she with him. They married and she became pregnant. But before she gave birth to the child she made up her mind to kill it, because the child would clearly be only half-human. The spirit-woman could not bear to have her secret revealed because she loved being adored by her husband and by the town.

So, after the child was born, she drowned it.

Instantly all of the spirits and God Himself became furious with her for the wickedness of her crime. She was punished by the heavens and was transformed into a hideous monster with taloned hands, the body of a hunting cat, horses hooves for feet, and a face pocked with oozing sores. In short she became the monster known as the Tulivieja.

But the transformation was not the end of her punishment. She was locked into the body of the Tulivieja and made immortal; and her true punishment was to spend the rest of eternity searching for the body of her murdered child. Like the tragic figure, Sisyphus, from Greek myth, the Tulivieja would never be allowed to complete her task. She will search forever.

To this day there are tales of her searching the banks of every river and every stream, calling out for her child in a voice like a screeching bird. To further mock her, she becomes the beautiful woman again during the days of the full moon, and has sometimes been seen bathing in the waters; but as the moon wanes she transforms once again into the cursed Tulivieja.

As legend has it, aside from her endless quest, the Tulivieja has become a spirit of vengeance and if a child behaves badly, then she may come for that child in the night and steal him or her right out their bed. It is a frightening story to tell children.

Hopefully it isn't true.

Tursas (also **Iki-Turso, Turisas, Turras)**   Tursas is an ancient Finnish sea monster who was believed to be both a War God and the Demon of Diseases. The root of its name "thurs" comes from the Finnish for "giant," and this malevolent behemoth has been behind countless floods, tidal waves, sea calamities, shipwrecks, and other disasters.

U

Uber   Uber is the Turkish word for "witch" but is also considered by many scholars to be the root of the word "vampire." This revenant rises from the grave of a person who died during an act of violence; or from the grave of a foreigner who was not a Muslim and died on Turkish soil. This latter belief is actually tied into the legend of the real Prince Vlad of Wallachia, who—though a cultural hero in Romania—is regarded as a bogeyman in Turkey. When they want children to go to bed or brush their teeth, parents threaten their kids with the fierce Uber Vlad.

In the fifteenth century, the Ottoman Empire invaded the three Romanian countries, Wallachia, Transylvania, and Moldavia. The Turks were bitterly repelled by Prince Vladislav III, son of Dracul,[71] more commonly known today as the historical Dracula. Vlad was a powerful ruler, a bloodthirsty warrior, and known as one of the most savage men of his day. He was responsible for the deaths of between 40,000 and 100,000 Turks.

It's no wonder they used Vlad as the model for the enduring legend of the eternally evil Uber.

Uentshukumishiteu   The Uentshukumishiteu is a terrible water monster of Inuit legend who travels beneath the icy waves and ice floes and can emerge anywhere when hungry for human flesh.

Ukoy   Though in films the supernatural beings of the deep, such as mermaids, are generally portrayed as friendly, attractive, and occasionally amusing, in folklore the people of the sea are seldom anything but nasty. The Ukoy of Filipino folklore is an odd blend of merman and octopus, with a human torso and head but in place of arms and legs he has at least eight (and sometimes as many as fifty) tentacles. This creature is enormously strong and can swim as fast as a dolphin, and though not an active hunter of humans, the Ukoy will indiscriminately kill swimmers and divers who chance to come too near to its underwater cave.

As powerful as it is beneath the waves, when the Ukoy lumbers up onto land it is relatively weak, just as a squid or octopus would be weak out of water.

---

71. Dracul means "dragon," and Vlad's father was part of a holy cadre of Christian knights called the Order of the Dragon. The suffix "a" means "son of," so Dracula is the Son of the Dragon.

Ukumar   Dwelling in the Andes of Peru the Ukumar is a huge and blood-thirsty creature whose evil nature is much like the *Shampe* or the *Shíta* of North America. The Ukumar is as big as a grizzly and twice as strong and when it hunts it can range as far as Bolivia and Argentina.

Like a typical predator, the Ukumar hunts the weak or helpless and generally attacks children, women, or the elderly. Though it seldom attacks a strong man, it can nevertheless rip a man to pieces with ease. It can be killed by nonmagical weapons such as guns or spears, but it is so fast and clever that no one has ever managed to bring one down. In those rare times when an Ukumar has been mortally wounded, its fellows will attack with terrible ferocity in order to recover the body.

Unicorn (also **Kirin, Ki-Lin)**   The Unicorn is a wild and untamable creature that appears in mythology from all over the world. Particularly in Asia the Unicorn is believed to be a bringer of good luck. In some stories in Europe the creature was lucky only when seen, but if someone attempted to capture it then either it would kill the person outright or curse him with ill fortune.

The first mention of the Unicorn in literature was by the Greek historian Ctesias in 398 BCE who described them as "wild asses which are as big as a horse, even bigger. Their bodies are white, their heads dark red and their eyes are deep blue. They have a single horn on their forehead which is approximately half-a-meter long."

The Unicorn is often held up as a symbol of purity and positivity. In Irish folklore, to attempt to harm a Unicorn is a sure way of incurring the very dangerous ire of the various faerie folk.

Upier (plural **Upierczi)**   The deadly Upier of Poland is one of the few "nesting" vampires in the world. Though a fairly typical revenant in most ways, the Upier builds a nest for itself, usually in a crypt or some other enduring and protected spot. It does not necessarily choose its own grave as its nesting place, but often moves far away from its own burial spot in order to escape detection.

The Upier is a daylight vampire and hunts during the hours of noon to midnight. When it finally returns to its resting place it fills its nesting basin with blood and sleeps immersed in the liquid.

Also known as the Wampir or Viesczy in Russia, the Upier of Poland uses a forked and barbed tongue for its attack rather than fangs, and when it attacks its insatiable hungers drive it to drain every last drop of blood from its victims.

The Upier is born from the graves of recently dead humans, typically those who had been born with teeth (a sign in many cultures of an unnatural hunger) or with a caul. During its human life the Upier is often hyperactive, agitated, and shows a constantly flushed and intense face, but while alive it is not necessarily evil. Only after death does it become the very embodiment of wickedness.

The single best way to prevent a corpse from rising as one of the Upierczi is to bury it face down. It will become confused and will consume its own flesh until it is too wasted to move. Another protection against the Upier is called "Blood Bread," which is made by locating the coffin of a vampire that has already been destroyed and gathering up some of its blood. This blood is mixed with water and flour and baked into a loaf, which is then shared among a family. Anyone eating the blood bread will be safe from the Upier's bite.

Upor   A slight variation of the Upyr is the Upor, also of Russia and surrounding countries—a blood-drinking revenant that preys mainly on children. Unlike its cousin, however, the Upor is a shape-shifter and can adopt many animal guises such as dogs, chickens, various small birds, insects, and rats. The Upor also possesses an empathic connection with different beasts and uses them as his spies and familiars.

In Russian folktales the Upor telepathically controls a family pet to make it run off so the kids who own it will go looking for it; sadly, though, when the children catch up with the pooch the monster is waiting. A variation of this has a Upor grabbing the family pet, keeping him for a day, and then knocking on the door of the house pretending to be a kind stranger returning the lost pet. The glad family invites the kindly stranger in and bloodshed ensues.

The Upor can only be killed using the standard Ritual of Exorcism, but finding its grave is exceptionally difficult and requires following one back to its resting place before dawn, which is also a great way of becoming the monster's bedtime snack.

Upyr   A Russian revenant vampire, the Upyr rises from its grave and goes hunting for entire families to destroy, first attacking the children in a family and then killing the adults. The Upyr[72] is the reanimated corpse of a witch or a suicide, because in either case that person's soul is damned. They are denied ascension and must remain on Earth—which seems a rather odd punishment

ᚻ CORPSE JUMPING ᚿ

There is a common tradition that any person or animal passing over a dead body may cause it to become a vampire. This stems from the belief that the spirit of the dead can snatch a portion of the life of any living creature and use it to rekindle its own unnatural life. The belief, in one form or another, is found in cultures as far apart as Eastern Europe, China, and the Navajo. Animals, such as dogs or cats, are easily capable of corpse jumping, but people, bats, birds, and insects should be restrained as well. In China, tigers are believed to possess what was known as a "soul-recalling hair" that hooks part of the spirit when it crosses over a grave.

---

72. The term "Upyr" is sometimes used as a general term for all kinds of Russian vampires, including the *Erestun* and *Eretiku*.

for spiritual crimes, considering that they then go out and attack the innocent.

Building on this theme of bad things happening for bizarre reasons, a Upyr
also can be created when a living person, dog, or cat walks over the grave of a
newly dead person, a dreadful mistake known in legends as "Corpse Jumping."

Ustrel   In Bulgaria one has to be careful not to offend the supernatural
world even when being born. For example, a child born on a Saturday but who
then died before he could be baptized the following Sunday was doomed to
become a type of vampire called an Ustrel. Though it dies while still an infant
it rises from the grave as a vampire the size of a small child, and can then grow
even larger and more powerful as long as it continues to feed. And if it can
manage to feed for ten consecutive nights it becomes so powerful that it no
longer needs to rest in its grave and then lives in the fields, resting during the
daylight hours between the horns of a ram or a young bull, or hidden between
the hind legs of a cow.

The Ustrel possesses demonic intelligence on a par with adult animal
predators like foxes and wolves, and generally avoids detection by eschewing
humans as preying on animals instead. Smart Ustrels disguise the signs of
their attacks by making them look like the signature bites of other animals.

On the other hand, Ustrels are not known for their enduring restraint and
often go too far, tipping off the locals who then call in a Vampirdzhija to set
about tracking down the blood-drinker. Only a skilled Vampirdzhija can actually sense the presence of the Ustrel and destroy it, using a complicated series
of rites and rituals beginning with the lighting of a pair of need-fires[73] in a field
and then having the village animals driven through the purifying smoke. The
passage between the flames makes the unseen Ustrel lose its grip on whatever
animal it is resting upon, and the creature drops helpless to the road, where

---

73. Also known as a Banfire, Bane-fire, or Bonfire.

the Vampirdzhija picks it up, places it in a bottle, and tosses the bottled monster into the flames.

The villagers all take flaming brands from the need-fire and use them to relight their home fires, which shares out the protective magic to every home.

Uthikoloshe (also **Oothikoloshe)**   Vampires and spirits that invade dreams and cause either mental or physical illness are not uncommon around the world. The Mara of Canada, Poland, and Scandinavia; the Incubus of Europe; and the Tengu of Japan are just a few examples of these "nightmares."[74]

Among the Bantu of South Africa there is legend of a nightmare creature called the Uthikoloshe, which invades the dreams of sleeping villagers and causes bad dreams of such intense ugliness and dread that the person becomes ill or, in some cases, dies. Those who have survived such dreams recall feeling like they were being strangled and were powerless to fight back.

These accounts also bear striking similarities to the *Old Hag*[75] tales.

The Uthikoloshe can be either male or female, and both sexes are similar in appearance. Most often they have been described as short, hairy hominids with heavily muscled shoulders and chests, sloping foreheads, and bandy legs—a description that also places them in the world's vast family of wildmen.

The Uthikoloshe live in mud huts along riverbanks or deep in the forests. They generally wear crude sheepskin clothing and carry very primitive tools. Though they do not make jewelry or other finery, they sometimes adorn themselves with bright and shiny items stolen from their victims.

These monsters practice a rudimentary but effective form of witchcraft, and even have familiars in their service. The creatures they most commonly favor are reptiles very similar to monitor lizards.

The Uthikoloshe have a language of their own, but they can speak Bantu and other languages, and their voices are slurred and lisping. They often speak

---

74. Nightmare is a contraction of the words Mara and nacht (night).
75. See sidebar on page 211 for more on this strange syndrome.

to children and coax them into playing with them, a recreation that seldom leads to anything but tears.

Among their magical talents is the art of invisibility, accomplished by placing enchanted pebbles in their mouths. When invisible they are able to enter the spirit world and from that place they can then enter the dreams of nearby sleeping villagers.

Opposed to the Uthikoloshe are "witch-sniffers" who are either Amagqirha (priests), or servants of Amagquirha, and who can sense evil in all its guises. Once the Amagqirha has diagnosed that a Uthikoloshe is at the root of an illness or a spate of bad dreams, he then prepares a bottle of Uthikoloshe fat that has been rendered down into a clarified oil. The victim drinks the oil and the spell is immediately broken.

If an Amagqirha were to confront the Uthikoloshe directly, he would use salt as his chief weapon as this is as fatal to this monster as garlic is to most of the world's other vampires. A handful of salt thrown into the face of an Uthikoloshe will kill it instantly. The priest must then work fast to recover the creature's body fat in order to prepare the curing oils.

Utukku   Spirits of vengeance abound in the folklore of Assyria and Babylon, and in the countries descended from those roots, including Iran and Iraq.

Among these many dreadful and unquiet ghost-vampires is the Utukku. This ghost is of someone who has been murdered and who simply cannot abide the peace of the grave until it has sought violent redress.

The creature rises as a spirit but manifests a physical form, either that of a human or an animal, and sets about tracking down its killer. However, the Utukku is not single-minded: it will kill any human it chances to meet. The more it kills, the more powerful it becomes, and the more it becomes seduced by its own power. An Utukku that kills enough will often choose to linger on Earth long after its initial prey has been killed.

There are also Babylonian stories of the Utukku, wherein the reasons for its resurrection from the grave are not always so noble. Sometimes the Utukku rises to simply prey on the living, satisfying nothing but its insatiable hunger for evil. It can also be invoked by ill will through curses or black magic spells.

Vadatajs   The Latvian Vadatajs is a vile trickster who uses a variety of ruses to lead travelers astray, often causing them to fall into crevasses, wander off cliffs, or sink into quicksand. Vadatajs often use shape-shifting in their trickery, taking both human and animal forms. The name Vadatajs means "leading to nowhere," and the creatures can also influence people to stray from their spiritual beliefs as well, resulting in them being "lost" in terms of redemption.

Vampir (also **Vampyr, Viper, Vepir,** and **Vapir)**   This is a general term used to describe any of the many vampire species of Bulgaria, and is derived from Opyr, the ancient Slavic word for vampire.

Vampiro   A general term for vampire used in Italy. Many of the vampire legends of Italy linger from ancient Roman times, but new stories and variations persisted well into the nineteenth century. One unusual variation on the belief was floated by the Franciscan monk Ludovico Maria Sinistrari of Pavia (1622–1701) who, in his study of demons and their practices, *De Aemonialitate, En Incubus Et Succubus,* argued that vampires were not actually reanimated corpses but another race of beings entirely: the Vampiro. He believed that these creatures were set apart from the descendants of Adam and Eve, much like the Neanderthals and Cro-Magnon evolved from similar roots but became separate species. Sinistrari believed that vampires even had souls, though he admitted that these souls were essentially flawed.

Varcolaci (Upirina and **Vrykolaka)**   Many Romanian vampires are unnaturally powerful, but the real powerhouse among them is the Varcolaci, who can travel as fast as the wind along invisible astral threads and can cause eclipses. The Varcolaci is a shape-shifter who can assume any form, changing its mass as well as its form, and is strong enough to punch through stone walls and hurl the broken bodies of its victims into the highest branches of the tallest trees. Preferred forms of the Varcolaci include small, black, winged ghosts; goat-legged demons; or even small dragons.

The Varcolaci look human and have pale skin, dark hair, and fierce deep-set eyes. They are night-hunters and generally hunt only in invisible astral form rather than in their corporeal bodies, preferring speed and deception to strength and an open attack. As strong as they are, there is a kind of spiritual Kryptonite that can substantially weaken them: garlic. Both the flower and the meat of this old reliable plant can cause the Varcolaci to become flesh again, and in that form it can be staked, beheaded, and incinerated.

Vengeance Ghosts (and other Unhappy Undead)   Many of the most ferocious supernatural predators are creatures that have come back from death to avenge some kind of wrong that had been done to them; often the wrong that led to their deaths. These monsters cannot rest until they find redress for these wrongs; though once satisfied many have been known to linger and continue to cause harm.

- The *Baka* of Benin has many aspects, but one is a vengeance demon who returns to kill his own murderer, and to do so spreads disease through the entire town in a kind of "kill 'em all, let God sort 'em out approach."

- *Bloody Mary* is an American legend about the ghost of a wronged woman looking for justice.

- The *Eloko* of Zaire are flesh-eating vengeance ghosts who cannot "cross over into the light" until they have balanced the scales.

- The Babylonian *Utukku* is the spirit of a murdered person who cannot rest until it has killed its own murderer.

VENGEANCE GHOSTS Lee Moyer

- The *Farkaskoldus* of Greece is usually the unnaturally resurrected spirit of a shepherd who has been abused or unfairly treated in life and has returned as a species of blood-sucking werewolf.

- The *Radiant Boys* are the angry ghosts of children that had been murdered by their mothers.

- The *Gayal* of India returns from the dead to avenge itself when its family members have not adhered strictly to the proper burial rites.

And there are many others scattered throughout the world and lurking within this book. (Be careful how you handle it . . . it might get angry and take a bite!)

Versipellis   Versipellis was the old Roman name, meaning "skin changer" for lycanthropes, whether *werewolves* or *wolf-men*. In some of the old stories, many of them adapted from even older Greek tales, the Versipellis were not always evil, and the "condition" of lycanthropy was merely regarded as an interesting facet of certain people's nature. It was the actions of the Versipellis that mattered: If he did not prey on humans, his lupine nature was not reviled; but if he developed a taste for human flesh, then he was regarded, quite properly, as a monster.

Vilkacis   The Latvian lycanthrope known as the Vilkacis ("wolf's eyes") is created when a person sins against Heaven, especially someone who speaks openly against God. Such a person is then damned for all eternity and will become a monster while still alive.

The Latvians believed that when a sinful person sleeps, the darker side of his personality separates from the human form and manifests as a shape-shifting Vilkacis, and runs off to kill and spread disease. This kind of astral projection is called "running with the wolf," and was often associated with werewolfism.

The Vilkacis is no more difficult to kill than an ordinary wolf, though this creature is smarter and more cunning than any animal. If the Vilkacis is killed then the sleeping person dies as well.

Vjestitiza   The Vjestitiza of Montenegro and nearby Serbia is a witch-vampire who preys mainly on children. Ordinarily she appears to be a simple old crone, but when hunting the Vjestitiza transforms into a glowing ball of pale blue light and in this form she hunts for young blood. The Vjestitiza can also shape-shift into a variety of animals, such as hens, black moths, or flies.

The Vjestitiza is a blood-drinker, though sometimes she craves more roughage and will cut out the heart and take it with her for a late snack.

The Vjestitiza may hunt alone but they like to form covens and when meeting in their secret places deep in the forests, the witches each take a different beast shape. Hearts stolen from children are often used as centerpieces for unholy feasts in these gatherings.

An old woman wishing to join the coven and gain supernatural powers must first swear a blood oath to uphold the rules and defend the coven's secrecy; and failing to maintain these dark bonds will result in an instant and agonizing death for the creature.

A Vjestitiza power is strongest during the first week of March. Knowing this, villagers stir the ashes in a home's hearth with two horns, then stick the horns into the pile of ashes, a ritual that creates a barrier shield against invasion by this vampire.

Vlkodlak (also **Volkodlak)**   The Serbian Vlkodlak is one of those rare creatures that begins its reign of terror as a werewolf but, once killed, returns to life as a vampire,[76] but then goes a step further and becomes human again!

As a werewolf it is simply a living human who transforms into a wolf, and though this transformation is unnatural, neither the human nor the wolf possesses any additional supernatural abilities. Once it rises from the dead as a Vlkodlak, the creature becomes more complex and far more dangerous.

Its vampiric appearance is that of a wretched and corrupt drunkard with florid skin the color of blood, and for seven years it exists as a blood-drinking revenant. However, if it makes it through those years, feeding continually, the Vlkodlak will undergo a second transformation and will become an ordinary human being once more.

Of course, when this new human grows old and dies . . . it will rise again from the grave as a new Vlkodlak and the bloody cycle starts over again.

---

76. The *Mjertovjec* of Belarus is another of these strange creatures.

The Vlkodlak can also be created when someone has fallen under what is known as the Serbian Curse, which states that if a person sees a werewolf and escapes then that person is doomed to become a vampire after death, no matter how that death occurs. Eating mutton from a sheep slaughtered by a werewolf will create the same cursed state. A person conceived through incest, who had committed incest with his own mother, or who died a violent death will also become a Vlkodlak.

To prevent a suspected corpse from rising as a Vlkodlak, the toes and thumbs of the body should be cut off and a nail driven into its neck to cripple the deceased. Garlic can also be thrown into the coffin to keep evil spirits from entering the corpse. The Vlkodlak can only be killed by piercing its navel with a hawthorn branch and then igniting it with candles obtained from a death-bed vigil.

Vodnik   The Vodnik is a Slavic killer-ghost that comes into being after a child drowns, and thereafter it takes the shape of a living child in order to lure other kids into the water to suffer the same fate. Sometimes it takes the form of a particularly attractive fish, or a coin lying at the bottom of a pool, or even a green-haired mermaid or merman. Essentially it takes whatever form it thinks will cause a child to venture too close to deep or fast-moving water, and when the youngster has tumbled in, the Vodnik holds the thrashing child under until it dies.

Vourdalak (also known as **Wurdalak)**   Russia's Vourdalak is an outgrowth of the legend of the *Eretitsa,* and is a vampire that rises from the grave of a heretic or blasphemer who, prior to death, made a deal with the Devil for immortality. These deals never turn out well for anyone, and the Vourdalak becomes a menace to every living soul in the vicinity, but at the same time its own hungers are so fierce that its entire life is eaten up by the need to hunt and feed. Immortality is wasted on a creature who has no time to enjoy it. This does not sweeten the disposition of the Vourdalak.

The Vourdalak is most frequently female, and can use her sorcery to appear young and desirable, but that is not her true appearance. When she gets her victim alone—either a young man, or a child—she reverts back to her true form: that of a rotting corpse.

Different versions of the Vourdalak legend appear in Russian songs and tales, most memorably in Leo Tolstoy's 1947 short story, "The Family of the Vourdalak"; and it was the basis for one of the segments of the 1964 Boris Karloff thriller *The Black Sabbath*.

Waillepen   The *Chonchon* is not the only supernatural monster that preys on the Mapuche Indians of South America; they also have to contend with a fierce and powerful shape-shifter called the Waillepen who can take any human or animal form but who most often appears as a bizarre amalgam of several animals at once. The creature also comprises vampire sub-types such as the essential vampire (it feeds on fear as it mercilessly taunts and then chases them for hours before killing them); the nosferatu (it spreads sickness and pestilence), a revenant (it is a resurrected corpse), a blood-drinker (it does love a gory draught once in a while), and a flesh-eater (sometimes it eats its prey).

Only a Machi, a wise-woman with great powers, and her familiar are needed to create charms to protect each house in a village, and to fashion talismans for travelers, farmers, and shepherds. These charms can only protect, however, and neither talismans nor weapons can kill this powerful monster. Only prayers invoked to Ñenechen (the God-ruler of the Mapuchen deities) uttered in the presence of the Waillepen can end the creature's unnatural life and send it back to the world of the dead.

Weetuck   When Dutch colonists first met the Mohawks in the 1600s they were told tales of a gigantic monster called Weetuck that was as tall as a pine tree and so fierce it hunted bears for sport. Naturally the Dutch were skeptical until 1705 when some monstrous bones were washed out of the eroding banks of the Hudson River. The bones were of a gigantic creature the likes of which were totally unknown to them. Even the Puritan Cotton Mather wrote of the legends of these monsters.

Today archaeologists have finally pinned a new name on the *Weetucks:* Woolly Mammoth!

Wendigo (also **Witigo, Witiko,** and **Wee-Tee-Go)**   The Wendigo is a fierce predatory monster created whenever a human resorts to cannibalism. A great number of stories exist about this creature from Ontario, Canada (as well as Minnesota in the United States).

According to legend the Wendigo is a demonic force that lays dormant in all men and never emerges unless a person commits the unpardonable sin of eating human flesh, at which point a transformation takes place that turns the cannibal into a gigantic monster of unthinkable strength and savagery. The name "Wendigo" translates as "the evil spirit that devours mankind." The monster is more than twice as tall as a man, with glowing eyes, long yellowed fangs, a lolling tongue, and a muscular body matted with coarse hair.

Werewolf   A general term for a person who changes from human form into a wolf. When transformed the wolf possesses no supernatural abilities beyond retaining some or all of its human intelligence. This transformation is deliberate and can happen at any time and is not, despite what appears in fiction, dependent on the cycles of the moon.

Some werewolves take on the predatory characteristics of a wolf though they don't actually change their physical form. Many dozens of these cases are documented in the historical records of murder trials in Europe, particularly Germany and France of the thirteenth through eighteenth centuries. Psychologists and social anthropologists believe that "werewolves" are nothing but the names given to what is now known as "serial killers."

⊰ WILDMEN: MODERN ⊱ NEANDERTHALS?

According to the fossil record the Neanderthal were supposed to have become extinct about 30,000 years ago. A popular misconception held by many people is that Neanderthals are our ancestors and that they evolved into the Cro-Magnon who in turned evolved into Homo Sapiens, but that is incorrect. The Neanderthals were a separate species that evolved more or less parallel to Cro-Magnon but which were not as successful in terms of developmental evolution, and they died out while the Cro-Magnon flourished.

Or is that really the case? Reports of creatures, generally referred to as "Wildmen," have been documented all around the world, in nearly every country and climate. These are reports of small humanoid creatures with largely simian faces who walk upright. These Wildmen are usually very hairy, though in some cases the reports suggest that they wear garments of shaggy animal hide and may not themselves be hirsute. Most descriptions of the Wildmen suggest that they are, on average, four to four and a half feet tall, with muscular arms and bandy legs.

Conjure in your mind a picture of the stereotypical Neanderthal and compare it to the typical Wildman. The similarities are obvious and thought provoking.

Could Neanderthals have survived into the modern era? Scientists have already discovered sea creatures that they thought to have been extinct for far longer than the Neanderthal. The best example is the coelacanth, found off the coast of Indonesia in 1998, and another earlier in 1938. The coelacanth was believed to have become extinct 65 million years ago; in comparison 30,000 years is nothing.

If any of the many thousands of reports of Wildmen are reliable, then perhaps the creatures spotted in forests and jungles around the world could be our distant cousins, the Neanderthal.

The Will-o'-the-Wisp Strange lights dancing in the woods have lured many a traveler off of their path and into trouble. It is a phenomenon written about in nearly every country around the world and back through history. Ghost lights, faerie lights, corpse candles, dead lights, demon-eyes, and jack o'-lanterns are just a handful of the many names given to these strange illuminations.

Everything from swamp gas to a mirage has been blamed for this spectacle, but no one really knows its origin for sure.

In the folklore of the supernatural, however, there are plenty of explanations. They are ghosts, spirits, demons, and vampires; and sometimes all of the above. Legends around the world speak of monsters that travel as balls of glowing light, dancing in the darkness, luring the unwary with their mysterious nature.

Will-o'-the-Wisp is the most common name given to these beings, and here it is used as a general category, though many of the creatures that fall under this heading bear little resemblance to each another.

In some cultures these Will-o'-the-Wisp beings are benign; but in many they are monsters. They lure travelers into deadfalls or lakes, or down wells. Or they change from glowing balls of faerie light into something far more dreadful.

Examples of supernatural predators that occasionally take on the appearance of a ball of light include the *Obayifo* of the Gold Coast, the *Loogaroo* of Haiti, the *Asema* of Surinam, the *Blue-Cap* of England, the *Zmeu* of Romania, the *Lidére Nadaly* of Hungary, the *Trazgos* of Spain, the *Soucouyan* of Dominica, and the *Vjestitiza* of Montenegro. Predators all.

The Latin for this phenomenon is *Ignis Fatuus,* which means "foolish fire," and it is a wry comment on the judgement of those persons who follow dancing lights into the unknown darkness.

Great Britain certainly has the largest number of Will-o'-the-Wisp variations, and each region has its own nickname for the creatures: Hobby Lantern (Hertfordshire and East Anglia), Peg-a-Lantern (Lancashire), Joan the Wad (Cornwall and Somerset), The Lantern Man (East Anglia), Hinky Punk (Somerset and Devon), Will the Smith (Shropshire), Pinket (Worcestershire), Jacky Lantern, Jack a Lantern (West Country), Spunkies (Lowland Scotland), Pwca and the Ellylldan (Wales), Will o the Wikes (Norfolk), Hobbedy's Lantern (Warwickshire Gloucestershire), and Jenny with the Lantern (North Yorkshire, Northumberland).

Wolf-Man　A variant of the werewolf legend, particularly in England, France, and Germany of the seventeenth through nineteenth centuries, in which a person transforms into a creature that is part human and part wolf. Wolf-men stand upright and have human torsos, but they are covered in fur, with monstrous faces that possess characteristics of both man and wolf.

The Wolf-man legend is the version most often represented in film, not the werewolf. The Wolf-man possesses enormous physical strength and is extremely difficult to kill. Aconite (Wolf's bane) drives this creature away much like garlic repels a vampire. Silver does not kill it, but is instead used as a treatment for the bite of the Wolf-man, and is applied by wrapping silver coins in clean linen and binding them around the wound. Silver is believed by many

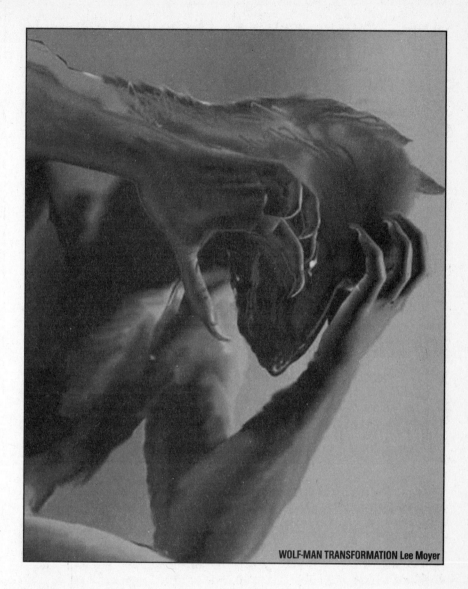

WOLF-MAN TRANSFORMATION Lee Moyer

cultures (and particularly Christianity of the late Middle Ages) to be the purest of metals and as such shares its purity with the victim, draining away any spiritual infection.

A Wolf-man can be killed by knives or guns, but it has great vitality and can sustain great harm before succumbing to its wounds.

⊰ THE MOST FEARED ⊱ WEREWOLF IN HISTORY

In 1589 Peter Stubbe (aka Peter Stube, Peeter Stubbe, or Peter Stumpf) is the subject of one of the most famous werewolf trials in history. After being tortured on the rack, Stubbe confessed to having practiced black magic since he was twelve years old. He claimed the Devil had given him a magical belt that enabled him to metamorphose into "the likenes of a greedy devouring Woolf, strong and mighty, with eyes great and large, which in the night sparkeled like unto brandes of fire, a month great and wide, with most sharpe and cruell teeth, A huge body, and mightye pawes." He also claims to have killed and eaten animals and humans for twenty-five years. The court, appalled by these crimes, sentenced him to having his skin torn off by red-hot pincers before being beheaded.

Wraith Derived from the Old Norse word vörthr, meaning guardian or watcher, a Wraith is a supernatural apparition of a person who is still alive but whose appearance foretells the death of that person.

Wume Despite what is seen in film and written in books, vampirism is seldom passed on through a bite or a sharing of blood. In most cases the nature of a person and his actions during his lifetime determine whether or not he'll rise from death as a vampire.

In some cases a person is doomed to become a monster if they were born with deformities, with a caul over their face, on certain holy days, or if they die before they can be properly blessed by clerics of their faith. Likewise many of the world's vampire species rise from the graves of those who have died sudden and violent deaths, or from the graves of those who were evil, sinful, or immoral during their lifetimes.

Such is the case with the Wume of Togo. This vampire rises from the buried corpse of a human being who either died under a curse or, more commonly, who was a criminal in life and is therefore doomed to damnation after death.

The Togolese are a very spiritual and moral people, and a good deal of their storytelling are fables of right and wrong behavior, and the consequences of one's actions even after death. The Wume appears frequently in these stories, often to make a stern point: live an evil life and you are damned to spend eternity as a hated and feared creature of evil.

In folklore, the Wume is an unrelenting and evil vampire that is always hungry and extremely hard to kill. The Wume is powerful and sly, and so skilled in fighting that no single human can overcome it. A small band of tough warriors is needed to confront the monster. These warriors must take ritual baths to spiritually cleanse themselves and be blessed by the village shamen. In this way they will have greater strength of purpose on their side.

Once these warriors are chosen, trained, cleansed, and blessed, they have the difficult task of locating and tracking the Wume—and often the priest will have to accompany them to look for spiritual signs when no Earthly spoor is visible to the hunters. If they find the Wume while it is awake, then the battle is likely to be bloody and long. The ideal time to catch this creature is after it has fed because it then lapses into a stuporous sleep. In that condition the warriors can overwhelm it and bind it with many dozens of turns of stout rope or vine. Then the monster is quickly carried to a secret place and buried deep in an unmarked grave.

After interment the hunters once again go through their ritual cleansing during which they forget the location of the buried Wume. The secret is kept by the shaman alone; if this secret ever leaks out, then whoever discovers the location may fall under a spell and be compelled to dig up the monster.

Xipe-Totec   Xipe-Totec, whose name means "Our Lord the Flayed One," is a blood-drinking god of the pre-Columbian Nahuatl Aztecs. He is also the god of spring, personifying life from death by causing the growing season to begin. These two qualities seem to be at odds with one another—savage murder and glorious rebirth, but then duality is not exactly a new paradigm, especially in the supernatural world.

The statues and stone masks of Xipe-Totec always show him wearing a freshly flayed human skin, symbolizing the "new skin" (vegetation) that covers the Earth in the spring. To celebrate the festival of Xipe-Totec, Aztec priests killed human victims by removing their hearts and then flaying the bodies and wearing the skins, which were dyed yellow and called teocuitlaquemitl ("golden clothes"). Other victims were strapped to a wooden frame and killed by a hail of sacred arrows. The dripping of their blood was believed to symbolize fertile spring rains.

Even with all of this, Xipe-Totec was actually considered a "gentle god" by Aztec standards.

Yagis   The Kwakiutl of Vancouver Island have an ancient legend of a sea monster called a Yagis that troubles the coastal waters. Variously described as a great snake, an aquatic fire-breathing horse, and a man-eating turtle (among others), the Yagis loves to overturn boats or cause waves big enough to swamp them, and then it attacks the foundering sailors and enjoys a tasty meal.

Yaguareté Abá   Some Argentinian Indian sorcerers have the power to transform themselves into were-jaguars called Yaguareté Abá. These great hunting cats retain their diabolical human intelligence, which gives them a greater advantage when hunting their human prey. The combination of conscious intellect, animal ferocity, and superhuman strength makes them one of the super-natural world's most fearsome predators.

Yara-Ma-Yha-Who   Australia has always been known as a go-to spot for strange creatures, from the kangaroo to the platypus; but the strangest by far is the Yara-Ma-Yha-Who, a short, red-skinned creature with an oversized head. This bizarre predator lurks in fig trees, clinging to the branches with oc-topoidal fingers and waiting for someone to pass beneath; then it grabs the poor unfortunate and drags them up into the shadows under the leaves and drains the victim's blood through suckers in the ends of its fingers and toes. Next it stretches wide its enormous mouth and swallows its victims whole. If a victim manages to escape before being killed, he will become a Yara-Ma-Yha-Who himself and the plague of terror will increase.

Yeren   The rocky northern territories of China are home to one of the world's least fierce species of hominid, the timid Yeren. Similar to the Yeti of the Himalayas, the Yeren stands over seven feet tall, has feet measuring close to sixteen inches, and is completely covered in thick hair.

Sightings of the Yeren have been documented for hundreds of years. By the twentieth century these sightings had become so common that in 1944 the Chinese government formed an organization, the Committee for the Search for Strange and Rare Creatures, comprising scientists in various fields (paleon-tology, cryptozoology, paleoanthropology, etc.) and has sent several official ex-peditions into the hills. The scientists returned with such artifacts as hair samples, feces, plaster casts of Yeren footprints; but no actual creatures were captured.

Yeti (also the Abominable Snowman of the Himalayas)   The most famous of all of the world's hairy wildmen is the Yeti, known as the Abom-inable Snowman, a frequently sighted creature (or race of creatures) that haunts the snow-swept peaks and passes of that remote mountain range. The Yeti is large and powerful, bestial in appearance and covered in coarse hair. Yeti

YETI Adam Garland

do not seem to be aggressive monsters. There are few reliable accounts of them even acting aggressive when surprised, and virtually no report tells of them hunting humans for food.

Though native to the Tibetan Himalayas, the Yeti (whose name means "magical creature") has been spotted in the mountain regions of several Russian provinces in what was once Soviet Central Asia. Mountain climbers have reported seeing the Yeti in the Pamiro-Alai mountain range in Tadzhik as recently as 1980. This creature also goes by a variety of regional names. In Russian Georgia the natives call it the Tkys-katsi; the Azerbaijani call it

Mesheadam; in Dagestan it is the Kaptar; the Balkas, Chechens, Kabardins, and Ungushes call it the Almasti.

Reports of the Yeti have been relayed for hundreds of years and it has been aggressively sought by amateur and professional explorers, scientists, and even the military. The most famous expedition was the 1960 search led by Sir Edmund Hillary, the first man to successfully climb Mount Everest, but he found nothing. Nine years earlier, though, an expedition found a clear footprint on the Menlung Glacier between Tibet and Nepal, at an altitude of 18,000 feet.

If legends are accurate, there are three separate species of Yeti, each of different heights and slightly different musculature: the Rimi (ten feet tall), the Nyalmot (twenty feet tall), and the Raksi-Bombo (four feet tall).

The Yeti are generally not violent, but there have been accounts of them attacking travelers. More often, though, the folktales suggest that the Yeti is timid and will flee from any confrontation with humans.

Yowie   The Yowie of Australia is probably the closest cousin to North America's Sasquatch, in both description and disposition: huge, lumbering, hirsute, and shy. However, unlike Sasquatch, there appear to be three distinct sub-species of this hominid.

The Dooligah is the sub-species that most resembles Bigfoot; it stands about seven feet tall, has apelike features, and can move very fast through the woods.

The Yuuri sub-species is only abut four feet tall and is very shy. Seldom seen, the Yuuri are, however, sometimes heard as they make a soft hooting sound that may be either a distress call or a kind of rudimentary language.

The real brute of the bunch is the Giant Quinkin who towers nine or ten feet in height and is quite menacing. There are reports of these beasts chasing hikers and tearing apart campsites in order to steal food. Nothing shy about them.

Like Sasquatch, scores of Yowie sightings occur every year, and there have been dozens of expeditions to try to find one. Though casts of footprints have been made and some locks of hair recovered, no one has captured a complete specimen.

Y-Pora The Guaranies Indians who live in and around the Delta of the Parana River in Argentina go in fear of a ghostly merman called the Y-Pora who attacks fishermen and travelers on that nation's remote waterways. The Y-Pora sometimes appears as a half-human, half-fish monster who possesses enormous physical strength, and sometimes takes the form of a thick mist that smells of sulfur.

Yurei A common name for the many different kinds of ghosts in Japanese folklore. Generally a Yurei comes into being when a person dies unexpectedly—generally through suicide or murder—and rises as a vengeance ghost. From then on the Yurei is driven to find redress for the wrong that was done to it.

Yurei often appear wearing a white kimono and headband—white being the color of mourning in Japan—and have a shock of wild hair. The Yurei are partial apparitions, fading from a solid upper body to transparent legs and no visible feet.

Zmeu The Zmeu of Transylvania is yet another of the many will-o'-the-wisp vampires who take the form of a floating fireball to hunt for female victims. However, unlike most of the other fiery creatures, the Zmeu only takes the form to target its victim. Once it has tracked a woman back to her home, the Zmeu enters her bedroom and then transforms into a handsome and charismatic young man who then seduces her and during sex drains her of her life essence.

In the Balkans the Zmeu is a different kind of monster, and one who is certainly no handsome charmer. This Zmeu is a kind of scaly ogre who could take the form of animals and birds of various kinds in order to move undetected among villagers.

ZMEU Bill Chancellor

Zombies These days the word "zombie" is often badly misused, and in modern films is used to describe a reanimated corpse that attacks humans and eats their flesh. This is pretty far removed, however, from the Zombie as he appears in the folklore and religions of Haiti.

In the religion of Vodoun (Voodoo) the Zombie is a dead person brought back to life through the use of magic and herbal chemistry by a priest (houngan) or priestess (mambo) of that religion. These clerics act as an intermediary between the physical world and the spiritual and use rituals to summon a loa (spiritual being), which then grants them the powers necessary to raise the dead. The power invested into the houngan or mambo is extraordinary and in Vodoun is the religious equivalent of being a cardinal or even a pope. A houngan capable of summoning a loa is often called papa or papa-loa, while the mambo is called mamman or mama.

These clerics are central figures in the community and serve as spiritual leaders, healers, educators, psychologists, and counselors to their people. Despite the prejudices and misrepresentations common in film and fiction, the religion of Vodoun is very positive and not at all associated with the powers of darkness.

So, what then is the role of the Zombie? There are a couple of different opinions. Largely the creation of a Zombie is the work of a bokor (also known as caplatas) who are priests of the religion who take a darker and more negative path, which is often referred to as left-handed Vodoun. The bokor raises the dead to use the Zombie as a tool or weapon, to terrorize, to perform tasks, and to serve as a bodyguard.

Once resurrected, a Zombie feels no pain, is immune to extremes of temperature, cannot be killed by guns or knives, and has no conscious will. There are a few ways of combating or controlling a Zombie, however. The easiest method is to lure it into a stone room (a crypt or cell will do) and close and chain the door. Strong as a Zombie is, it cannot break through iron or stone.

Another method is to catch the Zombie while it sleeps or is inactive and fill its mouth with salt and then sew up its lips. The salt somehow counteracts the magic that has animated its flesh, thereby rendering it truly lifeless again. Fire can destroy a Zombie only if it totally destroys its body.

And then there is the more modern take on what a Zombie is. Modern anthropologists and chemists have come to believe that a Zombie is merely a living person who has been given chemicals and herbs that diminish conscious control, make the victim highly susceptible to suggestion, and, for all intents and purposes, shut off the pain receptors. Wade Davis, Ph.D., an anthropologist and biologist, wrote a compelling investigative book on the subject of Vodoun and Zombies, *The Serpent and the Rainbow,* in which he discusses the chemistry used to create Zombies and the methods by which someone is chosen to become a Zombie. A film made from the book, though very interesting, bears little resemblance to the excellent and thought-provoking book.[77]

---

77. See also Wade Davis, Ph.D., *Passage of Darkness: The Ethnobiology of the Haitian Zombie,* University of North Carolina Press, 1988.

— Artist Index —

Vampire Universe is proud to include art and photography from some of the world's most talented artists.

JASON BEAM's illustrative story-telling of classic macabre tales have earned him worldwide popularity, and his work stands among some of the most unique artists of digital contemporary art. His frenetic attention to detail and creepy combination of sensual imagery and evocative settings give his work a graceful elegance bordering on the cryptically surreal. Jason Beam's work has been featured in numerous publications and displayed at noted galleries in Chicago, Philadelphia, Salem, and one piece in the permanent collection in the Centre Jeanne D'Arc Museum in Orleans, France.

Website: www.jasonbeamstudios.com.

STEVE BELDEN is the Hammered Wombat—an artist and armourer living in Ninilchik, Alaska. He specializes in "Sport Combat Artwork"—wearable art that aspires to be the ultimate in expression and protection for reenactment medieval fighting.

Website: www.hammeredwombat.com.

LILIAN BROCA is a Canadian visual artist. For thirteen years she was a Fine Arts Faculty member at Kwantlen College, teaching painting and drawing. Her art career spans thirty-four years during which she had more than sixty-five exhibitions in many parts of Canada, the United States, and Europe. Her work is included in important private and public collections around the world. The artist received the Lorenzo II Magnifico gold medal in the 2003 Florence Biennale International Exhibition.

Website: www.lilianbroca.com.

PETER BROWN is a thirty-seven-year-old dark artist/writer from New York who cites such artists as Giger, Vallejo, Dahli, Escher, Frazetta, Soroyama, and Bisley for inspiration.

Website: rayznhell.tripod.com.

MARTI BYES (aka Mardi Byrd) is new to the field of freelance art. She has always had a deep love of sci-fi and fantasy books filled with magical, supernatural, and strange creatures both good and evil.

E-mail: mardi_byrd@yahoo.com.

SANDRO CASTELLI was born in São Paulo, Brazil, thirty-two years ago. He still lives in the city, working as a freelance illustrator. Though mostly self-taught, he graduated from a comic book/illustration–oriented art school. Drawing professionally for more than ten years now, he collaborates with several national magazines, companies, and publishing houses. He grew a passion for dark and fantastic themes early in life; a deep obsession with human anatomy followed later.

E-mail: castelli@sandrocastelli.com; Website: www.sandrocastelli.com.

BILL CHANCELLOR has been doing covers for *Cult Movies Magazine* for years, specializing in classic monsters from the Universal Pictures era, as well as photo-real paintings of Vincent Price as Dr. Phibes, *Star Wars,* and even the Three Stooges. He has also produced DVD covers for cult horror films such as *The Asphyx,* and the legendary black vampire movie *Ganja and Hess.*

E-mail: bchance104@aol.com; Website: members.tripod.com/~chancellor35.

KELLY EVERAERT, of Vancouver, British Columbia, works on comic books, storyboards, and any other illustration project that comes his way.

Website: members.shaw.ca/kelticstudios/Keltic Studios.htm.

KRISHNA FU (aka Fu Xiaochen) was born in Hangzhou, the capital city of China's Zhejiang province. He graduated with a degree in Environmental Art, and after graduation set up an animation workroom where he held the post of the Director of Animation and oversees the development of a cartoon for French TV. He is also a lecturer at the Institute of Animation in China's Academy of Art. Currently he is working for a video game development company as a 2D majordomo for Monster and Scene's Conceptual design. He has provided art for many fantasy books and magazines.

E-mail krishna860@hotmail.com; Website: www.krishnafu.com.

ADAM GARLAND lives in British Columbia where he teaches in the digital animation field. His abiding interest in fantasy and the gothic side of art is reflected in his artwork.

E-mail: cowsmanaut@hotmail.com.

SHARON GEORGE has been a freelance illustrator since 1984. She worked for years in a prestigious San Diego advertising firm, and then in 1997 opened the virtual doors of Gorgeous George Graphics, her own computer-based design firm. She is widely known for her Fantasy and Goddess artworks.

E-mail: sharon_george@sbcglobal.net; Website: www.gorgeousgeorge.com.

MORBIDEUS W. GOODELL is an artist and illustrator, living in Maine with his wife and two children. Morbideus and wife Dee also own/run Postmortem Productions of Maine: www.Postmortem_Prod.com selling T-shirts, prints of his artwork, and Dee's photography.

E-mail: Morbideus@PostmortemProd.com or Morbideus@MorbideusGallery. com; Website: www.MorbideusGallery.com.

XRIS HANNAH was born in the United Kingdom in 1951, spending his early years in Liverpool on the west coast of England, amid the "Mersey Sound" scene of the 1960s era. He studied art in Scarborough College and Sunderland University and has exhibited his work through various galleries in Europe, including Paris (France) and Glasgow (Scotland). Xris currently lives in Scarborough on the east coast of England, where he presently teaches art and information computer technology skills while continuing with his illustration works.

E-mail: xrishannah@yahoo.com; Website: www.gfxartist.com.

ANDY JONES was born in England and currently lives in North Wales. Andy is a wildlife artist and recently expanded into digital art. He produces fantasy/horror illustrations, including concept art for movies.

E-mail: agi71@hotmail.com; Website: andy--jones.gfxartist.com/artworks.

RUTH LAMPI has been drawing fantastic creatures of all kinds since she could grip crayons. A BFA student at Moore College in Philadelphia, Ruth works in media ranging from pencil to linoleum to bronze, and shows her work at fantasy and science fiction conventions. She lives in Philadelphia with far too many sculptures, weapons, and imagined characters for her own good.

Website: www.thefivewits.net/ruth_lampi.htm.

GEORGE MARTZOUKOUS is a professional artist from Athens, Greece. His work has appeared in *Masters of Fantasy Vol. 3* (www.mastersoffantasy.com), *The New Masters of Fantasy 2004—A Collection of the Year's Best Science Fiction & Fantasy Artwork* (www.mastersoffantasy.com), *Fleshrot: Tales from the Dead Halloween Special* (www.fleshrot.com) and on various CD booklets for the Greek music industry.

E-mail: martzoukosarts@yahoo.gr; Website:georgemartz.deviantart.com/ store.

ZACH MCCAIN is a freelance illustrator and graphic designer currently living in Texas. His work focuses primarily on the horror genre but also ranges from science fiction to cryptozoology.

E-mail: zmccain@gmail.com or admin@zachmccain.com; Website: www.zachmccain.com.

KEN MEYER JR. has worked as an illustrator for twenty years, working in comics; paper and online games; educational media; books and magazines; and more. He has appeared in seven volumes of *Spectrum,* the best SF/Fantasy art of the year, *Heavy Metal Magazine,* and more. He produces the Tori Amos calendar each year for the RAINN organization. Commissions are available and freelance work is encouraged.

E-mail: kenmeyerjr@comcast.net; Website www.kenmeyerjr.com/portfolio.

LEE MOYER's award-winning work has been featured in *Spectrum 12,* D'Artiste-Digital Painting, *Design Graphics Magazine,* and in the Smithsonian Institution's Natural History Museum. Clients include: Paramount Pictures, 20th Century Fox, Sony Pictures, The Discovery Channel, Electronic Arts, Hasbro, Pharmacopeia, Career Builder, BET, McGraw-Hill, Philips Media, Dark Horse Entertainment, and the National Zoo. He lives in Portland, Oregon, with his talented photographer wife Annaliese and their dog Lego.

TIM E. OGLINE is a Greater Philadelphia–based illustrator and graphic designer. Ogline's work has appeared in the *Wall Street Journal,* the *Utne Reader, Outdoor Life,* and *Philadelphia Style,* among others. He is also the Graphic Stories editor as well as a contributor to the www.WildRiverReview.com, a literary e-zine. Ogline is an alumnus of, as well as a former instructor at, Temple University's Tyler School of Art. He is also principal of Ogline Design. Ogline Design works with a number of clients in the nonprofit and private and public sectors.

Websites: www.TimOgline.com (illustration gallery); www.OglineDesign.com (design work).

REYMOND PAGÉ is an artist from Winnipeg, Canada, who works best at night (mostly because he's afraid of something lurking in his bedroom closet). Growing up on a steady diet of comic books led to a keen interest in fantasy-based art. He avoids television if at all possible (what do his kids do? why, they read books!) and enjoys football, basketball, hockey, and fruit smoothies.

E-mail: reypage@shaw.ca.

ROBERT PAPP's award-winning art has appeared on hundreds of book covers around the world for virtually every major publisher. His detailed oil paintings have wide appeal and have been seen in projects as different as *American Girl* to *King Kong*. Currently, children's book illustrations now take up the majority of his schedule. Robert lives in Bucks County, Pennsylvania, with his wife Lisa who writes and illustrates children's books.

Website: www.RobertPapp.com.

JOHN WEST is a photographer and writer based in Bucks County, Pennsylvania, and Brooklyn, New York.

KIMBERLEY ZAGOREN is the author of the Mina St. Claire series of vampire novels as well as a photographer and artist. Kimberley's artwork is available at Gothic Creations in New Hope, Pennsylvania.

E-mail: nosfermina@hotmail.com; Website: www.Nosfermina.com.

JOE ZIERMAN's art has been seen on pages of comicbooks and newspaper editorials, and plastered along the sides of speeding trucks. He is currently developing a number of comic-related projects for release in 2006 and 2007. Joe lives in Illinois with his wife and children.

E-mail: zmancomix@yahoo.com.

— About the Author —

JONATHAN MABERRY is a professional writer, writing teacher, lecturer, and book doctor. He is the author of over a dozen books, including the Pine Deep trilogy (*Ghost Road Blues, Dead Man's Song,* and *Bad Moon Rising,* all from Pinnacle Books), and has sold over 900 articles as well as numerous short stories, poetry, plays, video scripts, workshop packets, and technical manuals.

Jonathan is the executive editor of *The Wild River Review,* an online literary magazine (www.wildriverreview.com) and the executive director of the Career Doctor for Writers, a company that provides writing workshops and classes as well as website design and editorial services. Jonathan is a founding partner for The Writers Corner USA, a group of professional writers and writing teachers based in Doylestown, Pennsylvania.

Jonathan is a frequent lecturer at writers' conferences, museums, universities, and other venues, speaking most often on writing, horror, or supernatural folklore. He is a board member of the Philadelphia Writers Conference and Moonstone, a nonprofit literary organization. Jonathan is an active member of the Mystery Writers of America, the Horror Writers Association, and a speaker for the National Writers Union.

Visit the official homepage for *Vampire Universe,* www.vampireuniverse.com, and the homepage for the Pine Deep trilogy, www.ghostroadblues.com.